The Trajectories of
the Indian State

AF515659

The Trajectories of the Indian State

Politics and Ideas

Sudipta Kaviraj

permanent black *and* ashoka UNIVERSITY

Published by

PERMANENT BLACK
'Himalayana', Mall Road, Ranikhet Cantt,
Ranikhet 263645

perblack@gmail.com

and

ashoka
UNIVERSITY

Distributed by

ORIENT BLACKSWAN
PRIVATE LTD

Bangalore Bhopal Bhubaneshwar Chandigarh Chennai
Ernakulam Guwahati Hyderabad Jaipur Kolkata
Lucknow Mumbai New Delhi Patna

www.orientblackswan.com

Copyright © 2010 SUDIPTA KAVIRAJ

ISBN 978-81-7824-352-8

Typeset in Agaramond
by Guru Typograph Technology, Dwarka, New Delhi 110075
Printed and bound by Manipal Technologies Limited, Manipal

for

Sugata

Contents

Introduction

This volume of my essays on Indian politics follows from those in an earlier work, *The Imaginary Institution of India*.[1] In the present book I move my argument about the present history of the Indian state into the period after Independence. The earlier work had sought to understand how a state with India's present-day boundaries came to be established in the collective imagination, how an idea that was initially unconventional turned imaginatively vivid, and eventually, through political action, came to be historically real. Behind the fearfully tangible institutions of the modern Indian state lies a long process of the elusive and contingent movement of political imagination. In the mid-nineteenth century, that imagination appeared to settle on regional linguistic cultures. But through a fascinating ideational change it eventually produced a complex and layered conception of political identity that subsumed, but did not cancel these regional cultures into a larger, second-order 'idea of India'. As against the essays in *Imaginary Institution*, the essays collected here deal with the more structural question of how the system of institutions of the modern Indian state was formed, and how these institutions actually functioned.

I hope that, behind the different and specific concerns of each essay here, a single general argument can be sufficiently discerned. Taken together, the essays suggest that to understand the baffling complexity of the present-day Indian state—the *strategies* of the elites who control power and the *tactics* of the groups who are the targets of these strategies—it is essential to develop a long-term historical analytic. This argument is linked to the one underlying *Imaginary Institution*: namely, that the imaginative unity of India is still historically recent,

[1] Sudipta Kaviraj, *The Imaginary Institution of India: Politics and Ideas* (Ranikhet: Permanent Black, and New York: Columbia University Press, 2010).

and historically contingent—which does not imply that it is not intense or durable—so the real functioning of the institutions of the modern state cannot be studied without constant reference to this genealogy. Instead of believing that we can understand without recourse to history why what is happening now is happening the way it is, we must look closely at the structures of social power existing over the long term—and even start the structural story of the state not at the time of Independence but much earlier. The essays here suggest that the beginning of the history of the contemporary Indian state lies in the political events and processes of India's pre-colonial past, in a period that is at times designated 'early pre-colonial modernity'—from the sixteenth century.

Two contradictory impulses appear to work in the history of this complex political 'field' called India. It is misleading to view this field as an unproblematically single political unity, even less a single political system, because it lacks the intentional direction and institutional coherence comparable to those of modern European nation-states. It is also misleading to treat it as a merely 'geographic' notion, as the British claimed, because political impulses of various kinds constantly intersect in this territorial region. And institutional structures which span this political field have, over the last century and a half, imparted to it an increasingly causally effective structure.

A primary impulse, at times overstressed in the academic literature, could be called the imperial impulse. Empires arise intermittently and seek to impose a relatively unified set of political institutions; but it is easy to overestimate the effectiveness of the imperial process, to regard the effects of imperialism's work as irreversibly final, and to view the intervals between imperial periods as mere interludes of anarchy—or as a period of waiting till another empire arises to restore order and a sense of India. This is an overstated picture because the intervals between empires are long, and during the interruptions stable, recognizable regional political formations rise and achieve impressive degrees of efficacy. Political unity, it must be recognized, is not a 'binary' fact—in the sense that it either exists or does not: so, we can make judgements about whether India is united or not. It is clearly a scalar fact: the judgement must be about whether, territorially, India is at any historical point more or less united than over the preceding period.

A second impulse, which pulls against the stability of empires, is the durability and intensity of feeling around definable regions—like

Banga or Kalinga or Vidarbha—which go back to Indian antiquity. Arjuna, unsatisfied by the wars of Kurukshetra, went out on an imperial campaign of conquest and brought under Pandava control regional kingdoms which have a remarkable similarity to the states of the federal union. Such military unifications were transient, and, except for a temporary militarily enforced territorial unity, they did not contain other durable features. In pre-modern times, therefore, these two impulses, working across this political field, contradicted and cancelled each other. Modern statecraft has found a way of balancing these two political logics, and the contemporary Indian state shows the workings of both these impulses in moderated form.

It appears from recent research by intellectual and economic historians that some more durable trends appeared during the period preceding the British entry into India. Politically, the Mughal empire was able to bring a substantial part of the subcontinent under its effective political control, and subject it to a more bureaucratically systematic and uniform administrative system. The researches of intellectual historians have shown that, partly because of Mughal tolerance towards a wide and diverse intellectual public sphere, intense intellectual exchanges took place between scholars and literary figures, not merely between North and South India, but also between territories falling within the Mughal dominions and outside. There is startling evidence that renowned scholars of Sanskrit grammar or literary figures were not merely patronized by the court, but received official stipends from both their Mughal patrons and rulers outside the Mughal empire. A vigorous public sphere of debate and interpretation seems to have existed independent of the political boundaries and conflicts attendant on them, which produced a busy circulation of ideas across distant regions. Finally, economic history has uncovered evidence of commercial transactions on an unprecedented scale in the 'long eighteenth century', which suggests greater monetization of the economy and exchanges across vast areas of the subcontinent.

Yet the end of Mughal rule demonstrated the power of the second fundamental impulse of Indian political life: the reassertion of regional kingdoms, when the grasp of the imperial centre slackened, and a transfer of both authority and resources back to smaller political entities which could depend on the cultural self-identification of peoples inhabiting flourishing vernacular cultures. Before the British administration created a stable unity of territories after the decline of the

Mughal state, powerful regional states had emerged in the Maratha, Mysore, and Punjab regions, indicating that the dual logic of political power in India was still powerfully active in the early eighteenth century. Political construction by the British followed the common logic of imperial states. For relatively fluctuating periods of time, empires united vast territories under a single centre of political control, but precisely the vastness of the dominions made it hard to aspire to impose on them a relentlessly uniform system of rules and regulative order. Following this imperial tradition, the British too experimented with different styles of revenue system as their empire expanded from the early control of Bengal to conquest of the North Indian kingdoms and Southern territorial acquisitions, and the shift from *zamindari*, *ryotwari*, and *mahalwari* systems. The actual processes of colonial governance thus struck a balance between the two impulses in the long term of Indian political history. These imposed central integrative techniques at times, and in the fields where they were needed, but left alone a great degree of regional specificity of political idiom and governing style. Political structures in India therefore continued to develop a complex pattern of rules and legislative orders, stretched across at least three planes—of 'locality, province and nation'—to express in modernist language a flexible structure that persisted over the *longue durée*. I suggest that the political structures truly comparable to the contemporary Indian state are not the European nation-states of the nineteenth and twentieth centuries, but the pre-modern empire-states of Indian and Islamic history, with the implication that we can find greater analytical assistance from studying not the history of Europe in the modern period—on which the social science studies focus obsessively—but pre-modern Indian history.

Political analysts often work with the wrong genealogy: the nation-state in India, after Independence, is not a structural descendant of modern European states but of pre-modern Indian empires. I believe that the studied ahistoricity of our political science thinking—the plausible but massively misleading convention of starting the story of modern Indian politics in 1947, or even 1858—encourages this misconstruction. There is no epistemically serious way into present politics except through the long past. The neglect of vernaculars, and of the cosmopolitan languages of Sanskrit and Persian, has rendered this exceedingly difficult. A revival of the study of the Indian state requires not the misguided epistemic selflessness of some dedicated devotion to the works of Weber and Marx or Foucault, but a painstaking reconnection with the vernacular facts of Indian political history. The exploration of Western theory is not unhelpful, but it can provide only oblique illumination to the history of Indian social power.

The essays of this book do not agree with the common periodizing of recent Indian political history. Politics after Indian Independence is usually periodized in terms of party governments. It is quite right, in one sense, to suggest that the long term of uninterrupted Congress rule, from 1947 to the early 1990s, was a continuous stage, disrupted by Congress' reduction to a minority government in the momentous elections of 1991, after which, for nearly fifteen years central governments depended on explicit or implicit alliances. Several of these essays claim that a more attentive analysis of the functioning of political structures would reveal a highly significant line of separation between the Nehru years and those that followed. At times, this is viewed misleadingly in entirely personal terms—by reference to the personal qualities of statesmanship to be found in Jawaharlal Nehru and Indira Gandhi. In fact, it is a combination of several significant changes: of higher political literacy in the electorate, of the new uses of political language, of structural changes in the economy, of the long-term reflexive effects of policies—that is, the manner in which policies, when pursued successfully over a long period of time, have effects that loop back and affect the structures of governance and social institutions. Although none of the essays directly addresses the question of periodizations of political history, collectively they call for a more attentive and minute characterization of historical change.

Regionality, Commonality, and Unity

A surprising result of this historicization is a more complex understanding of the constitution of the political field which we casually call 'India'. Obviously, this is a highly complex and layered terrain of facts which requires an appropriately complex methodological response. Though it is quite true that, within the varying levels of political power, regional kingdoms—equivalents of our modern federal states—are among the most durable, they are amenable to historical change. In the contemporary world these political regions are also subject to pressures from other forms of regionality—by which I mean a consistent historical process through which regions of varying kinds are formed and stabilized. Territorial regions acquire common features by being subjected to the same sets of laws and political practices, by being drawn into identical processes of economic production, circulation, and exchange, and by being affected by the same cultural and religious movements. All such processes produce determinate regionalities, they bring individuals and groups together into webs of common experience and control. The expansion of Mughal rule in most of northern and central India subjected varying territories to a similar pattern of revenue administration and principles of political governance. The rise of a Vaishnava religious movement united the territories of Bengal, Orissa, Mithila, and Manipur in a common artistic and cultural sensibility. Colonial economic processes created both clear divisions between coastal urban centres and extensive internal hinterlands—both connected and separated by the specific relations of economic production and exchange.

Region-forming processes of this kind are many in the modern period, and sometimes the economic and the cultural regionalities cross-cut political ones. In recent periods, economic and political regionalities have often accumulated different territorial configurations. In spite of UP being a single state, it is clear that—not merely in some socio-economic terms—it contained three different internal regions, and this was used as an argument for the creation of the new state of Uttaranchal (now renamed Uttarakhand) out of it: but eastern UP and Bihar also have significant common features. At the same time it is also quite clear that economic processes have created a common region incorporating the western parts of UP, the state of Delhi, parts of Haryana, and parts of Punjab. Faster economic growth in some states of India, compared to much slower change in others, creates political pressures, particularly if both growing and lagging states are territorially contiguous.

But Indian political space is also fragmented in other ways which need to be incorporated into an accurate picture of its topography. At times, regions may be quite diverse and geographically distant, yet demonstrate features or processes in common. The specific hierarchies of caste groups are quite different between varying regions, but show properties of inequality in common. Some processes are, however, more than just common: they unite territorial regions into unitary spaces for particular purposes. In some ways state processes and the growth of the capitalist economy have created such unities at a certain level of the Indian economy and polity. Thus, there is a stratum of Indian space which is united, which works as a single plane of acts and causalities; but there are also other strata which are divided into regionalities of various kinds.

The united space, created primarily by the efficacy of the upper levels of the state structure and the modern capitalist economy, is not however simply an upper storey which does not affect the lower levels of political life. Politicians who are based in their respective states often wield power in distinctly more authoritarian ways in state politics while demanding democratic rules of functioning when they operate at the national level. This is not a matter of mere inconsistency and hypocrisy: it is in a sense rational choice. As none of them can hope to dominate the national stage in the way they do the political stages of their regions, their best option is to guard against an unusual curtailing of their powers because of the possible emergence of political authoritarianism at the centre. The fact that these regions are parts of a democratic Indian union is not a fact external to their political life, but conditions and determines politics at state levels as well. To accommodate all such complexities into our conception of the political field, we need to think of a stratified political space.

Caste, Class, and Consciousness

These essays were written over quite a long stretch of time, and they contain significant methodological shifts. The early essays are marked by a much stronger imprint of Marxist techniques of analysis—though there can be disputes about what constitutes a decisively Marxist approaches to politics. Even the earlier pieces interpret Marxist theory to claim that economic structures are overdetermined by cultural and political causalities to produce specific historical outcomes. Pressures arising from economic structures underdetermine political acts and outcomes. The later essays, however, diverge from conventional Marxist analyses in more significant ways.

The Marxist analysis of politics faces an immediate dilemma in deciding between two alternative constructions of its method. It could be practised as a technique of resolute economic determinism, reducing political phenomena to underlying economically causal processes: if Marxists accepted this version of political analysis, there was little really to analyse; all that was required was simply to relate political events to appropriate economic triggers. Clearly, Marxist theory also contains a very different strand which recognizes the immense significance, even the 'primacy', of the political—usually in the context of analyses of revolutionary action. But it is not impossible to generalize this condition, and view politics as a highly significant activity which not merely subjugates and holds down subaltern groups, but shapes and gives form to the social world. Economic structures can be viewed as a set of constraints on political initiatives which limit political acts—in the sense of ruling out some options, constraining others, and imparting a direction to political choices consistent with the interests of basic social groups.

A second element of Marxist theory is the injunction to ask questions historically, i.e. instead of answering questions as they are, to give them a radically historical character. This requires that while seeking to understand relations between the state and social groups, or between dominant and subaltern communities, it is necessary first to historicize the question, i.e. to ask 'What is the history of the world about which we are asking such questions?' The impulse to historicize the study of Indian politics, seeking the precise nature and character of social groups, the nature of political conflicts, the precise mechanisms of social oppression, are in these essays drawn from this methodological impulse in Marxist historicism. This can lead to several problems when approaching Indian politics. It makes the standard forms of class analysis less relevant as we move from the relatively more industrialized regions of India to less industrial ones, and from the present to the past. In both cases, conflicts in political life happen primarily between agentive constellations of castes rather than classes specific to modern capitalist economies. In a sense, therefore, the consistent pursuit of the historicizing injunction within Marxist theory leads to a move away from class to caste as the basic category of political conflict.

A rejection of the idea that Marxism is 'a theory of everything' opens up the requirement to supplement its techniques by other theoretical and methodological apparatuses. In several essays, analysis by using the category of class is often supplemented by techniques for analysing strategic action. The dominance of social groups is seen primarily not in directly intentional but consequential terms—by comparing the varying efficacy of different classes in influencing political outcomes. The subalternity of particular groups does not imply that these groups do not act on the field of political action, but that their actions are less efficacious, which raises the question of why this is so. Some of the essays which focus on analysing the present historically—suggesting a major 'rupture' between the Nehru and Indira Gandhi years, for example—also suggest that, contrary to the conventional analysis of radical commentators which viewed the bourgeoisie and landed magnates as the two primarily dominant classes in Indian society, a more accurate picture should introduce two modifications. First, it should carefully register changes in the historical character of rural agrarian elites that have altered their patterns of economic activity, and often their modes of political control, over rural society. Second, it is important to see the managerial-bureaucratic elites as major participants in the structure and dynamics of political dominance: they do not merely participate in enjoying the fruits of political dominance, but at significant decisional moments play a major strategic and directive role among the dominant classes. This also implies a further splitting of the general notion of social dominance into socio-economic dominance, and dominance as directive capacity.

A collection of essays, though their separate arguments are interconnected, obviously cannot offer a coherent analytical picture of the complexity, vastness, and historical depth of Indian politics. These essays try to work on two fronts of political analysis: some try to sketch a long-term historical narrative of the political; and some seek to explore the logic of the specific constitutive phenomena of political life. I belong to a generation whose understanding of Marxist theory was transformed by the discovery of Gramsci and historicism on the one hand, and of French structuralism on the other. The effect of this double impact was to find the fact that the most creative moments of radical analysis emerged when theorists, after acknowledging that they lived in particular and not universal history, sought to theorize their own historical world by devising concepts appropriate to the surprises that their history threw at them. To follow Gramsci was therefore not to try to apply Gramsci everywhere, because that, paradoxically, would be to perversely misconstrue the high significance of Gramsci's work. Within the Marxist tradition, Gramsci was a theorist of difference, giving particular attention to those aspects of Italian politics which made it different from all others; and to follow him or to learn from him should lead to a discovery of historical difference in other specific contexts. Gramsci, for instance, turned his analysis different by addressing the peculiarities of the 'Southern question' in Italy, or the peculiar character of peasant culture. Although I must plead guilty to a simple transfer of concepts occasionally, I interpret the methodological injunction of historicity to imply that Indian analysts of politics should try to work out convincing analytical devices for forces which have shaped the history of our politics—such as language, caste, and religion—and meld them into a radical analysis of politics which captures the historical difference of the Indian lifeworld. Some of the essays here try to work out these smaller explanatory sketches, which could be fitted in as subsets of the larger picture.

Studying the modern state is astonishingly hard in some ways; and the theme that is repeated by most close observers of the modern state is that it is something new and unprecedented. Possibly the problem with the analysis of the state is one of semantic anachronism of a special kind. Long before the emergence of the mechanisms which we call the modern state, there were states composed of intricately connected institutions of rule, and there were also culturally specific stable meanings to the term 'state' (or rather terms which we would translate in English as the 'state') which referred to those institutional complexes. When the modern state arose historically in Europe, political analysts and popular discourse simply continued to use the old term for the new entity. In this case, the descriptive expectations folded into the older term 'state' continued to bear connotative effect, sliding the descriptions towards the past, suggesting that institutions and mechanisms existed which in fact did not.

At times, when trying to clarify what is involved in the rise of the modern state, theorists, not surprisingly, use metaphorical language—as Althusser says regarding Marx, this is quite common because there is a new perception of reality, but not a language which is prepared for it. In such cases, authors have to force the old language to do the work of the new, forcing the old concept to describe a new reality. In trying to explicate his difficult idea of 'governmentality' Foucault used a metaphor which captures this aspect of the unprecedented character of the modern state. A 'state of sovereignty', Foucault remarks, sets up a relation between the ruler and his subjects which resembles one between the shepherd and his flock. His relation to the flock is external: if the sovereign loses his territory, or his dominion is reduced, it has an external relation to him. By contrast, the relation between the ruler and the ruled in a 'state of governmentality'—the exact difference he was so interested in capturing—was like that between the passengers and the captain of the ship: the fates of the rulers and the ruled are inextricably connected, or at least intertwined in a new and quite different way. It is important note that what Foucault is trying to capture is not democracy, but a relation of reflexive power usually attendant on the modern state.

What I am trying to suggest might not be exactly the same as Foucault's idea, but it is significantly connected to it. The modern state is a new kind of instrumentality in its internal sovereignty, reflected in the crucial semantic alteration of the meaning of sovereignty under the European absolutist regimes. The state continued to perform its conventional—pre-modern—functions, such as defending the realm, fighting with enemy states, being unsubordinated to external command, etc; but gradually the internal functions of the state began to multiply and predominate: the state became involved more with doing things *to its own society* than to other states. Through taxation, finance, social engineering, the manifold tasks of the modern bureaucracy, the state became an agency primarily concerned with the most fundamental arrangements of its own society. In another way of speaking, it became the primary agency of reflexive social action: and this became its predominant function. Thus political groups try to lay hold of the state—not because they want to fight intruders or conquer territories, but because they intend urgently to do things to their own society. The history of both democratic and authoritarian states in modern times shows that the greatest transformations of the internal arrangements of social power have been made by modern states: the immense transformations wrought not merely by the Soviet state or the Nazi regime, but also the vast social engineering carried out by modern democratic welfare states.

By stressing the notion that the state was a mechanism which emerges out of society but is separated off from it, Marx was probably still thinking within the older language of the state—as an entity that is drawn out of, yet separated from, society; answering the first picture in Foucault, not the second. By contrast, as modern states developed nationalistic and then democratic institutions, this power, separated off from society, was sought to be reconnected to the whole society by devising new languages of universality, inclusion, and collective intentionality. Nationalism presented this power as not of the monarch, but of the country—of France or England. When a soldier fought in a military engagement the act, sometimes the sacrifice of death, did not carry the meaning that he was prepared to give up his life for a high ruler who owned his country, and to whom he was bound by rules of fealty. It meant, in contrast, that he was willing to lay down his life for a large collectivity which was ennobled precisely by its inclusiveness: he was dying for the French nation of which he was an indispensable part. Clearly, the rise of democratic institutions advances this picture of the power of the modern state stemming from its own people, who, under democratic conditions, procedurally sanction these wars in which soldiers fight. In a sense, therefore, the soldier is fighting in a war that he has played a role in launching, or, in a more elevated and unrealistic sense, has declared himself. Notice that in all these things there is a dual argument: an argument of inclusivity—all people are included and involved in these political acts or processes, and in the case of internal acts such as taxation (not war) there is a dominant quality of reflexivity—of a society sanctioning and enacting these changes to its own structure.

Liberal and Marxist theory appear to misconstrue the nature of this reflexive relation of power in two different directions. The trouble with ordinary liberal political theory is that it takes this picture of inclusivity and reflexivity as true in an excessively straightforward sense. In the common, i.e. extreme, liberal picture, even the captain of the ship is dispensed with: the passengers run the ship collectively through political equality; and this equality can only be seen as equality of opportunity—as at every election, in a legal sense, every citizen gets an exactly equal chance of shaping the decision of the political community. There are well-known difficulties in accepting this simple picture as true. Serious observers of liberal democratic societies would immediately observe inequalities not merely in non-political spheres like the economy and their distortive effects on the putative equality of political power; there exist real inequalities of power in a purely political sense, by implication, giving credence to the extreme Marxist idea that liberal democracy is a 'sham'. It is an unrealizable ideal, it is argued, and therefore the only reason for its persistence is ideological—to generate a false picture of liberal power, a powerfully plausible distortion of the way political power really operates in democratic societies.

I now believe that this is one of the major centres of modern political thought, in the sense that we should give more attention to this part of the problem; and it is possible to avoid the choice between two oversimple positions offered by versions of liberalism and Marxism (both of which are extreme), in the sense that they pick up a very significant feature of the real characteristics of the modern state, but generalize on that, ignoring other, equally significant features.

These essays are about a historically unprecedented activity called *politics*, an activity, if taken in this definition, that is available only in modern times, within the historical confines of modernity. It is hardly surprising that in many Indian languages this newness, the unprecedented quality of this activity, is captured by the fluent use, inside fully vernacular sentences, of what was originally an English word but is no more—a word which has decidedly lost its Englishness. People without any knowledge of English would today recognize the word, and its precise meaning. This is not because they know the English language, but because they know what that word indicates in their world. Thinking about the state—which is what these essays do—is to think about the historical advent of this activity. This is the indelible mark of modernity on history—the presence of the political in this sense. The least closely guarded secret of the modern world is that, although they do not make it as they please, men do make their own political history. I mean this in a much more narrowly and deeply political sense than Marx's famous remark. Over this particular field, politics, God has lost his sovereignty and the elites have lost their exclusive claim. In the modern world, all politicians, from devoted constitutionalists to radical fundamentalists, share a belief in the plasticity of the social world and feel the irresistible attraction of the activity called politics, the activity which, presupposing this plasticity, means to shape the structures of that malleable social world to their collective preferences. What makes a social world irretrievably modern, in the political sense, is not the appearance or possibility of some specific form of political power, democratic or totalitarian, but the presence of this activity. Modern state power is so universally sought because it is, when stripped of all pretences, the power to command the reflexive organization of society: turning, paradoxically, the power of a society towards itself to determine its nature and structure. These essays tell the story of how this activity produced a new set of governmental institutions in India, and how all social groups—elites, middle classes, and subalterns—are responding to its demands.

I am indebted to a long line of people, from friends and colleagues who helped me understand arguments by discussing or commenting on them, to students who often forced me clarify my own ideas by lively debates in seminars. I would like to thank Sobhanlal Dattagupta, Diptiman Ghosh, Partha Chatterjee, Dipesh Chakrabarty, Muzaffar Alam, Rajeev Bhargava, Sunil Khilnani, Satish Saberwal, Rajni Kothari, Ashis Nandy, D.L. Sheth, Bhikhu Parekh, and Pranab Bardhan for discussing Indian politics with me over a long period of intellectual friendship. I owe a deep debt to students and colleagues at the School of Oriental and African Studies (SOAS), University of London, where most of these essays were written, for stimulation and engagement with my arguments. I thank my colleagues at SOAS and Columbia for intense and active engagement with ideas and arguments, and for providing me with a stimulating academic atmosphere.

1

Modernity and Politics in India

This essay is in two parts. The first part suggests that conventional theoretical models about the structure of modernity and its historical extension across the world are faulty; to understand the historical unfolding of modernity, especially in the non-Western world, these theories need some revision. The second part tries to illustrate this point by analysing the role of 'the political' in India's modernity.

Theories of Modernity

Most influential theories of modernity in Western social theory, like the ones developed by Marx and Weber, contain two central ideas. The first is that what we describe as modernity is a single, homogeneous process and can be traced to a single causal principle. In the case of Marx, it is the rise of capitalist commodity production; for Weber, a more abstract principle of rationalization of the world. It is acknowledged that modernity has various distinct aspects: the rise of a capitalist industrial economy, the growth of modern state institutions and resultant transformations in the nature of social power, the emergence of democracy, the decline of the community and the rise of strong individualistic social conduct, the decline of religion and the secularization of ethics. Still, these are all parts of a historical structure animated by a single principle. This thesis comes in two versions. The first sees these as subsets of what is a single process of rationalization of the social world. A slightly different version would acknowledge that these processes are distinct and historically can emerge quite independently.

First published in *Daedalus*, Winter 2000, vol. 129, no. 1, pp. 137–62.

But it would still claim that these processes are functionally connected to each other in such a way that the historical emergence of any one tends to create conditions for all the others. Social individuation, for instance, is a prior condition for the successful operation of a capitalist economy. All these processes of modernity either stand or fall together.

A second idea usually accompanies this functionalist model of modernity. It is widely believed that as modernity spreads from the Western centres of economic and political power to other parts of the world, it tends to produce societies similar to those of the modern West. A corollary of this belief is that when we come across societies different from Western models, this is because they are not sufficiently modernized; they remain traditional. Modernity replicates Western social forms in other parts of the world; wherever it goes it produces a uniform 'modernity'. Both these theses appear to me to need some revision.

There are at least three different reasons why we should expect modernity not to be homogeneous, not to result in the same kind of social process and reconstitution of institutions in all historical and cultural contexts.

First, the coming of modernity is a massive alteration of social practices. Modern practices are not always historically unprecedented in the sense that the society was entirely unfamiliar with that kind of practice earlier. Most of the significant social practices transformed by modernity seem to fall into the spheres of political power (state), economic production, education, science, even religion. It is true that modernity often introduces a radical rupture in the way these social affairs are conducted. In all cases, the modern way of doing things is not written on a 'clean slate'. Practices are worked by social individuals who come from appropriate types of practical contexts, and these social actors have to undergo a process of coercive or elective willed transformation into a different way of doing things. What actually happens when such modernizing individuals learn new things can be suggestively likened to learning a language. Like the accents from our native languages that always stick to and embarrass our English, working from within or underneath, pulling our speech in the direction of a different speech, the background skills of earlier practices work inside and through the new ones to bend them into unfamiliar shapes. To take a simple example, one of the most startling cultural changes in nineteenth-century Bengal was the complete transformation of educational structures. The modern Bengali's conversion to Western educational ideals was so complete that traditional systems of instruction and the schools that imparted them disappeared within a very short time and were replaced by a modern educational system that, in its formal pedagogic doctrine, emphasized critical reasoning and extolled the virtues of extreme scepticism in the face of authority. Yet actual pedagogic practice retained the traditional emphasis on memory. Soon, more careful observers felt that one system of unquestioned authority had been replaced by another, and the reverence shown towards modern Western theories seemed particularly paradoxical.

The second reason lies in the plurality of the processes that constitute modernity by their historical combination. In modern social theory, there are various intellectual strategies that try to reduce this diversity into a homogeneous process or outcome. Some of them offer a theory of intellectual origin claiming that an intellectual principle like rationality expresses itself in and takes control of all spheres of modern life. So, the transformations in science, religion (secularization), political disciplines, industrialization, and commodification can all be seen as extensions of the single principle of rationality to these various spheres. Alternatively, some other theories suggest a functional connection among various spheres of modern social life, which often take a causally primacist form. Functionalist Marxism claims that the causal primacy of capitalist relations of production transforms other sectors of the economy, and subsequently other spheres of social life like politics and culture, to produce eventually a capitalist social formation. Alexis de Tocqueville's analysis of democracy appears to make a comparable primacist claim about the causal powers of the democratic principle. Historical accounts, however, show that the actual history of modernity does not manifest such strong functional characteristics. On the basis of historical evidence, it seems possible to make the opposite case. Not only is one process insufficient for the production of others, but the precise sequence in which these processes occur and the precise manner in which they are interconnected have a strong bearing on the form that modernity takes. Thus, to consider only the two most relevant to the Indian case—the temporal relation of capitalism and democracy—the absence of democracy might have assisted great spurts of capitalist growth in some East Asian societies, but under Indian conditions, when democracy is an established political practice, it seriously affects the actual structure and historical path of capitalist development. Similarly, if secular state institutions are subjected to determination by democratic decision-making processes, the outcome might be quite different from what an unworried theory of secularization might expect.

Third, the history of modernity is marked by a principle of reflexivity in two forms.[1] Modern societies are constantly engaged in devising more effective and expanded forms of collective agency. The growth of modern political 'disciplines', like a bureaucratic administration, the training of modern armies, and states of collective consciousness such as nationalism, all contribute to this obsessive search for forms of deliberate and well-directed collective action. The evolution of modern democratic mechanisms provides these societies with a new technique of collective will formation. When all these processes come together, it becomes possible to say that a government acts on behalf of the society, if only to translate its collective intentions into policy. These processes are reflexive in two senses. First, many of these modern devices of collective will and agency are directed not only towards 'others'— i.e., other states in wars, or subjected territories in colonial empires—but also, in crucial cases, towards the society itself. They are reflexive in the second sense in that these techniques require constant monitoring of their own effectiveness and are regularly reformed in response to perceived failures or in search of more effective solutions. This implies that concern for the rationality of systems and institutions generates a constantly recursive consideration of options open to societies and groups for ranging their own structures; societies, consequently, learn from an analysis of their own and others' experience. Because of the existence of this kind of recursive rationality at the heart of modern institutional forms, it is unpractical to expect that later so-

[1] Although societies may have possessed these capacities in earlier periods, they are greatly enhanced under modern conditions (see Beck, Giddens, and Lash 1995), and this transforms the nature of 'risk'. See Beck 1992. I think, however, that this was always one of the major distinguishing characteristics of modern societies and can be seen, as Michel Foucault's later work suggested, in political disciplines of the eighteenth century. See Foucault 1979; Foucault 1974.

cieties will blindly repeat the experiences of the West. The initial conditions of their modernity are different, and therefore they cannot imitate the West.[2] In other respects, these societies may not wish to emulate the West since the experience of Western modernity is diverse and not uniformly attractive.[3]

I shall now follow the story of political modernity in India through its three most significant aspects: the modern state, nationalism, and democracy. My argument will be that all three introduce distinctively modern ideas and institutions, but in each case these institutions or movements have evolved in ways that are different from recognized Western equivalents.

Colonialism and the State

The state is utterly central to the story of modernity in India. It is not merely one of the institutions that modernity brings with it, for all institutions in a sense come through the state and its selective mediation. However, some peculiarities of the entry of colonialism into Indian society ought to be noted because they make this history quite different from the principal narratives of state formation in the West. Curiously, British commercial enterprise initially entered India without a serious confrontation with the Mughal imperial authority. This happened because of the peculiar way social power was organized under the caste system. Everyday caste practice disciplined social conduct without frequent direct recourse to the power of the state; rather, the holders of political authority were themselves governed by the rules of caste order and barred by its regulations from exercising legislative power over

[2] If colonial empires provided a significant part of the capital required for industrialization, this is a condition that late modernizing societies cannot replicate—although some recent scholarship has sought to question the connection between colonialism and the early accumulation of capital.

[3] The experience of Western modernity appears attractive now if we adopt a resolutely short-sighted view and refuse to look beyond 1945. On a longer view, the rise of aggressive nationalism, militarism, fascism, death camps, and the repeated failures of democracy were essential parts of the modernity on offer, and, not surprisingly, Indian writers like Tagore and Gandhi had a deeply ambivalent and critical attitude towards its claims to provide a form of the good life unquestionably superior to traditional ones.

the productive arrangements of society. Royal authority is explicitly entrusted with the responsibility of upholding caste arrangements, which includes punishing infringement and restoring society to its normal form. But political authorities lacked the jurisdiction to alter individuals' caste membership or the ritual hierarchy between caste groups. In traditional Indian social order, political power is often distributed between several layers of legitimate authority stretching from the village or locality at the micro level, through regional kingdoms, to immense empires like the ones set up by the Mauryas or the Mughals. Historically, in India's political history constant shifts of power occurred from one level to another. With the emergence of empires, kingdoms were either overwhelmed or subsumed into their control, only to re-emerge as real centres of authority once the empires, usually rather short-lived, began to decline. The relation between these levels of authority is better described as one of subsumption or subsidiarity rather than sovereignty, as the powers of even the highest centres of power were circumscribed in two ways: the caste system set aside certain fundamentally important parts of social conduct from its legitimate field, and its relations with lower levels were often arranged in a way that was closer to modern federal arrangements than to the indivisibility implied by the Austinian definition of state sovereignty.

This explains the peculiarly stealthy entrance of British power in India. The British finally dispensed with the titular authority of the Mughal emperors only after the revolt of 1857. Control over the province of Bengal, which functioned as the indispensable platform for British imperial expansion into other regions, was achieved without formal assumption of 'sovereign' authority. Because traditional Indian society was not organized around the power of the state, the British administration in Bengal could start as a revenue-raising body and gradually extend its control over most other spheres of social life without overcoming or controlling the explicitly political authority of the Mughal empire.

In a paradoxical way, once they settled down in India, the British introduced two rather different types of ideas and practices: the first, the idea of state sovereignty; the second, which in part runs contrary to the absolutist demands of sovereignty, the idea of 'spheres' of social life, only one of which was in the narrow sense 'political'. Both of these ideas were fundamentally different from the conceptual schema governing traditional Indian social life. After British power was consolidated, it was forcefully used to create a replica of the kind of state authority that by this time dominated Europe. But here again we observe significant differences. This was a process of state formation in the entirely literal sense of the term; i.e. the complex of institutional mechanisms that we call the 'state' was in fact 'formed', literally brought into existence. This does not mean that earlier Indian society did not know social stratification or intricate organization of social power. It surely did. But this points to a central fact that is being demonstrated by trends towards globalization. The regulative functions that are now exclusively invested in the modern state, to the extent that we cannot easily imagine any other institution performing them, need not be concentrated in that manner under all circumstances.

This condensation of functions was a phenomenon of modern history—started by European absolutist states, carried forward at each stage by techniques of 'disciplinary power' and the rise of nationalism, democracy, and the welfare state. Although these processes are very different and are caused and sustained by enormously different circumstances, they led to a secular tendency towards a concentration of all regulatory functions in the instruments of the state. But, in principle, these regulatory functions can exist without being concentrated in a single institutional complex. Before modernity, such strange distributions were possible, as the British title to the Dewani of Bengal showed: even such important state functions as the collection of revenue could be handed over to a commercial body run by a group of foreigners. Colonialism does not come to India as one state invading or making demands on another. It presents itself and is taken seriously as a corporation, the East India Company. But the East India Company had to perform functions that were, in my sense, state functions—the collection of revenue, the introduction of statewide accountancy, and the production of statistics and cognitive registers like mapping, through which the territory could be made familiar to its foreign administrators.[4] After a lapse of a century, these state processes, introduced piecemeal, at different times, combine to create in a real sense a 'colonial state'. As a next step in our argument, it is necessary to compare the colonial state to the contemporary Western form.

[4] I have argued this in Kaviraj 1994.

The colonial state gradually instituted an enormous discursive project—an attempt to grasp cognitively this alien society and bring it under intellectual control. This knowledge was crucial in making use of the vast potentialities of this country in the economic and military fields. There is evidence of the introduction of disciplinary techniques in the bureaucracy, the military, and the colonial prison system. But this tendency is cut through and counteracted by an opposite one. Cognitive Orientalism, the development of a large body of cognitively disciplined material that documented what the nature of this land was like, often created a powerful intellectual tendency in the opposite direction. Orientalist knowledge might, inside the West, create prejudices against the Orient and make it appear inferior; but Edward Said's suggestion that it tended to show the Orient systematically as an object, passive and tractable, to be moulded by Western initiative is certainly partial and misleading.[5]

On the contrary, Orientalist knowledge about India quite often bore the opposite implication for policy-making. The more systematic knowledge was gathered about social conduct and forms of consciousness, the more edgy and anxious administrative opinion became about the amenability of this society to standard Western ruling practices. What is important is not the general point that Indian society was radically different, but the more specific question of how this difference was read, what this difference was seen to consist of. By this time, Western societies were significantly secularized; the central question of political life was class conflict. In Indian society, by contrast, religion provided the basis of primary and all-consuming group identities. Western societies were also regarded as broadly culturally homogeneous, unified by single languages and common cultures; Indian society was bewildering in its cultural and linguistic diversity. It was commonly argued that since Indian society was so fundamentally unlike Western society, none of the presuppositions of Western state practices applied there; policies that could be justified on abstract rational grounds, or by reference to sociological arguments in the West, were unlikely to work in India. Surely, the expression of this sense of intractable difference was usually in the form of regarding Indian society or its practices, including its art, as irrational and inferior; but the political

[5] Said 1978.

point was that administrative and governing rules, in order to be effective, must be appropriate to social conditions. Colonial power was thus influenced by a very complex, occasionally contradictory, set of ruling ideas: some showed the characteristic universalism of Enlightenment thought; others considered this hasty and uninformed.[6] In these circumstances, the colonial structure of political power eventually came to be modelled upon the British state only in some respects; in others it developed according to a substantially different logic. It was assumed that the Permanent Settlement Act, for example, introduced by Cornwallis in 1793, would encourage the growth of a class of progressive landowners and improve agriculture, a line of argument drawn directly from Adam Smith. Yet this experiment was not extended to other parts of India. This produced a social class entirely loyal to British rule, but the economic results were disappointing. Appreciation of the 'differences' of Indian society often stopped the colonial authorities from getting too deeply involved in the 'internal' matters of the society they now controlled; the objectives of colonialism were fulfilled by keeping control over the political sphere and allowing the traditional structure of subsidiarity to continue.

In the comparative study of colonialism, one striking fact is the different manner in which local religions responded to the colonial presence. European colonialism obviously invaded ideological structures of the societies they came to control. Certainly, British creators of new structures of knowledge based their work on the support of highly skilled, and at times unbelievably arrogant, native informants.[7] Still, colonialism triggered an immense intellectual assault on the culture of traditional societies. It undermined traditional knowledge about the world, not merely in natural science, but also about how society was conceived, in particular how to determine which social practices were just or unjust. Yet the results of the European intellectual impact were extremely variable across colonial societies. In Latin America and subsequently in Africa, indigenous religious structures

[6] Within colonial ruling groups, often there was bitter conflict between missionaries and colonial officials. Officials at times found the missionary universalism and enthusiasm for conversion troublesome. Missionaries accused administrators of turning their backs on both Christian and rationalist ideals.

[7] Bayly 1996.

collapsed and were replaced by Christianity, although it is often argued that there was subtle creolization of Christian beliefs with earlier religious practices. In India, remarkably, despite very energetic Christian missionary activity, the two major religions stood their ground. Hinduism and Islam remained largely undestroyed by colonialism, partly because English colonial rule was vastly different from the brutal excesses of Spanish conquests in Latin America.

The presence of Christianity, however, caused enormous internal transformations within Indian religious life. In Hinduism, it gave rise to at least two different trends with far-reaching consequences.[8] First, by drawing Hindu intellectuals into religious and doctrinal debates on rationalist terms with Protestant missionaries, it forced Hindu doctrinal justifications to change their character, leading to attempts to harmonize religion with a rationalist picture of the world. Consequently, it was difficult to tell whether the fundamental concession to rationalism was more significant than the defence of Hindu doctrines. Hindu society changed in fundamental ways. For instance, caste practices, clearly essential to traditional Hinduism, were seen by Hindu reformers as morally repugnant and doctrinally dispensable. Attacks on caste practice, which initially came only from outside Hindu society—from missionaries or from the small section of intellectual atheists—by the turn of the century came from figures who were in various ways quite central to the Hindu discourse: Vivekananda, Gandhi, and Tagore. The most significant fact was that indigenous religion, on which the entire intellectual life of society depended, did not decline, but rather restructured itself by using the European critique. The impact of Western civilization—not its power structures, but its immense intellectual presence—was tackled with a surprising degree of intellectual sophistication and confidence. Within thirty years of the introduction of this utterly new civilization, Bengali society produced an intellectual class that had acquired sufficient mastery not merely of the foreign language, but also of the entirely unprecedented conceptual language of rationalism, to engage in an uproarious discussion about what to take and what to reject of the proposals of Western modernity. This, incidentally, shows the inapplicability to Bengal and later to India of

[8] I am most familiar with the modern history of Hinduism, but this does not imply that such changes did not happen in other faiths.

Said's unguarded assertion that Orientalism reduced colonized societies to intellectual submission and silence.[9]

In any case, there were many reasons why the introduction of Western state practices to the Indian colony could not lead to an exact duplication of Western state-formation processes. First, the conditions in which processes were introduced in India and in the West were quite different. Absolutism in Europe had introduced a form of internal sovereignty dissolving all competing claims to political authority, the like of which Indian society had never seen. Second, the colonial state itself refracted its initiatives through Orientalist conceptions of Indian society, which emphasized the fact that the environment was basically different; therefore the colonial rulers withheld certain Western practices and modified others. Finally, even in those aspects of state practices under colonialism where Western patterns were introduced—in the judicial system, for instance—something like an accent-shift took place, especially if the practices relied heavily on Indian personnel taking the functioning away from their European models.

The Peculiarity of Indian Nationalism

Interestingly, some of the intellectual and organizational techniques of modern disciplinary power were enthusiastically embraced by the new Indian elites.[10] Traditional élites regarded these techniques with a sullen hostility. Yet the new elite created through modern education started taking an interest in disciplinary techniques almost immediately. There was an interest in instilling discipline into the human body through exercise, daily routine, and school curricula. Similarly, there were efforts to bring more discipline into the family and the lives of children through a science of domesticity. There was an urge to turn everything into discourse. Western-educated intellectualism produces a written world; it seems particularly important to write the social world down, to pin every practice down on paper, to give it a reliable image, a fixity required for subsequent reflection. Reflexivity on the part of the society, its capacity for acting upon its own structures for greater and more effective use (sociological reflexivity), seems to

[9] Said 1978.
[10] Chatterjee 1997.

depend on that social world being written down and being capable of cognitive recall.

A new ontology, based on the distinction between economy, polity, and society as three separate domains that had internally specific laws, appropriate to the intrinsic nature of each sphere, was introduced by the self-limiting impulses of the colonial state, justifying its claim that it could not be responsible for everything in that vast and complex society. The state's proper domain was the sphere of the political. Slowly, emergent nationalists came to appreciate the huge enticement of this distinction, to claim and mark out a sphere from which they could exclude the colonial regime's authority by using its own arguments.[11] The colonial administration applied this ontology of distinct spheres through their distinction between political and social activity, the latter indicating those aspects of social conduct that did not affect the state and were therefore outside its legitimate province. Indians, on their part, viewed this distinction as an extension of a traditional conceptual dichotomy between an 'inside' and the 'outside',[12] and claimed that religious activity on social reform fell within the internal affairs of Hindu society. The practical consequences of the distinctions were convergent and, for a time, convenient to both sides. Orientalism—the idea that Indian society was irreducibly different from the modern West, intractable to modern incentives and pressures, indeed in some senses incapable of modernity—gradually established the intellectual preconditions of early nationalism by enabling Indians to claim a kind of social autonomy within political colonialism. Such ideas led to a series of catachreses, slowly creating a sphere of subsidiary quasi-sovereignty over society within a colonial order in which political sovereignty was still firmly lodged in the British empire.[13]

But this only created the space in which nationalism was to emerge; it did not determine the exact form that Indian nationalism would take, or, to put it more exactly, which one out of its several configurations would eventually emerge dominant. The nationalism that emerged shows that all the clashing hypotheses of imposition, dissemination,

[11] Chatterjee 1993.

[12] Tagore's famous novel *The Home and the World* (in Bengali: *Ghare Baire*) played on this distinction.

[13] Chatterjee 1993.

emulation, and differentiation have significant points to contribute to its understanding. The first stirrings of nationalism are both emulative and oppositional. The modern elite naturally asked why India had become colonized. Eventually, the explanation of colonization is traced to three complex causes. The first, the most significant but also the most elusive, was the evident superiority of Western science, the West's cognitive grasp of the world through science and rationalist thinking. This meant that they could undertake and accomplish socially necessary things with greater deliberation and efficiency. But rationalist cognitive processes in themselves do not explain political mastery over the whole world. It is explained through a set of institutional structures of collective action, mostly associated with the state and its subsidiary organizations—particularly, modern techniques of political 'discipline'. However, quite distinct from the institutions themselves, Indian writers obsessively emphasized, there was a collective spirit of nationhood that animated Western political life. It is this spirit that helped the British to act with cohesion and come through the worst military and political calamities, while Indians started bickering at the slightest pretext and lacked, to use a common phrase, a 'public spirit'. Indians must, if they wish to flourish in the modern world in competition with modern European nations, develop these three things in their society: the control of modern knowledge, the techniques of creating and working modern institutions, and a spirit of collective cohesion called nationalism.

The Paradoxical Politics of Reform

The entrenchment of British rule gave rise to a strong associationism among modernizing elites. In traditional arrangements of power, demands or requests by individuals were usually made to the royal authority, and their justice was decided on the basis of various criteria of fairness and expediency. The British colonial authority, it became clear early on, acted on different principles. First, it carried with it an ideological affirmation of 'the rule of law', although high officials of the Company often slipped conveniently closer to autocracy when parliament was not looking. Yet the trials of senior officials like Clive or Hastings showed the significance of the procedural ideology. Second, it became clear that numbers were treated with a kind of occult respect by the colonial administration, and demands or complaints were taken more seriously if they were made on behalf of communities rather than individuals. Modern educated elites thus constituted themselves into associational groups of a peculiar kind. Educated members of caste communities sought to convert them into unified pressure groups of which they could claim to be the natural leaders and representatives. Thus, British rule brought in a logic of associationism that at first sight appears close to the creation of a kind of colonial 'civil society'.

Closer examination reveals that these groups lacked one important feature of modern associationism: membership or entry was segmentary, not universal. Only Kayasthas, for instance, could become members of the Kayastha sabhas; only Brahmos could benefit from opportunities given to the Brahmo Samaj. This associationism was therefore a peculiar but not historically incomprehensible mixture of universal and particularistic principles. It was not possible to welcome all men into them, but once the criterion of membership was specified these groups were expected to embrace every possible member. Clearly, this curiously mixed logic of collective behaviour was to have enormous consequences for modern politics. From the colonial period, representative government, either the restricted colonial variety or democratic rule after Independence, would have to cope with two types of group dynamics: groups based on interests and those based on identities. This also put a rather strange spin on traditional liberal principles like equality of treatment by the state. To take only the most contentious example, it was possible to argue that equality of treatment before the colonial state could imply the state's disregard for individuals' religious affiliation, i.e. being blind to their being Hindu or Muslim. Alternatively, and plausibly, as some early advocates of Muslim power argued, it must mean treating the two communities as equal communities, and thus giving them equal importance irrespective of the numerical weight of their membership. British administrators eventually adopted policies swayed by both types of considerations, as the community-equality argument could also be translated into one for the protection of minorities. Early reforms by British administrators inclined towards a solution that accepted a part of the second argument and offered Muslims and others separate electorates, flouting liberal tenets of universalism and leading to accusations of 'divide and rule'.

Nationalism is about fashioning self-representations. There are three stages of a complex evolution of self-identification. At the first stage, there is a spontaneous identification of people as Hindus or Mohammedans, as there are no other recognizable principles of collective identity. Soon it becomes clear that these traditional collective identities are being asserted in the context of a fundamentally different modern form of governance, and this generates an incongruous relation between the universality of the institutions and the particularism of the communities. A third stage is marked by a widespread dissatisfaction against this state of affairs and the conscious creation of a nationalist ideology that posits a stark dichotomy between nationalism and 'communalism'.

The Process of Imagining the Nation

To nationalist Indians, the combination of instrumentality and emotion in the modern nation-state had always appeared to be the secret of British power, and it was essential to understand and replicate it. Yet there was a major problem with the nationalist *imaginaire* when transposed to Indian conditions. With the emergence of modern vernacular languages there was a growth of regional patriotism. Under colonialism, because of the unifying structure of the British colonial administration, sentiments of patriotism took a strange turn. Alongside regional patriotism, a pattern of bilingual communication evolved, producing a political diglossia of vernaculars and English, by means of which elites from all regional cultures could form a political coalition within the Indian National Congress. Initially, a nationalist *imaginaire* was produced by a modern elite thinly spread over the urban space across British India. By the first decade of the twentieth century, however, the attraction of nationalism was pulling large masses of petit bourgeois and peasant elements into its fold who were primarily monolingual and whose cognitive political horizons never extended much beyond their region and its relatively local excitements. The great surprise of the story of Indian nationalism is how its internal ideological struggle went in favour of a most complex and non-Western construction.

Nationalism: Replication or Improvisation?

Indian nationalism needed a form of identity and ideology that was based on inclusivist and universal unifying principles, instead of the segmentation of traditional society. Two types of scepticism were expressed against the possibility of an Indian nationalism. European observers emphasized the fact that nothing seemed to hold India's immense social diversity together except the external frame of colonial power. The history of European nationalism, which modern Indians read avidly, seemed to suggest some preconditions for the establishment of successful nation-states: particularly, homogeneous cultures based on single languages and predominant religious communities. Hence, those who thought modernity had a single, uniform logic did not expect India would be able to solve this problem of finding a sufficiently single basis for its putative political community. One of the major internal debates within Indian nationalism took place over a long time on precisely this question of India's unmanageable diversity and the difficulty it constituted for a modern nation-state.

In the twentieth century, Indian nationalists developed two powerful but entirely opposed arguments to counteract this sceptical objection. It was inevitable that there would be an increasingly strong impression that successful emulation of the Western model of the nation-state must try to replicate all the conditions of the European experience as closely as possible. In India, this idea could have only two implications. The first idea, unattractive and unacceptable to nationalists, was that India as a whole could not form a nation-state; only its various linguistic regions could. A 'replication' argument asserted instead that despite India's cultural and religious diversity, if it wanted to be a modern nation-stare it must start to acknowledge the primacy of a single culture based on a majority religion and language. As Independence drew near, this argument took clearer shape, partly encouraged by the suggestion from the early 1940s that Muslims needed a separate state of Pakistan. Not unusually, the demand for a minority state for Muslims, by implication, seemed to turn the rump of India into a Hindu state with a distinctive culture, although the claim of linguistic majority for Hindi was distinctly less plausible. Hindi was still forming into a standardized language and was fraught with internal rivalries between regions and the central conflict between a bazaar Hindustani in which the people of North India actually communicated and a highly artificial Sanskritized Hindi that Hindu chauvinists sought to fashion out of political enthusiasm. In this view, an Indian nation-state could be securely based on a single culture of Hinduism, and the usual corollary of this was that Hindi of a particularly Sanskritized variety should be given precedence over other vernaculars as India's national language.

Remarkably, most of the leading intellectuals of Indian nationalism—Gandhi, Tagore, and Nehru—rejected this argument of replication. What they offered passionately against it could be regarded as an argument of 'improvisation', but in two substantially different forms. Gandhi and Tagore advanced an idea more consistent with the first type mentioned in my introductory section, asserting that the proper functioning of modern institutions depended on their chiming with traditional social understandings: only that could make modern institutions intelligible. Also, in their view, modernity's irrational bias towards pointless novelty was to be mistrusted: institutions and social conduct ought to be changed only if rational argument showed they needed to be, not for the sake of change or in emulation of the West. Tagore defiantly declared that it was the principle of autonomy of judgement that constituted modernity, not mere imitation of European practice. Autonomy of judgement about sociopolitical institutions might lead to the considered decision that some forms of traditional institutions suited Indian social life better than importing Western forms. If such practices were retained out of choice, it would be the result of a modern decision.

Nehru offered an argument based on modern principles of the reflexive constitution of society. For Nehru, the imposition of a homogenizing Western model of the nation-state was likely to fuel apprehensions of assimilation among religious and regional minorities; the imposition of a homogenizing form of Indian nationalism was therefore likely to disrupt a nation-state instead of cementing its cultural basis. In his political writings, Nehru absorbed a typical Tagorean idea that it was a mistake, following colonial thinking, to consider India's diversity a disadvantage: a diverse economy was less prone to scarcities, break-downs, and foreign pressures; a diverse culture offered greater imaginative and intellectual resources. Despite their differences, the Gandhi–Tagore and Nehru arguments converged to offer a powerful refutation of the replication thesis that called for a homogeneous Indian nationalism.

The practical consequences of this ideological disputation were enormous. Despite the creation of Pakistan, which raised fears of a quick balkanization, Indian nationalism retained its complex form over the singular and homogenizing one. It retained its confidence in the idea that identity and patriotism were necessarily a complex and multilayered affair and that there was no way of being an Indian without first being a Tamil or Maratha or Bengali. Indian nationalism was therefore a second-order identity, but not something insubstantial, fraudulent, or artificial. Thus, three processes were involved in the making of modern political India: a reasoned attention to the historical preconditions out of which modernity has to be created, the specific sequence of processes, and in particular the idea that modernization was not a blind imitation of Western history or institutions but a self-conscious process of reflexive construction of society that should rationally assess principles from all sources and improvise institutions suitable for particular societies.

Democracy and India's Modernity

After Independence, the central question of Indian politics was the construction not of nationalism but of democracy. The idea of social reflexivity is central to the politics of democracy. Political modernity consists of two parallel movements. On one side is the sociological fact of the plasticity of social orders, based on the increasingly widespread idea that the relations within which people are obliged to live out their lives can be radically altered by collective reflexive action. This sociological tendency, which explains the frequency of revolutions and large-scale Jacobinism in modern politics,[14] runs parallel to normative principles of autonomy extended from individuals to political communities, the moral justification of democratic rule.

Democracy is obviously the incontrovertibly modern feature of India's political life. In at least three different aspects, the evolution of democracy in India has shown the general tendency of modernity towards gradual differentiation. These aspects are (1) the lack of social individuation and the resultant tendency towards democracy being more focused on political equality of groups rather than individuals; (2) an assertion of electoral power by rural groups because of the specific sequence of economic modernization; and (3) the increasing conflicts of secular state principles as the idea of secularism is subject-

[14] Eisenstadt 1996.

ed to a democratic-electoral ratification. The 'strangeness' of Indian democracy is due, in my view, to the different sequence of historical events in India.

At the time of Independence, political institutions were chosen with explicit care, even including the rationalistic, autonomist idea that a people 'choose' and 'give to themselves' their constitution.[15] This involved a neglect of that other, more plausible idea that most people lived under political regimes out of habitual and historical compulsions. The idea of a deliberative adoption of structures of legitimate power was given a theatrical realization in the proceedings of the Constituent Assembly. In individuals like Ambedkar[16]—the author of many of the technical solutions in India's constitution—and Nehru, the Constituent Assembly had a rare combination of political experience, intellectual skills, and openness to international comparisons to provide at times startlingly innovative solutions to problems of political construction. But it seems in retrospect that Nehru and Ambedkar were wrong to disregard tradition entirely, taking the typical Enlightenment view of treating those ideas and practices as 'erroneous'. They also wrongly believed that to rescue people from tradition—their intellectual and practical habitus—all that was needed was simply to present a modern option; peoples' inherent rationality would do the rest.

I have argued elsewhere that this is based on the common but mistaken belief that traditions endured for long historical spans by simple obstinacy in the face of historical challenge, and, confronted with the light of reason, they would disappear. This ignored an equally plausible view that traditions were complex mechanisms that survived for long periods precisely because they could change insidiously.[17] In

[15] Preamble to the Constitution of India.

[16] B.R. Ambedkar, one of the most interesting figures of the nationalist movement in its last phase, came from an untouchable caste, was Western-educated, became a prominent lawyer, and eventually played a pre-eminent role in the drafting of India's constitution.

[17] Christianity survived for two millennia precisely because it changed its form and content quite radically: from early Christianity to its adoption by Rome; the adaptation after the discovery of Greek classical texts, especially Aristotle; Protestantism; and adaptation to a rationalist culture in modern times. My suggestion is, in the case of traditions, that this is the rule, not the exception.

another view, traditions, when faced with the challenge of entirely new structures like industrialism or electoral democracy, might seek to adapt to these, altering both the internal operation of traditional structures like caste or religious community and the elective institutions themselves. Actual political experience in India followed the more complex trajectories of the second type rather than the clear-cut oppositions of the first. Thus, instead of dying obediently with the introduction of elective mechanisms, caste groups simply adapted to new demands, turning caste itself into the basis of a search for majorities. Initially, the constitution produced an enormous innovation by affording the former untouchable castes a legal status as Scheduled Castes and making them beneficiaries of some legal advantages of reverse discrimination. Upper-caste groups, which were in control of the modern professions and understood the electoral significance of social solidarity, were unified by their modern loyalties and clearer perception of common interest. By the 1970s the 'intermediate castes'—those in between these two strata—recognized that by carrying on the traditional segmentary logic of the caste system they were proving incapable of exercising suitable leverage on the electoral system. Their response was to weld their parallel-status caste groups into vast electoral coalitions across the whole of North India—altering the nature of elective democracy and its operative logic unrecognizably.

During Nehru's time Indian democratic politics resembled politics as it was practised in the West, where the fundamental political identifications were on either class or ideological lines (which were internally connected). But, contrary to all historical scripts, as democratic awareness spread to the lower strata of society and formerly excluded groups began to voice their expectations, the outcomes began to grow 'strange'. Since these groups interpreted their disadvantage and indignity in caste terms, social antagonism and competition for state benefits expressed themselves increasingly in the form of intense caste rivalries. The dominance of caste politics in India is thus a direct result of modern politics, not a throwback to traditional behaviour. It appears strangely disorienting, as this kind of caste action is impossible to classify as either traditional or modern, leading to dark murmurings about the inexplicability of Indian history.

However, it is neither inexplicable nor indeed very surprising to accept that modernity is historically diversifying. Democratic institutions arrived in Western societies in their full form only at the start of the twentieth century, long after the corrosive effects of individualism on community loyalties had done their work. Democratic politics had to contend quite often in the classical cases of European democracy with the collective demands of various classes, particularly the early proletariat, but the logic of numbers on which democracy operates did not get tangled with a reassertion of communal groups. The logic of modern structures of electoral democracy does not automatically erase traditional forms of conduct, but manages to subsume them, or subordinate them to its own operations—changing them and changing its own character in the process. In fact, this is accompanied by a surprising fact. Precisely because the new elites who emerge into political power are quite often without the education that the colonial elite enjoyed, their understanding of the precedents of European modernity is tenuous, if not entirely absent. As they try to improvise and act reflexively on these institutions, their character is likely to change even further in uncharted and unexpected ways. They do not have the imposing script of European history before them when they are making their own. As a consequence, in trying to understand the current complexities and future prospects of Indian democracy, looking towards European precedents is not enough.[18] Instead, it is necessary to understand the historical logic internal to this process.

Such changes forcing the structure and tendencies of modern institutions in an unprecedented direction have not occurred only in politics. Briefly, I will point to two other fields with similar trends. Recent work on political economy has suggested that the trajectory of agrarian power in the context of Indian democracy is vastly different from the 'classic' European cases. In European modernity, by the time democratic voting was established, the process of industrialization had shrunk the agricultural sector into a secondary force. This resulted in two significant political effects in the West. First, since the rural interests were numerically and strategically weak, their impact on democratic politics was not dominant. The industrial proletariat and the professional middle classes wielded much greater electoral power and

[18] This does not at all mean falling over into indigenism. Indigenous traditions in India were utterly unfamiliar with democracy and cannot offer productive conceptual tools without much creative elaboration. Some parts of Western theory, evident in authors like Alexis de Tocqueville, remain particularly relevant in understanding the complexities of Indian democracy.

consequently had the capacity to dominate the political agenda. In purely economic terms, this difference in size made it possible for European economies to subsidize the agrarian sector, since this involved a resource transfer from a dominant sector to a smaller one. In India, by contrast, electoral democracy has arrived at a time when the agricultural sector is statistically, and in terms of its voting weight, enormous. Therefore, agrarian interests have the capacity to force state policies to concede their demands. Yet in purely economic terms the vastness of the agricultural sector makes it difficult for the state to force other sectors of the economy to subsidize the rural sector.[19] Democratic politics thus creates a huge contradiction in state policy towards the economy: sectoral constraints make it impossible for the state, or whichever party is in office, to ignore demands for agricultural subsidy; yet the size of the agricultural sector in comparison to others makes them increasingly difficult to sustain. Trying to learn from actual policies followed by Western democracies in these respects is unlikely to produce serious results, since the structure of the problem is historically unprecedented and requires new kinds of solutions.

A second case can be found in the politics of secularism. It has been plausibly argued that secular institutions in India have experienced increasing difficulty because they function in a society that is not secularized.[20] State secularism, it is argued, was an ideal intelligible only to the modernist elite, and it was because of the complete dominance of Congress modernists during constitution-making that secular principles were introduced without challenge.[21] Yet on this point too, careful observation shows interesting historical complexities. Undoubtedly, modernist authors of the constitution like Nehru and Ambedkar wished to establish institutional forms closely modelled on Western liberal democracies. But since they were practical politicians, they decided to acknowledge two types of constraints arising out of initial circumstances, tempering their extreme constructivism.[22] The constraints emerged from the immense uncertainty faced by Muslims who decided to remain in India after the Partition riots and the need

[19] Varshney 1994.
[20] Madan 1991.
[21] See Bhargava 1998 for detailed arguments on various sides.
[22] Eisenstadt 1996.

to reassure them that the constitution would protect their cultural identity. This conjunctural requirement to reassure Muslim minorities forced the framers of the constitution to improvise and to institute rights that individuals could enjoy only by virtue of their membership in communities.

In recent years, some liberal political theorists have sought to make room for cultural rights of communities within general liberal principles, but in the late 1940s this was a considerable innovation. I wish to make the historical-sociological case that the assertion of the distinctively modern right to form political institutions led the framers of the Indian constitution to produce a legal system that diverged significantly from standard Western liberal-individualist precedents. The primary reason for this again seems to be the differential historical sequence. In the West, institutions of the secular state were devised by a collective process of social thinking and institutional experimentation in response to the religious wars of the sixteenth and seventeenth centuries, and these arrangements for religious tolerance were unquestionably established long before democratic government arose in the twentieth century. In addition, by this time, the secularization of social conduct had made the question of religion and politics a rather minor affair for most Western states. In India, a secular state and democratic politics were introduced at the same time through a single constitutional settlement. As in democratic polities, eventually all significant questions of social life are either directly or by default ratified by the democratic reflexive process; the question of the secular state and its precise character thus becomes inevitably subjected to democratic processes. This opens up the intriguing possibility of a potential conflict between principles of secularism and a strongly majoritarian interpretation of democratic politics.

Conclusion

If we reject both a purely intellectualist teleological construction of modernity and a purely functionalist model and consider it—more realistically, in my view—as internally plural, this logic of plurality should be seen as intrinsic to the structure of modern civilization rather than as an exception to the historical rule. I would like to suggest that this is precisely what we find in the history of European modernity:

in the expanding panorama of modern transformations, the elements of industrialization, *étatisation*, individuation, and secularization are invariably present as constituent processes leading to a modern society. But their mutual articulation and combined effects, and, consequently, the structure of social life they produce through their combination, is vastly different between European societies. As European societies come under the deepening influence of these pressures, the political life of England–France, of Germany–Italy, and of Russia–Eastern Europe gets transformed, but in significantly different ways. What creates the misleading sense of similarity about political forms is a strange amnesia about imperial conflicts and wars. At the turn of the century, a comparison of European nations would have presented a vast spectacle of variation in the invention of modern life, from spheres of culture like painting and poetry to spheres of political experience. Indeed, some of the great conflicts of modern times happened precisely because modern politics gave rise to democratic and totalitarian forms of organizing the capacities of the state, and these opposing political forms came to a direct confrontation. It is difficult to accept that liberal democracy came to Germany by some kind of delayed spontaneous combustion in 1945 caused by underlying functional causes rather than by the simpler external fact of the war. Thus, the logic of modernity shows a diversifying and pluralizing tendency in Europe itself. How can its extension to different cultures and historical circumstances produce obediently uniform historical results?

References

Bayly, C.A. 1996. *Empire and Information*. Cambridge: Cambridge University Press.

Beck, U. 1992. *The Risk Society*. London: Sage Publications.

———, A. Giddens, and S. Lash. 1994 *Reflexive Modernisation*. Cambridge: Polity Press,.

Bhargava, Rajeev. Ed. 1998. *Secularism and Its Critics*. Delhi: Oxford University Press.

Chatterjee, Partha. 1993. *The Nation and Its Fragments*. Princeton: Princeton University Press.

———. Ed. 1997. *Texts of Power*. Minneapolis: Minnesota University Press.

Eisenstadt, S.N. 1996. The Jacobin Component in Fundamentalist Movement. *Contentions*, Spring, no. 5.

Foucault, M. 1974. *The Order of Things*. London: Tavistock.

———. 1979. *Discipline and Punish*. Harmondsworth: Penguin Books.

Kaviraj, S. 1994. Dilemmas of Democratic Development in India. In Leftwich 1994 (*vide infra*).

———. 1996. Religion and Identity in India. *Ethnic and Racial Studies*, vol. 20, no. 2, pp. 325–44.

Leftwich, Adrian. Ed. 1994. *Democracy and Development*. Cambridge: Polity Press.

Madan, T.N. Ed. 1991. *Sociology of Religion*. Delhi: Oxford University Press.

Said, E. 1978. *Orientalism*. London: Routledge.

Varshney, Ashutosh. 1994. *Democracy and the Countryside*. New York: Cambridge University Press.

2

On the Enchantment of the State: Indian Thought on the Role of the State in the Narrative of Modernity

One of the fundamental ideational changes brought by modernity into Indian intellectual culture was the transformation of the idea of the state. From an institution that was traditionally seen as a necessarily limited and distinctly unpleasant part of the basic furniture of any society, the idea of the state has been transformed into a central moral force, producing an immense enchantment in India's intellectual life. Indeed, in the Indian context, as distinct from the European one, it has been the primary source of modernity.[1] This essay seeks to present an absurdly short history of the curious adventures of

This essay was originally presented at a seminar on the state at Columbia University, organised by the Centre for the Study of Political Thought (CSPT) in April 2005. It was first published in the *European Journal of Sociology*, 2005, vol. 46, pp. 263–96. I am grateful to David Armitage and David Johnston who organized the conference and to those who contributed to the discussion.

[1] In the European context, Marxist historians would view the role of economic transformations towards capitalism as a primary process, bearing a causal influence on changes in the state. Others may disagree with the Marxist ascription of a causal role exclusively to the economy, but it is generally acknowledged that the story of European modernity is driven by economic as well as political forces. I wish to suggest that in India the primary causal impulses towards modernity came mainly from the state and political transformations around its control. Significant economic changes were conditional on changes in the structure of political power. In other words, it is the changes in the structure of the state that explain changes in the economy, not the other way

this idea. It also seeks to explain why, despite the global dominance of ideas of liberalization, and a reduction of the state's interference in social and economic life, this enchantment is still undiminished in India.

I look at the movement of the idea of the state in the broadest sense, and my study includes very different forms of 'thinking'—from the highly self-conscious thinking of theorists to the far more practical, sketchy, but powerful conceptions that animate ordinary actions in the political world—the ideas carried in the minds of ordinary politicians, voters, bureaucrats, dissenters. Although these ideas do not possess the form of political theory, they cannot be neglected by political theory. In fact, the task of political theory must be to make sense of these ideas, and give them more consistent and definite shape so that they become thinkable in a theoretical fashion. In understanding the very different trajectories of the imaginary of the state in India and Europe, it is useful to look contextually at these ideas. I think the Skinnerian injunction about a strict contextualist reading of ideas holds not merely when we are studying the theoretical work of individual theorists and the meanings of their atomic statements, but also when we are trying to pursue a much more elusive beast: what a ragged and complex collectivity like 'political Indians' (with all the necessary ambiguity of that phrase) 'think' of an entity called the state. The boundaries and content of the idea of the state are likely to vary between intellectuals and common people, and also between literate and illiterate actors in the political world, between elites and underprivileged populations. All this can be gathered together into something like a 'political imaginary' or a state imaginary. So, this essay is not only about thinking in the form of political theory in its ordinarily recognizable form, but also about thinking in many other unorthodox shapes and forms, ordinary people's powerful but inchoate expectations, moral understandings, and 'habits of the heart'.[2]

---

round. That does not mean, however, that once the structures of a capitalist economy are established in various parts of the productive system, they do not exert important and independent causal influence.

[2] Charles Taylor (2004) has used the concept of an imaginary, following the earlier discussions in Castoriadis 1987. 'Habits of the heart' of course is Tocqueville's wonderfully evocative and capacious phrase.

The first part in what follows below offers an elementary distinction, necessary for my argument, between pre-modern and modern conceptions of the 'state'.[3] It gives two separate examples of pre-modern conceptions: an image of the state from Hindu antiquity, and an Islamic-Aristotelian one associated with the Mughal empire. It suggests, against common understanding, fundamental similarities between the two. It then describes how the peculiarity of British rule—particularly its long and staggered inception—introduced the *modern* idea of the state, how Indians responded to it, and began to conceive it as central to the social organization of modernity. It then shows how through almost a century (from the 1860s to the 1950s) two broad strands of thinking about the nature of modern power struggled for imaginative dominance.[4] One produced a serious, searching critique of the European version of the modern state and warned against its unmodified installation in India on the grounds that, in its view, would impede a realization of the good life.[5] The other strand, which eventually triumphed, advocated a comprehensive reliance on the modern state—based precisely on the European model—for the remaking of Indian society according to just and democratic principles, and viewed that precisely as the particular form of the 'good life' which modernity had rendered possible. For reasons of space, I shall disregard finer differences and inflections of emphasis. Instead I shall focus on four influential thinkers who presented fundamental ideas that have gone into the making of Indian intellectual discourse on the fascinating fate of the modern state. It must be noted that any judgement about victory and

[3] I readily acknowledge the frailties of the notion of a 'pre-modern' state, because there was more than one form of the state before the coming of modernity. The use of this distinction does not deny the diversity of historical forms, but is strictly limited to this kind of discussion where the contrast is important—not the internal variations within the 'traditional' side of the contrast.

[4] This is of course a considerable oversimplification: there were major differences of principles and inflection amongst theorists who belonged to these two strands. But these are disregarded here in the interests of a broader intellectual narrative.

[5] I have chosen Bhudev Mukhopadhyay (1827–94) and M.K. Gandhi (1869–1948) as the two examples of this strand—a point of departure and a point of arrival, to echo Partha Chatterjee's terms. See Chatterjee 1989.

defeat in the political imagination is partly artificial. While there is no doubt that the state-centred view gradually 'won', these theories offered dense, intricate, considerably detailed, and subtle ideas on thinking about the modern state, and many of these 'elements' are in constant circulation. They provide, in a certain sense, the underlying repertoire—of concepts and arguments—by which Indians have thought about the state for nearly two centuries. This story should also illustrate a separate and more general argument in which I am interested: the need for bending middle-level principles of social/political theory away from their familiar architecture historically centred on Western history; bending the whole enterprise of theory—with its major methodological principles, theoretical hypotheses, large taxonomies, central concepts, and minute patterns of detailed analytical inquiry—away towards other historical formations (not cultures),[6] in a fundamental diversification of political theory.[7]

I: Subsidiarity/Sovereignty

Two Conceptions of the State

First, although we generally tend to speak about the pre-modern and the modern state, this way of speaking has a major conceptual shortcoming: it implicitly contains an unavoidable suggestion that we are talking about two historically different versions of the same object, though this precisely is to be seen as a *problem.* In fact we are talking about two very different types of organization of political authority. However, for other theoretical reasons it is plausible to house them inside a capacious general category. If the state designates *any* coherent, distinct organization of power such that it identifies a group of people and an institutional structure that lays down the rules which members of a society must follow, it can perform the conceptual function of that

[6] This is an important difference: I do not wish to offer a culturally relativist position. However, I think what is true and compelling in cultural relativist arguments is derived from the historical peculiarities of cultural formations. Cultural differences are central to understanding politics, but they are produced historically, they are not essential differences which defy standard forms of historical explanation.

[7] I have developed this argument elsewhere: see Kaviraj 2005.

generic category. It would be clear however that this definition is much wider than the definition we conventionally draw from Max Weber because it omits two crucial Weberian features: it makes no reference to the anonymity or impersonality of the powers of the state; nor does it demand that the state should exercise a monopoly on the legitimate uses of violence.[8] The Weberian idea is in any case undeniably local in historical terms, as the feudal order in Europe would not fit his more stringent definition. Weber's definition of the state, which forms such a central, self-evident basis of modern social science, is in fact the definition of a modern European conception of the state. To try to understand the precise nature of political authority in other contexts of time and space thus involves suspending reflex uses of that definition.

States of Subsidiarity/Subsumption: The Idea of the Pre-Modern Indian State— The Manusmrti[9]

Ancient Hindu philosophy produced two styles of reflection on the nature of royal power.[10] Some theoretical treatises contained detailed dogmatic compendia of the principles governing royal conduct.[11]

[8] Weber 1978 [1925]; for an excellent account of how this idea developed historically, see Skinner 1988.

[9] One of the most celebrated texts of social rules in the Hindu tradition is the compendium *Manusmrti*, attributed to a legendary sage Manu. It provides the most detailed description of rules to be observed in the Hindu life-cycle, with two chapters 7 and 8 dealing with *raja-dharma*—the rules to be observed by rulers. See Doniger and Smith 1991.

[10] There can be legitimate questions about the ways by which we can really understand how ordinary Indians think about and practically orient themselves towards the state. Clearly, the reading of theoretical texts is one particular way of capturing only one particular form of thinking: this approach certainly privileges a highly intellectual, and thus brahminical, form of thinking. How ordinary Indians think about the state cannot be simply deduced from textual arguments, especially from the highly esoteric Sanskrit canon. Secondly, the Sanskrit canon itself is internally diverse, with some differences of emphasis between major canonical texts.

[11] Three of the most famous of these were, first, the two chapters dealing with royal power in the *Manusmrti*, the great dogmatic digest of rule of Hindu

Reflective discussions on the nature of royal power were generated by a perpetual interweaving of two kinds of thinking. One strand contained in *theoretical* texts—like the *Manusmrti* and the *Arthasastra*—setting out high principles, and the other suggested by the *narrative* complications offered to those principles by the epic and puranic narratives.[12] The *Manusmrti*, in its seventh and eighth chapters, provides detailed dogmatics about the norms surrounding the power of the ruler. Although Manu conceives of only a single royal form of state power, and does not refer to the republican traditions of Hindu and Buddhist antiquity, his disputation on the character of state power advances some subtle suggestions. In *sloka* 3 of chapter 7, Manu begins with a demonstration of the necessity of political authority which resembles an elementary Hobbesian picture: 'Since in a condition of anarchy, ordinary human beings are terrified by the powerful, for the preservation/security of all people, the Creator has created kingship.'[13] He represents social order: even though the king is a child, he should be treated like a god, that is, as an agent different from ordinary human beings.[14] The central move in Manu's theory of kingship is made, in my view, in this *sloka*:

> In the interest of the king / for the good of the king, God first created *danda* [an abstract conception of 'order'] in his own image, for the preservation of all beings. *(Manusmrti*, chapter 7, *sloka* 14)

---

social life which detailed the rules that should govern the conduct of both ordinary members of a principality and of the ruler; second, the *Arthasastra*, the treatise composed according to legend by Chanakya, the shrewd counsellor to the first Mauryan emperor Chandragupta who defeated Alexander's successor Seleucus and established a Hindu empire. The empire was inherited and morally transformed by Asoka, Chandragupta's grandson, who converted to Buddhism. Third, the almost entirely self-standing disquisition on royal power given by the great elder statesman Bhishma on his bed of arrows, before his death, to the new king after the great battle in the late canto of the *Mahabharata*.

[12] In the Hindu tradition, scholars were exhorted to read the theoretical texts along with the epic narratives because they contained exercises on application of the principles.

[13] *Manusmrti*, ch. 7, *sloka* 3, Doniger and Smith 1991.

[14] *Manusmrti*, ch. 7, *sloka* 8, ibid.

This 'law' (or order) which combines the attributes of both a divine and a natural conception, is central to Manu's theory of kingship. By distinguishing between 'the law' (*danda*) and a fallible human agent (the king), Manu is able to construct a theoretical structure in which the king does not enjoy unconditionally absolute power over the lives of his subjects. It is absolute in the sense that there is no other human authority which can contest it, but it is not absolute in a more fundamental sense as there exists a moral framework to which it is, in turn, subordinate. The king's power is simply the translation into the human scale of 'the law', the logic of a divinely given natural and social order. The *Manusmrti* makes it entirely clear that the locus of sovereignty is in the *danda*, not in the person of the king or his adventitious intentions:

> In essence, it is the law [*danda*] that is the king, the person with authority, the person who keeps the order of the realm, and provides leadership to it. (*Manusmrti*, chapter 7, *sloka* 17)

Entirely consistent with this theory is the corollary that if a king goes against the rules of this abstract and super-personal order, he is 'destroyed by the order itself' (*dandenaiva nihanyate*).[15] This *danda* is truly 'the source of immense power' (*sumahattejah*), and is impossible to control and use by those 'rulers who have not learnt to govern their own selves' (*durdharasakrtatmabhih*).[16] The fundamental distinction between the king as the human agent and the law as the superhuman abstract order leads to a theory of restrained rulership and a conception of fairness of treatment towards different types of subjects. Early Hindu reflections on the state produced a theory which, while recognizing the requirement of unrestricted royal authority, sought to impose restrictions upon it by positing an order that was morally transcendent—an order to which it was both subject and in complex ways eventually responsible.

Two aspects of this brahminical theory are significant for a long-term historical understanding of conceptions of the state. The first is simply an implication that follows from the last observation. A central feature of Hindu society is the curious, complex interrelation among the

[15] *Manusmrti*, ch. 7, *sloka* 27, ibid.

[16] For the relevant passages, see ibid.: 129–31.

upper castes of the *varna* order of antiquity. The order of the ancient varnas is based, as is well known, on a division between the great goods of human life: pure social prestige associated with knowledge; political power vested in royal authority; and wealth produced by commerce. Interestingly, the social order of the varnas separates these great goods of human life radically by making them the legitimate province of the life activity of specific and separate castes (varnas). By radically separating them, the varna structure also brings into play a subtle but persistent logic of coalitional interdependence between these groups, making them interdependent on each others' assets. The dominance of a complex caste-based social order can be achieved, this theory clearly implies, not by the exclusive use of any of these assets—of prestige, power, or wealth—but by their combination: only a combination of these assets and their social possessors could be sufficient for social dominance. Yet, curiously, even these upper castes live according to general rules of hierarchy, and the Brahmins retained their ritual superiority over the two other upper castes (the Kshatriyas and the Vaishyas) primarily because they are regarded as the human representatives of this overarching transcendental order.[17] In a certain sense, of course, a well-ordered society is ruled by abstract principles, but these principles need constant reinterpretation in the face of historical change and complexity of circumstance; the Brahmins are the repositories of this essential form of social knowledge.

This might serve to explain certain peculiar rhetorical characteristics of the *Manusmrti*. Traditionally, nationalists illegitimately assimilated Indian forms of writing to European ones, often suggesting that texts like the *Manusmrti, Arthasastra*, and the Santiparva of the *Mahabharata* were similar to European literature in relation to advice given to princes. Closer attention to the technical rhetorics of address, the manner of writing, and even the use of the grammatical forms of the imperative reveals a significant difference. The *Manusmrti* is written in an imperative mood, a mood of command; it is not friendly, avuncular

[17] Louis Dumont's celebrated but contested reading of the caste system, *Homo Hierarchicus*, makes this point by insisting that there is a deep connection between social hierarchy, or more strictly the claim to social precedence, and a logic of 'encompassing'. The general order that the Brahmins represent is on this view higher than the political order that the ruler sustains, because its abstract moral principles encompass the rules of mundane political authority.

advice from a wise, intelligent, widely experienced counsellor. There is correspondingly very little use of concrete historical examples, as these are not items of advice but rules created by a transcendent authority—accessible, because of their cognitive specialization, only to the thin stratum of the Brahmin intelligentsia—to be followed, without hesitation or defiance, by wielders of political authority. The *Smrti* is written in the grand, unanswerable tone of a divine decree simply recorded by its human amenuensis. The central idea of this form of political theory is that social order is not subordinate to the king's legislative function; rather, he is subordinate to the social order.

Another central idea in the *Manusmrti*, entirely consistent with this line of reasoning, is the relation between the political ruler and the social practices of the caste order. The ruler's power is executive or administrative; it cannot make fundamental rules of social conduct or change them. The rules of the caste order as a system of social relations are thus impervious to the constant fluctuations of royal power. The constant ebb and flow of power from dynasties or kingdoms or individual rulers constitutes a stratum of events that occur at the insignificant surface of deep social life, affecting the lives of a very small number of individuals who are born, by their caste fate, to endure the impermanence and aggravations of a life of political power. Narrative traditions of the Hindu epics—the *Ramayana* and the *Mahabharata*—merely accentuate this sense of the excessive and exorbitant mortality of political power, of the extraordinarily volatile existence of rulership, and emphasize the extraordinary gifts required of individuals who have the miraculous moral skills for making such lives fulfilling. The two primary features of the brahminical theory of rulership therefore restrained the power of the state by subjecting it to a transcendent divine order, and divesting the state of all legislative authority over society. This seems to me to explain an unusual feature of Indian history: the general absence of political rebellions against political rulers similar to the slave or peasant rebellions of ancient or medieval Europe. By contrast, the major upheavals of Indian social history were directed against this supposedly transcendent order and its primary intellectual custodians and mediators: the brahminical intelligentsia. Indian society saw a succession of social reform movements directed against the classical brahminical social order, starting with Buddhism and Jainism in ancient times, down to bhakti movements in the middle period which responded to the political and religious challenge of Islam.

The Islamic State in India

As religious systems, Islam and Hinduism contained antithetical principles in many respects, for example in relation to idolatry and the nature of God. However, in terms of the relation between the power of political rulers and what I have called the 'social constitution', they obeyed surprisingly similar rules. Islam was a religion of the book, unlike Hinduism, and its social constitution, it could be argued, was far more explicitly laid down in the Koran and Hadith in contrast to the messy diversity of sectarian texts within Hindu society. Yet, in response to the significant question of whether the temporary possessor of political power could alter the fundamental tenets of the social constitution, Islam suggested a remarkably similar answer. A plausible functionalist suggestion could be that in traditional agrarian societies political power was so fragile and volatile that the necessary social stability could not be maintained if legislative power of a serious kind was given to the political ruler. To impart stability to norms of social life and save them from arbitrary rule, most religions in agrarian societies probably followed a similar logic of ascribing the power of the legislative constitution of society to divine authority, with a crucial mediating role played by religious intellectuals—the very similar function performed by Brahmins in Hinduism and the ulema in Islam. After the eleventh century, most of the territory of northern India was politically subordinated to Islamic dynasties; yet, strangely, this stable Islamic empire made little effort at systematic conversion of the Hindu society over which it exercised uncontested political dominion. Recent historical scholarship has provided some intellectual clarification for this extraordinary behaviour on the part of Islamic empires in South Asia (Alam 2004). The Mughals, the most powerful of the Islamic dynasties in South Asia, followed a theory of rule drawn from a tradition of Persianate Islam which developed under entirely exceptional circumstances in the Khorasan region. Unlike the rest of the Islamic world, in Khorasan a highly developed Islamic society had to submit to the conquest of non-Islamic rulers. Using a reading of Aristotle, Islamic intellectuals claimed that the responsibility of the ruler, irrespective of his own personal faith, was to provide the conditions that would allow his subjects to flourish. The task of the ruler was not just to ensure that his subjects were able 'to live', but 'to live in a way fit for human beings'. Living as human beings—not just *zoe* but *bios*—required conditions in which subjects could use their intellectual and spiritual capacities. On the basis of this interesting derivation from Aristotle, they were able to assert that the task of the non-Islamic ruler was to preserve the religious practice of his Islamic subjects. By a generous application of this principle to its own non-Muslim subjects, the Mughal dynasty extended a *rule* of tolerance to the surrounding Hindu society. From our angle, what is significant is that Islamic political *rulers* implicitly accepted limitations on political authority in relation to the *social* constitution, which were parallel to those of Hindu rulers. In terms of the historical long term, the entry of Islam into Indian society triggered highly significant changes in many other fields of social life, but not in the structure of its political order.

The Islamic state saw itself as limited and socially distant as the Hindu state. Crucially, because of this, neither the Hindu nor the Islamic state employed a conception of what domination entailed that was strictly similar to modern European notions of sovereignty. In terms of their external relations with other kingdoms or empires, these states were certainly 'sovereign' over their territories; but we cannot simply assume that in their internal relation with their subjects these states exercised the familiar rights of sovereignty. It is essential to understand the difference between actual weakness of a state and its marginality in principle. The relative autonomy of the social constitution from the state did not arise because the state was weak, and would have invaded social rules if it could muster the necessary strength. Rather, it accepted a marginality that was a consequence of its own normative principles. The marginality of the pre-modern state was a social fact precisely because it followed from a moral principle which guided the relation between rulers and subjects.

II: States of Sovereignty: Colonialism and the Early Modern State

In recent years the history of India from the sixteenth century has become a field of astonishingly fertile contestation, with strikingly revisionist suggestions on both historical and conceptual questions. Historians working on vernacular textual sources have suggested an autochthonous process of 'early modernity' which was partly accelerated and partly negated by the arrival of colonialism, which introduced institutional forms from modern Europe (Pollock 2003, 2006). According to a new strand of historiography, there was a demonstrable impulse of indigenous modernity from the sixteenth century onwards which was defeated and channelled in different directions by the triumph of British power in the mid-eighteenth century.

British colonial power entered India in a peculiar fashion. This has made it difficult to recover it with historical accuracy, because the immensely powerful narratives of British imperial histories and Indian nationalism both tend to occlude its complex and unusual character. Both imperial histories and nationalist narratives saw it as a cataclysmic struggle between two societies—their normative principles and their collective institutions—though the actual historical process was far more limited, uneven, and messy. The establishment of colonial domination was not a result of a comprehensive conflict between these two societies, though its eventual consequences were certainly far-reaching. British power did not enter Indian society as a conquering colonial power: in fact secrecy, stealth, and imperceptibility were the conditions of its conquest. The British were eventually able to conquer India precisely because they did not conquer it all at once, and the entire process did not look, at least initially, like a conventional imperial conquest. Similarly, nationalist torment about the loss of sovereignty to a distant and alien power was also based on a misdescription. The British did not conquer an India which existed before their conquest; rather, they conquered a series of independent kingdoms that became political India during, and in part as a response to, their dominion. Schematically, all states before the coming of colonial modernity in India answered the description of a *state of subsumption / subsidiarity*: they dominated society as a group of rulers distinct from the society below them, untied to their subjects by any strong common emotive or institutional bond; correspondingly, their ability to affect society's basic structure of the organization of everyday life was seriously restricted.[18]

The idea of the modern state in the West was first of all the object of a long tradition of theoretical reflection. In contrast, in India, there

[18] This might appear similar to the distinction in Foucault's work between a state of sovereignty and of governmentality; but that distinction was quite specific to a particular period of European history, and should not be casually imported into the Indian case.

was a disconnection between the earlier theory and the nature of the modern state.[19] In Europe, the rise of the modern state occurred within an intellectual context of major theoretical interventions (by Hobbes and Locke, for instance) which emphasized both the necessity of the modern state and expressed suspicion of its overexpansion into areas of 'civil society'.[20] Western political theorists drew upon a long tradition from Greek and Roman antiquity of reflecting philosophically on questions of the state, the nature of political obligation, the idea of the *res publica,* and the more recent traditions of Italian republican political thought. By contrast, when the modern state arrived in India, despite the considerable sophistication of its intellectual life, Indian society could not draw upon an existing body of conceptual and theoretical resources to make sense of, describe, and evaluate the new institutional and practical forms of political power.

From the point of view of comparative history, the rise of the institutions of modern European states was also marked by the emergence of strands of thought and behaviour deeply mistrustful of this monstrously powerful new institution of the absolutist state which, for the first time, entirely subdued all other centres of competing authority. As one particular line of political theory associated with Bodin and Hobbes pressed for a prudential and moral recognition of its authority, there were parallel intellectual lines of reasoning which suggested that restraints should be placed on its potentially destructive powers—for instance, Locke and Montesquieu in vastly different but equally influential ways (Taylor 1990). Additionally, in the emerging capitalist social form, powerful social classes like the emerging bourgeoisie deeply mistrusted the absolutist state and its potentially predatory instincts. Guizot's elegant thesis that European modernity was made possible because in its long history none of the three principles—royal, aristocratic, and popular—was ever completely destroyed, and each balanced the other, in a sense reflected this historical reality.[21] Crucially, Indian society had never seen a state form which remotely resembled

[19] For the state of traditional political theory immediately before the arrival of the modern colonial state—in the compendia of the *dharmasastras* in the seventeenth century, see Pollock 2006.

[20] The second line of reasoning is distinctive of Locke's theory.

[21] Guizot 1997.

the unprecedented powers of the modern state: its intellectual culture, therefore, did not feel an urgent need to either define and understand the powers of the modern state, or to produce a strong argument that urged that people treat this new institution with caution.

In fact, the study of the peculiar process by which the colonial state emerged illustrates an important theoretical fact: the various functions which are systematically bundled together in the modern state were not institutionally conjoined in earlier times in a necessarily singular structure. British power entered into Indian society almost unnoticed, when the East India Company became one of the major players in a situation of political uncertainty and flux. As the Company established its hold over specific levels of the economy and administration of various regions of India, it introduced, in segments, and as its requirements demanded, various military and administrative functions to its indescribable collection of diverse activities. Its power was initially based, on the one hand, on a legal permission to trade granted by the Mughal authority which was already normatively fading and politically ineffective, and on the other by its military capacity to protect its own territorial and commercial establishments. As its territory expanded, and as it obtained further permission to collect revenue on behalf of the empire, it had to bring in accounting practices, which then led to greater cultural contact with the native population and cautious cultural moves to introduce the natives to modern education. Eventually, over a period of about seventy years, these new ruling practices came together to form what became the recognizable figure of a colonial state.

As it established itself on Indian soil, the colonial authority continued to display the distinctive outward insignia of a state of subsumption. First, initially, the functions it partly inherited and partly usurped were indeed those of a subsumption state. Second, in its early stages, the Company was anxious not to produce an exaggerated image of its own control—for fear of triggering a rebellion. Third, those who ran the Company administration and those who exercised increasingly substantial supervision over its expanding operations, on behalf of the British government, followed what they considered Roman precedents, before the British empire found its own true principles and a suitable rhetoric to accompany them. Finally, there was a strong current of opinion in English political thinking, represented by Burke, that was deeply mistrustful of its actions in India and feared that its lawless conduct in the colony would slowly invade the rules of metropolitan governance.

Eventually, when British power was consolidated, the state that emerged was something of an intermediate form, a hybrid between an empire state of the older type and a sovereign state in the European pattern. Some of its features came to demonstrate distinct marks of the relation of sovereignty that binds subjects to their sovereign state authority; however, its colonial character prevented it from developing other aspects of a state of sovereignty or its evolution into what Foucault has called 'governmentality'. The relation of sovereignty characteristically marked the relation between the state and its nation. As modern research in nationalism has demonstrated, it was the state that established fixed territories, introduced new cultural practices, and 'produced' their nations—contrary to the earlier view that it was pre-existent nations which demanded and eventually obtained their states.[22] The Italian and German cases, where something like the conventional narrative was credible, were in fact the exceptions and not the rule.

It was soon evident that the British empire was fundamentally different from its Mughal predecessor. The nature of its power, the purposes for which it was used, and its long-term historical consequences were all immeasurably different from earlier empire states. British colonial rule, because of its unprecedented supremacy in military technology, gave a new kind of fixity to political territoriality. Except for the outlying regions in the north-west, most of the subcontinent came under a stable, single, uniform administrative authority. Territorial fixity was followed by slowly expanding moral claims of sovereign power. In European discourse, British rule over India was often justified by a dubious 'right of conquest'. However, within India it was ideologically anchored more effectively in a typically utilitarian line of reasoning. That theory maintained that the legitimacy of a government should be judged *consequentially*: not by some vague and indeterminable right of natives to rule, but by the historical results of a form of governance. By this criterion, it was possible, if not plausible, to provide an effective justification of colonial rule.

[22] Despite their considerable difference on other points, the two arguments by Gellner (1983) and Anderson (1983) converge on this one.

Early colonial policy proceeded from an acknowledgement of the alienness of British power and showed excessive anxiety over interference in the social habits of its Indian subjects. British missionaries often pursued energetic campaigns for conversion from Hindu society, and chided the government for not performing its Christian duty of spreading rationalism and enlightened beliefs by interventionist legislation. Officials, on their side, responded coolly to such proposals of expeditious moral improvement, and regarded them as meddlesome distractions from calculations of colonial policy. By the middle of the nineteenth century, such claims of sovereignty were beginning to be embedded in early modern Indian culture, and the large-scale rebellion of 1857–8 in northern India, which the British called the Sepoy Mutiny,[23] can be seen as a desperate attempt at rejection of this new definition of an alien but sovereign state by appealing to a more conventional language of power. The rebellion failed ideologically as well as politically. Except for a small revivalist Muslim elite in northern India which believed in the vague possibility of a return to Mughal power, it had ambivalent support from ordinary people. The majority of the peasantry were too alienated from the world of political power to respond widely to contests against the legitimacy of foreign rule. The modernist elites based in Calcutta saw their own economic prospects as being too deeply entangled with British rule to welcome such a ruinous retreat into the past.

After the rebellion of the mid-nineteenth century, and in part as its consequence, the character of colonial rule changed in major ways. First, the metropolitan government assumed direct responsibility of the Indian empire, abandoning the earlier policy of ambivalent exploitation of the colonial connection.[24] When the Company ruled India, British official policy was a mixture of quiet enjoyment of the financial benefits of Company rule and a casual denial of responsibility

[23] The large-scale mutiny of British Indian troops started from camps in Bengal and spread to the major cities of northern India. It was eventually put down by the British with the help of those parts of the army that remained loyal to colonial authorities. Interestingly, the emerging modern elites sided entirely with the British, though much later nationalists reinterpreted the events anachronistically as the first war of independence.

[24] For excellent accounts of the nature of British power and the ambiguities of colonial rule, see Bayly 1989 and Washbrook 1999.

if things went wrong. With the direct assumption of empire by the home government, the British establishment had to be more directly involved in the affairs of the colony, and it had to take far more seriously progressive demands that emerging liberal rules of governance should be applied to the government of India. Secondly, colonial authorities had a clearer perception of the political need for Indian collaboration, bringing a group of modernist Indians into the business of colonial administration in subordinate roles, so that they could work to provide an ideological relay into Indian society, performing a quasi-hegemonic connection with at least the ambitious, modernist segment of the Indian upper class.[25] It is fair to say that, in the early period of British rule, even before direct governance by the crown, the Indian upper classes saw the expanding claims of sovereignty of the British state as a way of intensifying their own control over Indian society. The case of the abolition of sati is an excellent example. Social reformers like Ram Mohan Roy despaired of persuading conservative Hindu society to support a rejection of sati on rationalistic grounds, and gradually shifted their strategy to persuade the reluctant colonial administration to interfere in stamping out barbaric practices from Hindu society.

The sati episode illustrated the emergence of attitudes that were to characterize Indian political discourse for a long time. The controversy split Indian intellectuals and public opinion into three ideological camps. The first supported the abolition unconditionally and argued that since Hindu society was unwilling to abolish the practice, the only rational solution to the problem was to bring in the power of the colonial state. Rationalist reform was historically necessary, even though the cost was colonial intervention into Indian social practices. Some Hindu reformers agreed that sati was morally abhorrent but insisted that it must be eradicated by Hindu society itself—through a process of self-correction. To allow the colonial state to rectify the undoubted barbarisms of indigenous society was to give it an illegitimate jurisdiction

[25] There is a long and interesting discussion about whether the Gramscian concept of hegemony, in some appropriately modified form, can be applied to colonial India. For some direct interventions in that discussion, see the work of Shula Marks and Dagmar Engels (1994); for a dissenting view by a distinguished historian, see the work of Ranajit Guha (1997).

for interference without consultation and went against the fundamental notions of self-rule. A third strand of Hindu opinion was more coherently conservative: it opposed the jurisdiction of the state to initiate reform and rejected normative criticisms of sati as a social practice.[26]

The second strand of argument was the most interesting, in a sense, and also contained an ambiguity. It was not clear at that stage if the objection to the use of the state as a reforming power against society was based on the fact that it was a foreign power, or because it was the state. In other words, the basis of the objection was ambiguous: whether it was the state's claim to interfere into social rules that was unacceptable, or the fact that the state was in the hands of an alien power. The distinction was fundamental. The first argument would merge into a Gandhian scepticism about the state in general; the second would eventually evolve into the Nehruvian reliance on the nationalist state. In later periods, these would increasingly diverge into two separate strands of political reflection—one rejecting the foreignness of the intervention; the other, more radical one, objecting to the power of the modern state to intervene in the rules of society. All these strands would for the time being use the idea of swaraj/swarajya—self-rule or autonomy—but in significantly different, often contradictory directions. I shall try to illustrate this by reference to three intellectual positions in the evolving discourse about the nature and role of the modern state.

Intellectual reflection on the peculiarities of imperial control brought the question of the state gradually to the centre of the political field of vision. Something like a shift of horizon in a Gadamerian sense began to occur from the mid-nineteenth century onwards. In the nineteenth century, the central puzzle for Indian intellectuals in their recent history was the question of subjugation: how such a small number of alien rulers, from such a distant base, could control a country of such immense size and diversity. By the early twentieth century, this was transformed into the question of independence: a consideration of how this power could be effectively contested and ultimately removed. The answer to

[26] In the Bengali controversies about the abolition of sati, and more generally the role of the state in initiating social reform, Ram Mohan Roy articulated the first position, Bankimchandra Chattopadhyay the second, and Hindu conservatives the third.

the first question went through several stages, and Indian intellectuals eventually provided increasingly complex and 'political' answers to this central puzzle of modern Indian history. Initially, Indians were inclined to blame the victory of the British simply on an unusually long run of military misfortunes. But British military victories were too numerous, and too consistent to be explained away as a statistical quirk. A second version of the explanation focused on military technology and organization; but Indian rulers like Tipu Sultan of Mysore eventually succumbed to British power even though they employed European military organization and technology. When these two explanations appeared implausible, Indian discussions moved towards a more sociological form of analysis, suggesting that the obvious invincibility of British power arose not from material things like superior technology, or simple organization of their armed forces, but something deeper, more comprehensive, and subtle—which Indian intellectuals slowly identified as 'a national spirit'. By this they usually meant the historically peculiar device of the modern nation-state, which produced a new constitutive relationship between a people and their state. Early Indian nationalist thinking is replete with references to the virtues of discipline and what Foucault has termed 'governmentality'. For that was what the British possessed, and the Indians lacked. The discourse of Indian nationalism was thus born with a strangely contradictory relation with European nation-states: clearly, the only way of prising open the colonial grip of the British nation-state on its Indian empire was to generate a sense of nationalism, and the eventual creation of an Indian nation-state.

III: Thinking about the State

A Discourse of Disillusionment: Bhudev Mukhopadhyay

A major strand of theoretical reflection emerged in the 1860s in the work of several Bengali authors, among whom Bhudev Mukhopadhyay's essays on sociology (Mukhopadhyay 1892 [1981]) were the most incisive and consistent.[27] Bhudev wrote a powerful treatise which

[27] A major problem in studying modern Indian intellectual history is that academic attention is invariably given disproportionally to authors who wrote

asserted that Indian and European societies were providentially joined by history, but the simple power of colonialism could not erase the fundamental fact that the two societies were organized around demonstrably different principles—in the normative and organizational sense. Indian society, by which he primarily meant the Hindu social order based on caste, was characterized by an '*interior organization*' (*antah-sasane sasita*): this form of social ordering was interior, and anterior to the external authority of the state.[28] Its normative principles derived from a collectively accepted and intelligible normative order of dharma,[29] and it ran according to those 'internal' principles, in other words, disqualifying the claims of 'internal sovereignty' of the modern state. Modern European societies alienated this power of social organization to a state which then assumed legitimate external authority to provide societies and communities embedded in them with their normative and practical order. External interference into the settled habits of Hindu society—its *sittlichkeit*[30]—was therefore perceived as normatively unjustified, and for this reason likely to be ineffectual if attempted by pure force (Mukhopadhyay 1981 [1892]); for interpretations, see Raychaudhuri 1989, Kaviraj 1995). Bhudev was

---

primarily in English. Authors who chose vernaculars as their exclusive vehicle often have extremely interesting ideas: at times, they can afford to be more explicit in the political implications of their arguments. Bhudev Mukhopadhyay is undoubtedly one of the most insightful 'theoretical' thinkers in nineteenth-century Bengal, but there is no serious translation of his major works into English.

[28] The idea that Indian society was ordered internally—not by the state—becomes a major argument in much social reflection associated with Indian nationalism, and is echoed, with appropriate inflections of emphasis, by thinkers like Gandhi and Rabindranath Tagore. For Gandhi's version, see *Hind Swaraj* in Gandhi 1997. For Tagore, see his political essays in Thakur 2003, in particular the essay 'Bharatvarshe Itihaser Dhara' (The Course of Indian History).

[29] The meaning of the term dharma is notoriously difficult to capture in translation, but the closest equivalent in the context of this discussion is 'right'—encompassing both the sense of what is right, and what the rights are, the proper ways of acting, that is, by different social agents.

[30] I am not suggesting a direct reference to Hegel, though Bhudev was extremely well acquainted with contemporary European theory and commented on Hegel in a separate part of his work: Mukhopadhyay 1981 [1892].

among the early thinkers who offered, from an explicitly Hindu point of view, a comprehensive sociology of modern European civilization, and built an unappealing Hobbesian picture of modern European society.[31] Societies in modern Europe were based on a new kind of fundamental acquisitiveness and expansion of individuality which had three negative effects when judged from a rationalistic humanist perspective. It destroyed the unconditional affection which traditionally held families together and introduced forces that were bound to turn this basic social unit into an increasingly contractual institution. It turned the world of work, the field of interaction between productive persons, into a field of unceasing conflict: a war of all against all. For Bhudev, Hobbes's solution, however, was delusive: the creation of a sovereign would not reduce or eliminate incessant conflict; it simply gave it a more civilized disguise. Modern European societies did not have real moral cement because of the apotheosis of competition. 'Civil society', or its economic version in the modern market, appeared to him to create a condition of utter instability of fortunes and insidiously persuaded modern Europeans to accept that as a natural and desirable condition induced by a false theory of 'human nature'. Finally, European colonialism was simply the application of this logic of conflict to the level of world society. From altering the norms and institutions of their own societies, European societies now had the collective power to extend them to all others; to impose these norms artificially on all their dominions and pretend that this forced universality confirmed their 'natural' character. Modern societies did not emerge in other cultures through spontaneous combustion but by the forcible reforms of European colonial rule.

Modern states were unprecedented devices by which the entire social universe in the colonies was restructured by European imperialism into a form of society that was excessively materialistic, individualistic, and competitive, and which eventually made any real conception of 'community' unsustainable.[32] In Bhudev's critique—which was echoed and elaborated by a long line of subsequent nationalist writers—this

[31] For a discussion, see Kaviraj 1995.

[32] Bhudev was writing in a period when Bengali fascination with French theories, particularly Rousseau, was at its peak. Some of his arguments may have come from a reading of Rousseau as much as from Hindu philosophical reflection.

eventually led to a comprehensive moral rejection of the modern Western social form. Bhudev's succinct assessment of the historical consequences of expanding modernity over the world was interesting: society would eventually undermine its own bonds of basic sociality by encouraging individuals to treat all others instrumentally (to borrow Kantian language) and make both collective and individual life unfulfilling. States based on these forms of competitive sociality would reproduce similar relations of hostility and competition towards other states, which would lead to interminable wars among nation-states. The European mastery of modern military technology made such wars more destructive than ever before. In an intriguing critique of emerging international law in the nineteenth century, Bhudev suggested that modern European societies periodically sought to impose such quasi-legal restraints on their own states because the history of European modernity was an incomprehensible story of building and destruction. Modern European societies constructed an unprecedentedly opulent civilization in periods of peace but were unable to control state conflicts that swiftly annihilated what was achieved. But Europeans were showing signs of tiring of the repeated mutual destruction of their own economic prosperity. Attempts at the creation of modern international law to restrain wars were primarily aimed at avoiding future wars *within* the European continent. If that version of international law succeeded, it would reduce military destruction within the territory of the European continent. However, as the militaristic and aggressive nationalist nature of these states could not be changed, this would simply mean the transference of devastating wars from the European centre to the peripheral world of the colonies. It would be the rest of the world that would have to pay the price for European propensity towards aggression. Interestingly, although Bhudev was sharply critical of modern European statecraft, he showed deep admiration for two achievements of European modernity: political economy—the European science of improving the wealth of nations; and the growth of modern science. Apart from these two spheres, Indian society had nothing to learn from Europe.

Despite their power and complexity, Bhudev's reflections on the modern state remained fatally incomplete on several counts. First, his thought, though insightful and critically incisive on the centrality of the state in European modernity, recorded this simply as a brute historical fact, without any suggestions for strategic opposition. He had no answer to its power, except for refined disapproval.[33] Without a counter-strategy, his response to colonialism was simply a technique of what Bhabha has termed 'sly civility'—accepting British rule as providentially given while waiting for some future fundamental change in the field of political power.[34] What is notable about Bhudev's early modern critique of Western modernity is its pervading sense that the modern West was a new kind of historical force that would not merely transform Western societies but that also carried a universalist proposal for moral and institutional change in all civilizations: that the civilization of the modern West was 'universalistic' in a different way from the hopeful, putative universalism of proselytizing religions like Christianity and Islam. Central to his thought was also a deep reflective conviction that 'the form of life' that Western modernity proposed to the rest of the world could be shown through rationalistic argument to be morally indefensible and causally dangerous. Although the ideology of Western modernity assumed that it had philosophical implements to secure other cultures' dialogic conversion to its superior principles, it had acquired the political power necessary for a monologic imposition of transformation according to its own preferred rules. Colonialism was not a rational conversation over principles, but an unequal exchange of power between societies. The trouble with modern Western civilization was that it talked about the dialogic persuasion of norms, but actually relied more on the coercion of unanswerable power—which must remind us of contemporary parallels.[35]

After close inspection, he rejected the Western proposals of modernity on four fundamental grounds: capitalist modernity depleted the emotional bonds within the family by making them illegitimately

[33] Indeed, the disappointing conclusion of all his sophisticated analysis was *netrpratiksha*—a wistful 'waiting for leadership'. Bhudev's (1892) conclusion was ironically called *kartavya-nirnaya*—deciding what is to be done.

[34] His essays begin with a fascinating report of a conversation with an Irish official of the British bureaucracy, who, after some youthful flirtation with Irish nationalism, joined the service of the empire, and subsumed his Irish identity into British nationalism. But Bhudev claimed that this subsumption was inauthentic, and under conversational provocation 'the fire' of his Irishness flared up again. See Mukhopadhyay 1892: Introduction.

[35] It is odd how isomorphic the present situation in Iraq is to the one Bhudev described.

contractual; capitalist economies destroyed all sense of community by rendering human relations competitive and aggressive; modern states were primarily effective engines of comprehensive wars against other states; and the search for self-interest by states drove modern European nations into a denial of self-determination—which they valued for themselves—for others, thereby justifying modern imperialism. The very universality of the proposals of European modernity forced reflective individuals of other societies, who wished to live thoughtfully in history, to adopt a partly relativistic vision of an increasingly interdependent world that did not allow the traditional separateness of cultures. The intellectual and political power of European modernity irreversibly ended the era of isolated civilizations. Evaluative isolationism was rendered impossible in a world dominated by European empires. The work of social theory—conceiving in their most general abstract form the principles on which one's society runs, and making comparative judgements about different societies—was an inevitable task for modern intellectuals. Bhudev was convinced that Hindu society had to be subjected to scrutiny by abstract rational principles, but confident that it could win such an argument with modern European social philosophy. Implicit in his thinking was the idea of the unavoidable centrality of social philosophy to the human condition in modernity. To defend Hindu society against Western cultural imperialism required social theory as much as the modernist argument of assimilation into a single homogeneous modern culture ruled from a Western imperial centre.

I give more room to an elaboration of Bhudev Mukhopadhyay's thought for several parochial reasons. First, in recent historiography of Indian intellectual modernity, vernacular reflection has been relatively neglected in favour of authors who wrote in English. Yet, the ideas of English writers were often derived from strands of reasoning which were already powerfully articulated in the odd secrecy of vernacular discourse. In some ways, vernacular critical thought was in fact more original and more intransigent towards Western reasoning than what appeared in English.[36] Secondly, a discussion of Bhudev shows that

[36] No serious study has been done on the question of the 'self-translation' of Gandhi's autobiography, *My Experiments with Truth*, a central text which was composed in Gujarati and translated into English. The English version of course utterly overshadowed the Gujarati original; but some interpreters

Gandhi's startling interventions on the question of modernity and the state had a long indigenous pan-Indian history.

IV: The Discourse of Disillusion—Gandhi

Gandhi's unusually intransigent rejection of modernity's material, technical, and political attractions made this critical political vision internationally known—though originally it simply attracted amused derision from Western sources (Parel 1997). Gandhi's elaboration of this position (Parekh 1986, Brown 1989) however introduced some crucial disjunctions with Bhudev. Gandhi revoked the two concessions even a historical conservative like Bhudev had made to European modernity—on the crucial questions of science and political economy. By doing this he would add a new dimension to the critique. Gandhi asserted that the central feature of modern Western society was the substitution of the traditional principles of moral restraint—in the desires of the individual and in the economic acquisitiveness of society—*vis-à-vis* the human exploitation of nature by technology. He deployed the resonant Hindu-Buddhist idea of *himsa*—violence in a complex, vastly capacious sense—which could extend from personal jealousy against others, to meat-eating, the ill-treatment of animals, aggressive behaviour in market society, modern wars which extended the full capacity of modern science and technology towards a rationalist project of destruction against other states and peoples. By outlining the ramifications of this concept Gandhi believed he could bring the entire architecture of European modernity into a single intelligible theoretical grid, and in a manner that would be entirely persuasive to religious-minded Indians. He simply appealed innovatively to a concept deeply embedded in reformist traditions of Indic religion—in Buddhism, Jainism, and all versions of the Vaishnava sects. In Gandhi's hands, and partly in the works of his friend Rabindranath Tagore, this critique of

---

believe a close textual scrutiny would reveal serious and significant differences of emphasis and inflection between the two texts. Exactly parallel to this, Tagore wrote in far more complex ways about nationalism—both Indian and European—in his copious Bengali essays on this theme, than in the simplified presentation in his English text, *Nationalism.* Little serious work, however, has been done on this crucial problem of self-translation.

modernity assumed a different kind of dignity and coherence. The major predicament of modern European culture (Gandhi disagreed with its description as a 'modern civilisation'[37]) arose from its reversal of the ideal of restraint, which was a central normative ideal common to all pre-modern civilizations. For Gandhi the primary principle of human life was restraint, what he would call *swaraj*—using a theme of dominant reflection in Indic religions on the government of the self, especially sensual desires.[38] In his thought there was a distinction and inverse relation between *internal* and *external* government. If the individual could govern, restrain, control his self, especially his material desires, he would find contentment and require less external control. The extent of intrusion of the state in the lives of individuals and local communities was directly proportional to their failure to exercise self-restraint. If we observe closely, we will find a direct elaboration of the Bhudev argument that traditional Indian society was *ruled from inside,* ordered by the operation of internal restraint—only this is now elaborated by Gandhi into a much more comprehensive and multi-level doctrine explaining adversities common to modern life. European modernity has turned human ideals upside down. Its ideology reinterpreted a fulfilling human life as not one in which desires are restrained and 'stilled' (a very Indic concept running powerfully through both the *Gita* and the teachings of the Buddha, the *Dhammapada*), and through which he can live in solidarity and compassion with others; rather, it has turned the abandonment of restraint itself into the ideal of human life. Thus, to produce social order it is forced increasingly to depend exclusively on the external powers of the state. As individual acquisitiveness is encouraged and crosses all traditional restraint, the ordering powers of the state have to expand to impose legal prohibitions:

[37] When asked by a journalist what he thought of 'Western civilisation', Gandhi said 'it would be a good idea'.

[38] It must be emphasized that in Gandhi's thought the junction of the two morphemes *sva* and *raj* produces a compound with two distinct, but crucially interrelated connotations. Swaraj undoubtedly means rule by the self, taking this in the direction of political autonomy. However, it crucially means rule over the self as well: for Gandhi, willed acceptance of punishment or suffering is an indispensable instrument for making foreign rule ethically unworkable, and this brings independence through non-violent non-cooperation.

for Gandhi therefore there was a clear explanatory solution to the paradoxical simultaneity of the expansion of liberal ideals of individual freedom and the inevitable expansion of the powers of the state. It was a failure of liberal theory not to see the deep connection between these two parallel developments in Western modernity. The more the atomistic individual is encouraged by the modern social imaginary to invade others' interests, the more the state would be called upon to restrain and mediate between them. Finally, the enslavement of the individual to his/her own desires leads necessarily to the enslavement of societies to their states and ruling mechanisms of an external institutional order. This historically conservative theory of the state therefore had two defining characteristics: it accepted as ideal the conventional belief in an order which was divinely given, but rationally intelligible to ordinary human beings, which reduced the function of the state to the merest preservation of that order. Its conception was also of a 'minimal' state, but minimal in a radically different sense from laissez faire liberalism. This vision questioned the need of the modern state altogether: what it sought was not a minimal version of the modern state, but the state minimized in a pre-modern way.

But Gandhi's theory of 'the government of the self and government of society' failed to answer several questions. His writings implicitly acknowledged an idea central to Tocqueville's analysis of the European state. The powers of the modern state were so vast and intrusive that individual defiance to this state was ineffectual. The only form of resistance to the power of the modern state was another typically modern form of collective agency: the political mass movement. This was already a fundamental concession to political modernity. Besides, Gandhi's thinking had no simple answer to the question of how to practically evict the power of the state from Indian society once British colonialism was removed. His historical conservatism eventually failed due to three reasons. First, the modern form of the state was attractive to modern elites because they saw in it an immense expedient for the expansion of their own power over society; modern elites were not satisfied with segmentary forms of domination: only the mediation of the modern state could provide it. Subaltern groups in Indian society, especially the lower castes and untouchables and, in a different but parallel movement, working class parties, also saw in the modern state the only instrumentality which could provide them with some reasonable chance of emancipation from traditional subordination to social elites. Finally, it was clear to the political and intellectual elites that whatever the undesirable associations of the modern state, the international order was irreversibly an order of states and no national group could exist viably without employing this transactively mandatory form of political organization. Historical conservatism therefore offered a powerful critique and an ineliminable utopia, which bothered, troubled, and inconvenienced the irresistible march of the idea of the modern state, but eventually could not resist it.

V: The Enchantment of the State: The Modernist Political Imaginary

No other thinkers in the Indian nationalist tradition could match Gandhi and Tagore in intellectual significance. Yet, paradoxically, the *political* imagination of independent India—both of the elite and of subaltern groups—turned decisively in an opposite direction. Their ideas were accorded a hollow reverence, while actual political reasoning fell deeper into an abiding enchantment by the state. Gandhi brought independence to India, but it was Nehru—an entirely unrepentant modernist—who obtained the historical opportunity to decide what to do with that independence, and how the powers of this newly acquired sovereignty should be used. In any case, there was a contradiction at the heart of the Gandhian political project. After all, the Independence movement was about the capture of the state, and it was anomalous to suggest that the state that was captured with such effort should then be reduced to insignificance. Sociologically, the crucial reason for the state's triumph in the Indian political imaginary was the manner in which it captured the imagination of both elites and the masses. Eventually, even the conservative elites who initially held back from the seduction of the state succumbed to it, partly because of the strange paradox of modern political rationality—for even those who wish to restrict the inroads of the state in society's affairs have to use the state to legislate that prohibition.[39] Our comparisons are usually utterly one-sided—always measuring modern India against the history of modern Europe. If India is compared with other societies of the South,

[39] From that point of view, it is entirely misleading to liken the limitation of the state that conservatives desired with the capitalist limitation on state interference proposed by neo-liberals.

probably the most striking thing we observe is the depth that the modern idea of the state and its institutional practices have gained in the political imaginary of ordinary Indian people.

The most consistent and eloquent presentation of the modern *statist* vision of the future came of course from Jawaharlal Nehru, who consistently represented a different theoretical view inside the national movement.[40] Nehru considered Gandhi's vision of the quiet, idyllic Indian village community historically romantic and practically unworkable. In contrast to Gandhi, he had a vivid and thoroughly modernist political imagination based on the conception of an elective self, of an economically atomistic individual who would go out in a life of work. His work would be carried out within an open economy in which individuals could choose their occupation and emerge from the crippling continuity of hereditary occupations, and a democratic state which would confer on its citizens the right to act in a participatory public sphere. In his vision, this state must also accept responsibility for the reduction of extreme social and economic inequality, and work actively for income redistribution. Emancipation from European control was essential, because colonialism blocked the realization of true modernity.[41] For Gandhi, independence meant the historical opportunity to move out of the forcible imposition of European modernity on India; for Nehru, modernity was a universally desirable condition, but imperialism created a two-speed world in which serious modernity in the colonies was either partially realized or perpetually deferred. Colonies required independence precisely because they wanted to break out of the systemic imperialist provision of inferior versions of modern life. Gandhi remained indispensable for Indian nationalism during the anti-colonial movement; after freedom, his political imagination went into abeyance with a peculiar rapidity. After Independence the nation-state ignored Gandhi's politics in exchange for a ritual celebration of his life and death.

[40] Nehru himself has offered a frank assessment of his theoretical differences with Gandhi in his *Autobiography* (1936).

[41] Nehru did not write a systematic treatise on the questions of the state and the economy, but his ideas on these issues were presented with great expressive force in a series of essays and speeches in the 1930s, 1940s, and 1950s. See Nehru 1962.

This modernist elite, which assumed power through somewhat fortuitous circumstances, had an entirely Jacobin conception of the state.[42] They used a strong distinction between the state and the society it governed precisely to view the state as an instrumentality, rather than as an organic growth that should reflect society's cultural habits.[43] The state was conceived in really revolutionary terms—its task was precisely to drag into a modern age a largely reluctant, conservative society by directly attacking its unjust and reactionary practices. In his pedagogic version of nationalism, Nehru conceived of the state as a vast, bureaucratic instrument of collectively-willed, elite-directed social change, drawing the sanction for this proposal of radical social transformation from philosophical readings of history rather than instant support of his people (although during his tenure as prime minister he enjoyed entirely secure elective majorities). The state's role was particularly critical in two major areas of reform. First, India's economic backwardness was attributed to imperialist exploitation, but more strictly to the neglect of industrial development under colonial rule. In Nehru's clever mixture of Marxist and Fabian political ideals, political sovereignty was never secure without serious industrial development, particularly the growth of heavy industries. Continuing dependence on former colonial powers for complex technology and capital goods seemed to Nehru to threaten the real core of sovereignty.[44]

Accordingly, after Independence the Indian state began to expand its economic role frenetically—with serious long-term historical consequences.[45] True, Nehru inherited the framework of the British colonial

[42] I am using the term Jacobin not in the sense in which it is used in the context of French political history, but to refer to a much broader idea that through the adoption of a new constitution, enforced by the state, modern people could achieve something like a 'refoundation' of society, a fundamental overhauling of the basic principles of social co-operation.

[43] To refer to the distinction in chapter 1 of J.S. Mill's *Consideration of Representative Government,* which exercised a strong influence on the language of state-making in modern India.

[44] For a more detailed exposition of Nehru's arguments on political economy, see Kaviraj 1994.

[45] Though there can be finer periodizations of this process; and the serious expansion of the state began after 1955, with the start of the Second Five Year Plan in the next year.

state; but in the next two decades this state changed its character in several fundamental respects. First, from a state concerned primarily with political order and tax collection, it turned into a vast bureaucratic machine striving to affect the functioning of the entire productive economy in two ways. Nehru's government legislated a huge framework of protective laws that would shield Indian industry from foreign competition, but it also exacted a heavy price by imposing an intricate network of rules of bureaucratic approval.[46] By using the reformist imaginary of the state, Nehru's government easily established a firm directive control over Indian industries—which was to turn destructive in later decades. Secondly, the Nehruvian state was not content with merely directing industrial investments of the private sector by public economic policy; it decided that the Indian bourgeoisie lacked the capital required for establishing large-scale industries and purchasing advanced technology. Starting from slightly experimental moves in the early years, from the 1956 Second Five Year Plan it rapidly constructed a large public sector of directly state-run industries. Commonly, observers emphasize the continuity between the colonial and the Nehruvian state; but their discontinuities are at least equally significant. The political history of Asia and Africa is full of examples of states which simply inherited colonial bureaucracies, with a tired political imagination, which could not achieve any significant imaginative integration with their peoples. As they moved away from contact with popular aspirations, these states degenerated into personal or military tyrannies, or simply crumbled. The Indian state was an exception to this general dismal fate. After Independence, the Indian nationalist state produced a new, powerful imagination for itself which reconnected it to popular aspirations, and which allowed the Indian state to continue its successful career despite disapproval from both camps in the Cold War. There were two crucial factors in this unusual success of a state which managed to install democracy without conditions of economic prosperity. The first was the manner in which it captured the imagination of the emergent modern elites. Despite its stark and obvious failures in various fields—the removal of poverty, the provision of primary education, achieving respectable rates of long-term economic growth,

[46] For an excellent recent discussion of India's political economy, see Chibber 2003. Two earlier studies provide much interesting analysis of Nehru's economic strategies: Frankel 1978, and Rudolph and Rudolph 1987.

distributive justice—the state supervised the rapid growth of a modern middle class which, paradoxically, benefited from the expansion of both the market and the state. This might have accentuated internal inequality, but the absolute size of this middle class created a substantial enclave of contentment with the state's performance. By allowing the market economy to develop, albeit slowly, and by creating a rapidly expanding state sector of the economy which required the expansion of a supervising bureaucracy, this state earned the gratitude of the new middle classes—the aspiring and confident entrants into this modern mixed economy. At the same time, the Nehruvian state retained at least an ideological commitment to social reform and distributive justice, though slow and insubstantial economic growth threw the state increasingly upon the resources of the modern elites and slowed the prospect of any serious income redistribution.

Interestingly, the Nehruvian state also appealed powerfully to the subaltern political imagination. Through the design of the new constitution, it undertook an immense project of social reform, using the state as the primary instrument for tearing down the millennial indignities of the caste system. This caught the imagination of the lower orders of Indian society in a different but equally potent fashion. All previous states had accepted defeat in the face of the historical persistence of the caste order, although the colonial state had begun to provide for limited political representation to the lowest castes. By adopting a reformist constitutional system, the Nehruvian state declared the 'sovereignty' of the state in deciding social principles and legislated the basic rules of the caste system invalid—an unprecedented move unachieved either by any previous state or by the sporadic efforts of religious reformers. By the constitutional abolition of untouchability, and a system of reservation in three sectors—electoral representation, government employment, and educational institutions—the independent state made the first fundamental attack against the normative legitimacy and institutional power of the caste system. The constitutional initiative on caste eventually yielded two consequences. It is now generally accepted that there was a large gap between legal rhetoric and social conduct. The actual ameliorative results of the reservation policies were very slow, affected a small segment of the lowest castes, and were consequently seen as largely symbolic—conferring on the lowest sections of Indian society a ritualistic formal citizenship which the state could not actually translate into effective redistribution of dignity, not to speak of incomes. But this small segment of the upwardly mobile elite from low castes secured for their communities a symbolic dignity, a staged equality with other bearers of power in state institutions. It is remarkable that, despite the formal openness of the competitive market, this did not produce lower-caste or untouchable millionaires or business magnates.[47] Despite all the failings of the ponderous state, it produced a real stratum of bureaucrats from the lowest castes and, eventually, the elective apparatuses of the state also produced a stratum of important politicians who sat on the central cabinet and ruled large states as chief ministers—one of them eventually occupied the post of president of the republic. Despite the undoubtedly nominal character of this elevation, the process changed the normative template of Hindu society. Paradoxically, the slowness of this process and its largely ritualistic character also produced among vast masses of the lower castes an indignant sense of urgency in demanding their rights. This has expressed itself in a strange transformation of the basic language of Indian politics—its intriguing turn since the 1970s towards the vernacular. Electoral politics in India now mainly occurs in the vernacular—both in a literal and a symbolic sense. Since the late 1970s, parliamentary politics has gone through an amazing transformation—in its personnel and language. During the Nehru period, politics was almost entirely an arena for upper-middle-class politicians who were wedded to ideologies like liberalism and socialism, disputing their claims in chaste English in India's numerous legislative chambers. By the late 1970s, they were substantially replaced by politicians from lower social strata, with less or more vernacular education, whose political imaginations and practical preoccupations were startlingly different. Western ideologies like liberalism and socialism disappeared from the language of political contestation, which acquired a new kind of intensity and was entirely concerned with the question of dignity and resentment against the unacceptable sluggishness of caste emancipation.[48] Thus, while politics from the 1970s became undoubtedly more participatory, and in that sense democratic, it also became

[47] A point argued most recently in Damodaran 2008.

[48] This does not mean that the basic principles of liberal and socialist politics—liberty, equality, justice—lost their significance. Rather they were translated increasingly into terms that were central to the Indian social system.

unmistakably more vernacular, caste-oriented, and non-Western. The movement of democracy in India has become historically peculiar: it has become more Indian while it has become more democratic.

From the point of view of comparative political theory, the Indian case illustrates an interesting point. In modern Indian political life the central conflict was about two views of the state, represented broadly by Gandhi and Nehru. One of them demanded a limitation of the state's powers; the other an unambiguous expansion. Yet, this was not a re-enactment of the European conflict between liberal and socialist theory. The limitation that Gandhi wanted was very different from liberal theory. What Nehruvianism eventually came to represent was also quite distinct from socialism: because the state had little success in its redistributive agenda. Yet it was not a failed socialist state, as it is often represented: it succeeded in something else. The correct characterization for this would be a pure 'statism', without a strong redistributive expectation. It was literally a poor people's version of the welfare state, which had too little revenue to provide them with normal everyday welfare but came to their rescue via the desperate mitigation of crises.

It has been suggested that 'the Congress system' (Kothari 1970)—or what I have more grandly called the Nehruvian state—was based upon a consensus. This is misleading if consensus implies different political groups reaching agreement on the same principles. It is more accurate to say that in the Nehruvian state there was a historic convergence of radically different expectations. The upper classes saw it as an instrument of economic growth—naturally, primarily for themselves, and in the immediate future. Lower strata in Indian society were drawn to it by the promise of social dignity, an end of the caste system, and a distant dream of economic redistribution. The two dreams, and their divergent justifications, were equally real for the relevant groups to repose their faith in the modern nation-state.

But, in a certain sense, a distinction between the Congress government and 'the Nehruvian state' is crucial for understanding what is now happening in Indian politics. 'The Congress system' fell into decay by the 1970s, and Congress' fortunes were revived briefly by Indira Gandhi through a quite different kind of political system.[49]

[49] This is a contentious issue in the interpretation of recent Indian history.

By the 1980s, even the restructured system had failed Congress, and Congress's conception of a pluralist Indian nation was being seriously challenged by an aggressive Hindu nationalism. A subtle and interesting shift has taken place in the imaginative universe of Indian politics through these political changes. All forms of collective belonging—the Hindu community, the secular Indian nation, pluralist Indic civilization—have come under increasing sceptical criticism. In some parts of India's territorial boundaries there are movements of radical separation from the conventional idea of the Indian union. Since the early 1990s successive Indian governments run by various political parties have implemented an expanding programme of economic liberalization which necessarily wants to shrink the powers and the spheres of operation of the state.

VI: Reading the State

All these confusing and conflicting aspirations and the inevitable disappointments that historical experience has brought along have impaired the legitimacy of the state, and done something strange to the exact location of its image in the political imagination. The sense of the state that has survived, despite unexpected historical twists in politics and the widening effects of economic liberalization, can be clarified by a series of negations in popular discourse.[50] It is seen as distinct from governments at the central or the state level, run by the Congress or the BJP, which are generally seen as corrupt, inefficient, and, in cases like Gujarat, murderous. It is distinct from the bureaucracy, which

---

Some scholars see the state under Indira Gandhi as a continuation of the Nehruvian state. I believe the differences between Nehru's rule and Indira Gandhi's were highly significant.

[50] This last section moves away from 'political thought' in the formal sense. Ways of viewing the political world had major theoretical exponents like Jawaharlal Nehru, or the dalit leader B.R. Ambedkar in the years after Independence. Since the 1970s it is hard to identify such large-scale positions in the world of politics in general. The picture presented in this section is a composite one drawn primarily from parliamentary discussions, debates in the political public sphere, and the results of surveys of popular attitudes.

is widely regarded as elitist, indifferent, and always carrying a faint stench of corruption. It is not the army and the police, the coercive apparatuses, which are dreaded and hated by large parts of the population for being violent and venal. In standard academic discourse, the state comprises the army, the bureaucracy, and the government; in Indian popular imagination, it is made strangely distinct from all these institutions. This has made it difficult to read the precise locus of this popular conception of the state—it is not to be found in the places where we are accustomed to search for it. Yet its distinctive presence as a powerful regulatory idea is unmistakable. It is implicitly invoked in every demand for justice, equality, dignity, and assistance—because all such demands can be made only in its name; and it is the state's responsibility to meet all these expectations. Ordinary Indians see the operation of this state in many tangible events which could not have happened without it. The poor, for whom this state should have been the most difficult to discern, see its presence in the way the right to property is put in abeyance when they squat on government land, or encroach on private property (Chatterjee 2004: ch. I). They see it as the obvious provider of relief after natural calamities such as the earthquake in Gujarat or the tsunami in South India. They see it as the provider of education and as their recourse during extreme distress. What is significant in a narrative of the state is that disadvantaged groups, who often volubly declare their disillusionment with the Indian nation—its offer of common citizenship—and are bitterly resentful of all incumbent or potential governments, still need something like a strangely disembodied idea of the state to articulate their grievances in the modern social world.

So the idea of the state has gone through an astonishing transformation. It has cut itself loose from its attachment to conceptions of the nation but has attained a strange apotheosis as the only repository, though elusively present, of people's moral aspirations. All other normal repositories of public and collective life—governments, bureaucracies, communities, the nation—have lost some of their legitimacy in a rising tide of undirected and uncontrollable social aspiration, except for a distant, second-order, spectral, and moral idea of the modern state. Its attributes are strangely familiar: it is capable of knowing everything, doing everything, removing all obstacles, punishing wrongs, showing mercy, averting evil; it is expected to be nearly omniscient and omnipotent. There is no end in sight of Indian society's strange enchantment with the modern state.

References

Alam, Muzaffar. 2004. *The Languages of Political Islam: India 1200–1800.* New Delhi and Chicago: Permanent Black and Chicago University Press.

Anderson, Benedict. 1983. *Imagined Communities.* London: Verso.

Bayly, C.A. 1989. *Indian Society and the Making of the British Empire.* Cambridge: Cambridge University Press.

Brown, Judith. 1989. *Gandhi: Prisoner of Hope.* New Haven: Yale University Press.

Castoriadis, Cornelius. 1987. *The Imaginary Institution of Society.* Cambridge: Polity Press.

Chatterjee, Partha. 1989. *Nationalist Thought and the Colonial World.* London: Zed Press.

———. 2004. *The Politics of the Governed.* New York: Columbia University Press.

Chibber, V. 2003. *Locked in Place.* Princeton: Princeton University Press.

Damodaran, Harish, 2008. *India's New Capitalists: Caste, Business, and Industry in a Modern Nation.* Ranikhet: Permanent Black.

Doniger, Wendy, and Brian K. Smith. Eds. 1991. *The Laws of Manu.* Harmondsworth: Penguin.

Dumont, Louis. 1970. *Homo Hierarchicus.* London: Weidenfeld and Nicolson.

Frankel, F. 1978. *India's Political Economy.* Princeton: Princeton University Press.

Gandhi, M.K. 1997. *Hind Swaraj and Other Writings.* Ed. Anthony J. Parel. Cambridge: Cambridge University Press.

Gellner, Ernest. 1983. *Nations and Nationalism.* Oxford: Blackwell.

Guha, Ranajit. 1997. *Dominance without Hegemony.* Cambridge, Mass.: Harvard University Press.

Guizot, F. 1997. *The History of Civilisation in Europe.* Ed. and trans. L. Seidentop. Harmondsworth: Penguin.

Kaviraj, Sudipta. 1994. Dilemmas of Democratic Development. In A. Leftwich, ed. *Democracy and Development.* Cambridge: Polity Press.

———. 1994. A Reversal of Orientalism. In H. von Stietencron and V. Dalmia, eds. *Representing Hinduism.* New Delhi: Sage Publications.

———. 2005. Outline of a Revisionist Theory of Modernity. *European Journal of Sociology.*

Kothari, Rajni. 1970. *Politics in India.* Boston: Little, Brown.

Marks, Shula, and Dagmar Engels. 1994. *Contesting Colonial Hegemony*. London: I.B. Tauris.

Mill, J.S. 1962 [1861]. Considerations on Representative Government. In A.D. Lindsay, ed., *Utilitarianism, Liberty, Representative Government*. London: Dent (pp. 175–6).

Mukhopadhyay, Bhudev. 1981 [1892]. *Samajik Prabandha* (Social Essays). Calcutta: Paschim Banga Pustak Parishad.

Nehru, J. 1936. *Autobiography*. London: Bodley Head.

———. 1962. *India's Freedom*. London: George Allen and Unwin.

Parekh, Bhikhu. 1986. *Colonialism, Tradition and Reform*. New Delhi: Sage Publications.

Parel, Anthony. 1997. Introduction to *Hind Swaraj*. Cambridge: Cambridge University Press.

Pollock, Sheldon. Ed. 2003. *Literary Cultures in History: Reflections from South Asia*. Berkeley: University of California Press.

———. 2006. *Ends of Man at the End of Premodernity*. Amsterdam: Royal Netherlands Academy of Arts and Sciences.

Raychaudhuri, Tapan. 1989. *Europe Reconsidered*. Delhi: Oxford University Press.

Rudolph, L.I. and S.H. Rudolph. 1987. *In Pursuit of Lakshmi*. Chicago: Chicago University Press.

Skinner, Q. 1988. The State. In James Tully, ed. *Meaning and Context*. Cambridge: Polity Press.

Taylor, Charles, 1990. Modes of Civil Society. In *Public Culture*, vol. 3, no. 1, Fall 1990, pp. 95–118.

———. 2004. *Modern Social Imaginaries*. Durham: Duke University Press.

Thakur, Rabindranath. 2003. *Kalantar*. Kolkata: Visvabharati.

Von Stietencron, Heinrich, and Vasudha Dalmia. Eds. 1995. *Representing Hinduism*. New Delhi: Sage Publications.

Washbrook, D. 1999. India: 1818–1860. In A. Porter, ed. *Oxford History of the British Empire*. Oxford: Oxford University Press.

Weber, Max. 1978 [1925]. *Economy and Society*. Berkeley: University of California Press.

3

Political Culture in Independent India

An Anti-Romantic View

Professor Rajni Kothari has offered an excellent account of Indian politics as we would like it to be, not as it really is.[1] Indian society would have been a lot more humane, political life much less meaningless if what he said were true. The struggle for winning democracy for India would then have been in the past, and not, as I believe, in the future. I am afraid what he says, though pleasant, is not quite the case. In the rest of this essay I shall state why.

I

This essay is explicitly negative. It sets down some reasons for not considering Professor Kothari's view of ideological structures as the only possible one.[2] I have stated my case in four parts. In the first I have

This essay first appeared in *Teaching Politics*, Delhi, 1979.

[1] Kothari 1978. Substantially similar to ch. 7 minus the section on political socialization in Kothari 1970s. One is a little disappointed, since one cannot know how Professor Kothari feels about the alterations, if any, in our political culture since the early 1970s. From his other work it appears that he thinks his 'consensual model' is cracking up. Cf. his articles in *Seminar* and Kothari 1976. Though democratic institutions were revived after the emergency, the 'consensual model', in its strict sense, has hardly survived. Can there be two parties that are consensual in the same way in which the earlier Congress was? Is Janata a consensual party of the same type? Unfortunately, all such interesting questions have to be kept in suspension.

[2] The ones that Kuhn had called translation problems. These are not exactly translation problems of the same order.

set out what I take to be Professor Kothari's 'problem', in the form in which he has constituted it. In the second I present what I take to be the logic of his 'solution', and state why I find it difficult to agree with his view. In the third part I agree that there is a fundamental question implicit in his analysis, though, in my view, he does not see it in its correct form. I shall, finally, suggest some ways in which this problem can be reconstituted; but I do not suggest any firm answer.

Both in the critique and the incidental remarks, my preference for a marxist analysis will, I think, be apparent. I shall suggest however, that a theory of the electoral process, as distinct from electoral institutions and parliamentary democracy, is still a major gap in marxist political theory.[3] Marxists have yet not given systematic attention to this crucial aspect of political life. Much greater attention is paid to more alluring abstractions like state and class power.

II

Let me state first what I take to be the underlying problem in Professor Kothari's argument. I shall take some liberties with his language and present it in a form closer to my concepts. There will therefore be some problems of shifting an idea across the frontiers of one conceptual system to another. But this is unavoidable.

At the centre of the Indian political experience, Professor Kothari argues, lies the wonder of Indian democracy. It is a wonder in a rigorous sense. For the establishment of a stable democratic state in India went against all established laws of political history. Theoretically, both classical political scientists and marxists had been sceptical about the success of the democratic experiment in India. Followers of Mill would have been appalled at the prospect of universal suffrage in a country with an extremely low rate of literacy. Classical marxists too

[3] Most Comintern documents since the late 1920s discounted the possibility of stable democratic post-colonial states in these regions, including India. One could sample the analyses of M.N. Roy, Rajni Palme Dutt, and other less-known people. There was a similar theoretical ambivalence towards democratic institutions in communist party documents upto the mid 1950s: an interesting mixture of apprehension that it could not last long with the relief that it was still working. For concrete examples, Sen 1978.

would have been sceptical about the prospect of bourgeois democracy on historical grounds. Historically, modern democracies have been associated with certain economic conditions. It was only in the countries of Western Europe, in the period of expanding colonial control and uninterrupted capitalist expansion, that liberal democratic political forms first appeared.[4] For roughly the same reasons, it was only in those countries that they acquired historical stability. The possible objection that such countries as US or Sweden were not imperialist powers is too formal. Forms of capitalist economic control can be direct or mediated, explicit or covert. At least historically, there is a constant association of democracy with expanding industrial capitalism, preferably reinforced by colonial empires.

I think the structure of this problem is implicit in much of Professor Kothari's analysis of Indian democracy.[5] Democracy is not seen normatively as a system that ought to exist; and one that can exist if men could be logically convinced and mobilized to work for it. Rather, it is seen as something that historically seems to require objective circumstances for its sustenance. The entire interest in a 'theory' of Indian democracy stems from the fact that here these conditions are not present; at least not to an equal degree. So, both from the functionalist and the marxist point of view, a conventional answer is ruled out. For India, one must look for an alternative sustaining factor. Professor Kothari finds this in the pre-existing pluralist political culture of our traditional society. This is clearly a significant question for anyone trying

[4] Liberal states, or their prefigurations, had come into existence in England in the seventeenth century; in France, a hundred years later. Liberal-oligarchic government assumed a purer form in the United States, because there it did not encounter feudal resistance. But liberal democratic practices in the strict sense started only by the middle of the nineteenth century, still later in most cases. Two long spells of economic expansion of industrial capitalism, 1815–71 and 1875–1910 helped this to a great extent.

[5] Though it is latent in Kothari's work, it is quite explicit in a lot of other 'behavioralist' literature. This specific argument was used to justify imperialist intervention in the politics of the third world. Since purely endogenous factors could not sustain democracy, it was obviously the responsibility of Western democratic states to shore up weaker members of the free world. Finally, they had to advance from a simple assistance to virtual superintendence. The Americans went down this slope in Vietnam.

to understand how Indian democracy works, and to evaluate its prospects.

I think Professor Kothari's answer can be schematically presented in terms of three related formulations:

(i) The happily imprecise 'traditional' society of India had a pluralistic way of life, particularly in the organization of its culture. Indian unity had been a cultural, not a political, phenomenon. A people that has practised tolerance (= pluralism) in one field, can also do so in another. Indians had practised pluralism (= tolerance) for long. True they had not been pluralistic in their politics. But it is simply a question of transferring the same logic to another field.

(ii) Political institutions in post-Independence India are based on pluralism=tolerance. Concretely, this principle involves constitutionally limited, impersonal powers of the political elite, and the corresponding rights of all citizens (tolerance in this sense).

(iii) A democratic political system based on pluralism and tolerance can exist in India precisely because it does not go against, but takes the assistance of, our pre-existing cultural tradition.

III

Unfortunately, I disagree both with Professor Kothari's description and his analysis. There is an initial difficulty about what is exactly meant by tradition. 'Traditionalism' is explicit only in a negative sense.[6] By a 'traditional society' we mean one that is fundamentally different from a modern, industrial bourgeois society. But a society can be non-modern in many ways. Akbar's India was traditional; so was Asoka's. But they were based on different principles of organization. We should, therefore, not assume an undifferentiated and homogeneous 'tradition'. We can then find out which aspect of the present traditional structures is derived from which particular period of our history. Though I believe

[6] Apart from the theoretical criticisms that one can advance against the term 'modernization', it indicates another interesting problem with a logical structure similar to that of ethnocentric prejudices. In maps of the world, one tends to put one's own country at the obvious centre. In thinking about history, there is a remarkably similar tendency to regard one's own time as being obviously 'central' to human experience.

our traditional structures were uniformly repressive, the ingenuity of the ancient and medieval ruling classes cannot be doubted. They showed great inventiveness in engineering their repressive system and its moral code to suit the requirements of particular situations. The social structure showed a curious mixture of rigidity and elasticity. Through a constant elasticity of interpretations, the repressive function was kept uniform. Despite formally rigid rules, the structure was not the same from one stage of feudalism to another. When a tradition is merely referred to as 'traditional', I find it difficult to understand which specific social practice is meant—pre-feudal, feudal, medieval, colonial, or any of the numerous discrete forms of feudal society. All such forms do of course have some common distinguishing qualities in contrast to modern capitalist societies. Still, this mode of reference hides their specificity and distinct organizational principles.

My disagreement with Professor Kothari's argument is not only methodological. It has to do mainly with his content. Traditional India certainly lacked a stable political centre. No one would disagree with him that the Indian sense of identity was primarily cultural. A North Indian and a South Indian may not have lived under the same political regime, or a similar set of laws. Still, they would have regarded themselves as having some common identity. This identity must therefore be extra-political. How this happens—why political disintegration did not lead to cultural diversification—is a much larger question. But I find it difficult to accept Professor Kothari's implicit argument that this represented a case of pluralism; and pluralism of this sort is equal to tolerance; and, finally, that pluralism of this kind can function as the cultural understructure to modern democracy. I do not think what we consider pluralism in the context of democratic politics is the same thing as pluralism in the context of ancient or medieval India.

Certainly, in traditional Indian society there was a large variety of cultural and political forms. We can call that society pluralistic in the sense that there were numerous coexistent political units, and sometimes a certain variety of lifestyles. But that is simply a registration of variation. Indian animal life or plant life also shows great variation. We do not, however, call it pluralism in the sense of democratic tolerance. Using euphemisms, we can perhaps call it a principle of 'mutual respect'. But let us examine what we mean by this term.

Suppose, in a cultural system X, you have political units P, Q, R. A population of individuals, say a to z, is distributed among these political territorial units.

P (a b c d e f)
Q (g h i j k l m)
R (n o p q r s t u v w x y z)

Suppose, further, that all these are princely autocratic states, that is, we imagine them to be as close to the traditional Indian states as possible: a rules P; g rules Q; and n rules R. In ruling, that is, taking the most significant decisions affecting these units, a never consults b, c, d, e, f, and so on. How do we characterize the situation? In fact we have chosen an uncharacteristically civilized specimen, because it includes only political inequality. It could be rendered *more* realistic and more complex by introducing other elements like caste and sex inequality. But let us continue with this relatively simpler model. Would we be entitled to characterize this situation as pluralistic = tolerant = culturally democratic? If I understand Professor Kothari's argument correctly, he would reply in the affirmative: pluralistic = tolerant, and if not = democratic, at least conducive to democracy in the long run. I, however, do not see quite how.

Political democracy refers, I think, to a quality of relationships existing between the rulers and the ruled. It finds expression in universal consultation, accountability,[7] majority rule, rights of citizens, and definitive restrictions on the powers of the governors. None of these conditions obtain in our model of traditional society.

The conditions that do exist reveal two equally significant characteristics. There is a certain pluralism in the sense of existence of variation. Equally certainly, there is no democracy, and no conscious, rational tolerance for other modes of behaviour. The coexistence

[7] Universal consultation is not an abstract constant. Both in democratic theory and in practice its content is differential. Democratic theory can be divided into three clear stages: a liberal-oligarchic, or liberal constitutionalist stage; a liberal democratic-stage; and an elite-democratic stage. In the first stage, the legal principle of responsibility of the government to the propertied was explicitly sanctioned. In the second stage the formal right to participation was extended to all citizens. In the third stage, although the general universal right to political participation was not explicitly denied, the meaning of 'participation' was constantly watered down.

of numerous local communities, which would have liked to impose their ways on others had they the power to do so, cannot be regarded as pluralism = tolerance. It is a pluralism which represents a powerless intolerance. Several contiguous and mutually independent autocracies do not represent a democratic culture. At best, one can argue for an antecedent *federal* tendency in our tradition. But I think the idea that federalism is intrinsically democratic is not self-evident. Federalism does ensure greater equality among rulers in a lateral division of powers. It does not ensure that the relations between the rulers and the ruled within each unit possess a democratic quality. The US is a democratic state; but I doubt that its democracy is the result of its federalism. Historically, I think, one can make a case that the reverse is true. Real democracy emerged in the US after the initial or 'real' federalism had disappeared as a result of the development of large-scale industrial capitalism.[8] Conversely, the United Arab Emirates, may be regarded truly federal. But the nation is hardly democratic. I understand the argument that antecedent plural cultural forms made federalism necessary for India. But I do not understand how a pluralism which does not involve any theory of consent or responsibility can even remotely be called democratic, or how it can be an apprenticeship for democratic government.

Traditional Indian culture was deeply aristocratic, repressive, and massively violent towards the oppressed. It is of course a remarkable feature of the Indian system that there was rarely a challenge to the repressive system from the lower orders. But this again is not an expression of democracy. The fact that the lower orders acquiesce, either because they are faced with an overwhelming force, or because there is an effective legitimation system, does not make the system democratic, though this certainly calls for an explanation of the behaviour of the oppressed. The argument of acquiescence is actually rather dangerous. British rule in India was not effectively challenged for a long spell after 1857. It had not suddenly become democratic. It represented the peace of the graveyard.

Let us put this argument now in a second form. The Indian tradition accepted pluralism (in the sense of variation, or deviation from a

[8] For a rare application of the theory of capitalist development to the study of American politics, and particularly to the unlikely field of judicial behaviour, cf. Lerner 1958.

general norm) in matters of secondary importance. There were surely variations in the subcaste systems of different regions. There were differences in the detailed practices of Hindu religious ritual. It is important to note these variations for certain types of social science research. An anthropologist, for instance, should not fall into the error of believing that the active caste system means the *varnas* and overlook the complexities of the *jatis*. But, for a political scientist seeking to understand the political functioning of the traditional society, I think it is equally dangerous to overstress the plurality of subcaste formations; for him the more fundamental fact is the unity of their legitimation function. To give a dramatic example of what I mean: Hindu society in south Bengal may have respected the right of north Bengali society to burn its widows in its own way. North Bengali upper-caste men may have reciprocated by tolerating the pluralistic principle that, when a low-caste man was to be punished, scrupulous regard was to be paid to local custom. But I am sure Professor Kothari would not expect us to regard these as examples of pluralism.[9] This, unfortunately makes it all the more difficult for me to understand precisely what he has in mind when he refers to our traditional pluralistic culture. Pluralism in a democratic sense would involve asking the widow and the Harijan their views on the matter. It is difficult to believe that this was done on a large scale in India.

There can I think be another argument against this part of Professor Kothari's case. Democratic tolerance is not based on political ineffectiveness. When a case is made for political autonomy to individuals or groups, its premise is not that the central government is unable to control them administratively. You cannot give away what you never had in the first place. Professor Kothari's traditional pluralists were most of the time politically ineffective. Perhaps historical circumstances imposed pluralist behaviour on them. On the few occasions some of them were able to establish relatively stable empires, they shed their pluralism. A similar argument would apply to Hinduism. Certainly, Hindu society did put up with external interference, and developed very interesting mechanisms of social and cultural absorption. But here too I think one should not be romantic. Hinduism is not a homogeneous religion. Its internal structure is marked more by ineffective intolerance, than

[9] Etymologically, these variations should be termed plural, or plurality. Ism denotes an element of consciousness that is entirely lacking in this case.

ideological tolerance of a positive kind. This has led to peevishness and irritation more than mass violence. The early Buddhists, who overrated the effectiveness of an ideology of tolerance, had to pay heavily for their mistake. They were thrown out of the Indian mainland and had to look for shelter elsewhere. In this connection I find Professor Kothari's mention of Shankara's tolerance puzzling.

The attitude of tolerance that goes with political democracy does not come out of lack of political power. It is a rational and conscious decision flowing from the idea that even if you do have the power to impose your way of life on others, you choose not to do so. It is a different situation from one in which you would like to impose your will on others but cannot—because you lack the means of doing so. I am afraid Professor Kothari does not make adequate conceptual distinctions between these two meanings of pluralism. Consequently, he has an incorrect understanding of our culture. He interprets what I think are the least democratic elements in our culture as democratic elements. This has large implications for political practice. It will lead to confusion about the allies and enemies of the democratic process.

IV

Professor Kothari's second general proposition is that today we have a political structure based on the principle of pluralist tolerance. This pluralism is revealed in two ways. First, any democratic system is of course based on the abstract principle of pluralism and bargaining. But Indian politics is distinguished by pluralism of another variety. It is based on a political culture of consensus—a tendency to sort out issues by bargaining, not by forcing issues. Most significant is the fact that this bargaining is entered into by a party which has no need to so bargain, because of its overwhelming electoral preponderance.

On the first question, one would agree with Professor Kothari. Democratic government involves a formal equality of treatment and an open system of political articulation. The only problem here would be to judge how much of this abstract notion is realized in practice. I tend to think that the Indian record has not been particularly impressive. Social tensions have not disappeared. Communalism, provincialism, and linguism have used political channels offered them by political democracy to mobilize essentially undemocratic social forces. Even today, some Hindus in Aligarh find it difficult to tolerate the existence of Muslims. Some Assamese are not quite reconciled to Bengali residents in Assam. Members of Parliament from North India consider it rather unreasonable that southerners insist on speaking in a different language.

The record of the state has not been encouraging either. The police officer from the upper caste is insufficiently reconciled to the idea that his victims can now formally claim some rights. In most cases of communal rioting and police firing, violence by the state is sought to be condoned by the leaders. One can refer to incidents at Pantnagar, Aligarh, and the two districts of Andhra Pradesh where the state has not only tolerated violence, its executive wing has actually organized it.

We must therefore keep abstract formulae distinct from the facts of the political process. Formal rules of democratic government enjoin that there should be equality of rights. Repeating this does not really help us understand Indian reality. A critical question rarely asked by academics is about the depth of the democratic process. Curiously, however, most academic enquiries, while proclaiming an empiricist epistemology, actually start with definitions. In textbooks, democracy is defined as a system of equal rights, but in the real world these rights are not enjoyed equally by all.

A democratic system is certainly preferable on rational grounds. But political decisions of social groups are not always guided by logical considerations. They are dictated by interests. Land-owning classes in England consistently obstructed the growth of democratic institutions. The early bourgeoisie also opposed first the inclusion of the petty bourgeois and then of the proletariat into the political process. Early bourgeois parties fought against any hint of democracy, against the conversion of a narrow property-based liberal scheme of government to a universalistic liberal-democratic form. The good bourgeois of the eighteenth century would have remonstrated against any suspicion of democratic ideas. The rise of democracy was partly the result of a strategic historical defeat of the bourgeoisie. Democracy was won in the teeth of bourgeois opposition, wrenched bit by bit from its clenched fist by bloody mass protests in the streets of London and Paris. No ruling class is persuaded by arguments to give up its power.

It would have been surprising had the Indian rural elite given in to democratic assaults on their traditional fortresses without a fight. They did not. The bourgeoisie made it easier for them by opting for a fabian, instead of a radical bourgeois, strategy of social change by accepting an incomplete bourgeois transformation of agrarian relations. On all accounts, the democratic processes have not yet percolated to the countryside.[10] They have come up against traditional power structures. British rule fortified the undemocratic power of feudal landed interests through land reforms and other types of political engineering. Colonial intervention reinforced earlier hierarchies in rural societies where they existed. Occasionally, they also created new forms of inegalitarian structures. Democratic norms encounter organized resistance from these interests. This is because political relationships in pre-independence India were organized on antithetic principles. Democratic processes have to be established by overcoming the opposition of these interests and not, as Professor Kothari suggests, with their help.

The rural elite in India has responded to democracy through a complex strategic mix. On the surface, there is an acceptance of electoral power as long as it helps legitimize the power of the traditional elite. The rural elite has bent, more or less successfully, institutions of formal democracy to the service of existing power structures. Formerly the village tyrant had a paternalistic claim to authority. Now he wins elections. The moment electoral channels threaten existing hierarchies, they are resisted with force. In case there is a possibility of those lower down the hierarchy winning the elections, there are either no elections or, in extreme cases, there are no candidates left to contest them.

Other shifts have also occurred, shifts that are subtler and easier to neglect in analysis. The composition of the rural elite has changed since the colonial days. The place of feudal landlords and moneylenders

[10] Ordinary behaviouralists are not usually bothered by such unscientific obstacles in the road to science. One cannot pose a questionnaire to people on the balance of liberty and terror in the village. In any case no 'community leader' is going to answer questions on how many Harijans he has prevented from voting. So we normally work on the assumption that all is well. An extreme example was an electoral study which sought to prove that the 1971 elections in West Bengal were 'free and fair'. One can perhaps ignore such cases because the motives inspiring the study were probably more directly political than political-scientific. But this is part of the epistemological paradox of behavioural election studies. Questions that are amenable to its procedures are trivial—it amounts to a latent theory of the inevitability of trivialization of political studies.

has sometimes been taken up by rich farmers. The Congress government's policy of fabian capitalism has given full scope to the rural rich to manoeuvre the situation to their advantage. They have not merely flouted the land ceilings. They have largely escaped the rules of democratic conduct. Local government institutions are controlled by those who own land. At the lower levels, there is a simple and visible transitivity of economic into political power, with few mediations. There are no screens. Mediations increase and become more complex as one moves up towards the state and central governments. But even at the intermediate levels—in state cabinets and administration, for instance[11]—pressure from the land lobbies is usually decisive. The interweaving of the economically powerful and the officially important is symbiotic, often personal. At each remove, the political representatives of this group become a little more presentable, the connections a little more difficult to guess. Still, life processes in the village are not altered fundamentally. Murders of recalcitrant peasants, the burning down of lower-caste dwellings, rapes, every form of violation of humanity which is part of a feudal and not a bourgeois political order, are all daily occurrences.

City newspapers, reconciled to these natural phenomena, give them little attention, or simply and misleadingly classify them as 'crimes'.[12]

[11] The personnel for these bureaucracies are drawn increasingly from the rich peasant, first-generation educated strata, announcing the arrival of the economically powerful into the precincts of cultural privilege and formal power. This has changed the character of the educational process. These strata have a frank power orientation towards education, emphasizing the degree which legitimizes their assumption of jobs that they secure by social pressure and connections. They are apt to look upon the old-fashioned British-trained, rationalistic emphasis on skills and knowledge with contempt. In the colonial period these functionaries were supplied to an imperialism of clerkships from Bengal, Bombay, and Madras. The new functionaries are sometimes more repressive than their predecessors. The earlier groups of officials were not immediately involved in the local social conflicts. This is no apology for the former official. Only, the new tyrants are hardly better.

[12] In Indian society and its press one is immediately struck by the differential reception of crimes. Crime against children or adolescents of the upper middle class create an instant sensation—an insecurity and revulsion among articulate city dwellers. Similar crimes against children of less fortunately salaried parents

In fact, to deserve the attention of the cultured city, the brutality has to be monumental. Only a Pantnagar, or Belchhi, or Aligarh ruffles the placid conscience of the city, and the democratic citizen tolerates its interference with his morning coffee for just a few days. Usually, there is a ceremonial elegy from the city, little sustained action. The city apparently feels good at proving to itself that it has a conscience. It is very rarely realized that violence is a continuum. Small and big violence are organically related. Every act of violence that you tolerate without protest, because it is remote from you, brings it a step closer to your doorstep. It is because small violence is tolerated that big violence is rendered possible.

Democracy consequently has become a commodity that can be had in urban housing areas with a middle-class income. This has happened not because Indians cannot run democracy; but because of the survival of feudal elements in the superstructures. Our political culture not only permits ruling-class violence, it reconciles its victims of the naturalness and inevitability of this treatment.

V

Professor Kothari also believes that Indian democratic politics has followed a consensual style with unlimited opportunity for bargaining over political demands. I both agree with him, and do not. It depends on what exactly we mean by this consensus and how we define its limits. In all democratic forms, there is a market-like operation of political forces. However, the significant claim is not in the market-like nature of political transactions, but in the unstated assumption that this market is perfectly competitive. And it must be kept in view that Professor Kothari's use of the perfect competition assumption is not a simplifying device for the early stages of the argument, which could be dropped when the argument gets more complex. The argument,

---

are taken with equanimity and make three-line items on the fourth page. Criminals may violate legal codes; but they often instinctively abide by the social codes of a social form. What is remarkable in this contrast is the fact that the revulsion of the city middle class is not against the crime as a violation of humanity, but against the violation of its own security as a *class*.

unfortunately, never gets more complex. No one denies that there is some bargaining. But the notion that all groups come into the market-place with an initial equality of resources or leverage is simply misleading.

Professor Kothari also uses the term consensual model to denote a specific way of handling conflicts. According to him, Indian ruling groups have shown an unwillingness to settle matters by a showdown. They have settled conflicts before these could turn into deep cleavages.

Certainly, under specific conditions, ruling groups in India did not take matters to a breaking point.[13] In others, however, they have. I shall argue that there is a certain logic in the distinction between these two types of situations. Those conditions which encouraged them to be tolerant are therefore important. Take the politics of the Constituent Assembly. The composition of the assembly surprised even some Congressmen. Several extreme conservative politicians, who had collaborated with the British and had consistently opposed Congress agitations, were beneficiaries of the consensual largeheartedness of the Congress leaders. Representatives of feudal interests were also made members of the assembly.[14] Not surprisingly, the work of the Constituent Assembly was full of wrangles. And it turned out a document that was somewhat different from the programmes which Congress had placed before the people. It was considerably less radical. The tussles were no mere legal quibbles. They reflected a conflict between those who, naïvely, wanted to carry forward the programmes of the Congress, and those others who, realistically, wanted to back out of them towards a more regressive social compromise. There were also those who thought that this opportunity could be used to fling the Congress back on to a fully feudal or fully nineteenth century bourgeois social programme. In the event, the Constituent Assembly sanctified a non-aggression pact between the bourgeois and the feudal interests This was curious. For, the landed aristocracy had tried to ensure that the occasion for such independent constitution-making did not arise. Princes, who had an unblemished record of collaboration with colonial authorities, were given generous

[13] As Kothari admits elsewhere, this does not apply to Mrs Gandhi's treatment of the opposition between 1974 and 1977; nor to Janata's treatment of Mrs Gandhi since then. Kothari 1976: *passim.*

[14] Cf. Kothari 1970: *passim*, specifically 106.

terms.[15] The colonial bureaucracy, instead of being attacked or dismantled, was given a key role in the new set-up. The government was not so considerate in other cases. An example is the treatment meted out to radical forces. In Telengana it not only crushed a communist insurgency, it also took away from the rebellious peasantry the purely anti-feudal gains of the land struggle.[16] Later, it tried to work a counterfeit land reform through the Bhoodan and Gramdan movements, outflanking the militant land struggles. These two instances—generosity to pro-colonial princes, and harshness to the radical peasantry—have been taken from the same period.

The tolerance of the state had clear and specific limits. It was organized around a definite principle. After Independence, because it felt weak and apprehensive, the Congress leadership gradually evolved a strategy of coalition of all owning classes.[17] Thus, the feudals got a

[15] This was astonishing in the context of earlier declaration of the Congress. The non-aggression pact between the feudals and the bourgeoisie was a definite retrogression from its earlier programmatic vision; programmes since Karachi had led people to expect better things. The radicalism of the Congress was declining in exact proportion as independence drew nearer. Some believe that the compromise with feudal elements was due to Congress nervousness on assumption of power. However, even after Congress power was evidently consolidated, it showed no urgency in attacking feudal structures—proving that this was a policy, not a tactical retreat. Eventually, this offered Mrs Gandhi a gratuitous opportunity to claim radical legitimacy by liquidating these ridiculous anachronisms.

[16] For a detailed historical account, see Sundarayya 1972.

[17] In a crucial passage, Marx (1975) makes a distinction between two types of revolutions, one following an ascending line, the other a descending one: 'In the first French revolution the rule of the constitutionalists is followed by the rule of the Girondists and the rule of the Girondists by the rule of the Jacobins. Each of these parties relies on the more progressive party for support. As soon as it has brought the revolution far enough to be unable to follow it further, still less to go ahead of it, it is thrust aside by its bolder ally that stands behind it and sent to the guillotine. The revolution thus moves along an ascending line . . . It is the reverse with the revolution of 1848 . . . Each party kicks from behind at that driving forward and leans over towards the party which presses backwards. No wonder that in this ridiculous posture it loses its balance, and having made the inevitable grimaces collapses with curious capers.

prize for obstructing national freedom. Communists were punished because they tried to take it too far. The Congress surely followed a policy of consensus, but a limited consensus accommodating certain groups at the expense of others.

It is in this sense that a consensus both did exist and did not. This is not a literary paradox. To claim an unqualified consensus, as Kothari does, is to exhibit a highly selective memory. If we mean by consensus the rapprochement between feudal elements and the rising bourgeoisie, then the Indian model was certainly consensual. Whereas Marxists call it the bourgeois-feudal coalition, Professor Kothari calls it a consensual model.

Of course, all bourgeois democracies show internal unevenness.[18] Britain has Northern Ireland, the US had Detroit. And these unevennesses are not static, they shift according to the historical situation. Infringements of formal democratic rules become more serious in periods of economic stress. There are, therefore, specific limits to democracy. Geographically, democratic rules do not extend much beyond the cities. Marx referred to French democracy in the nineteenth century as a system of freedom in the general sense, but its abrogation in the margins.[19] We can similarly characterize Indian democracy as a system of freedom in the city, and violation in the outskirts. Secondly,

---

The revolution thus moves in a descending line. It finds itself in this state of retrogressive motion . . .' There is also an interesting supporting argument on why the bourgeoisie may prefer 'impure' forms of its rule in certain contexts: 'instinct taught them that the republic, true enough, makes their political rule complete, but at the same time undermines its social foundation, since they must now confront the subjugated classes and contend against them without mediation . . . It was a feeling of weakness that caused them to recoil from the pure conditions of their own class rule and to yearn for the former more incomplete, more undeveloped, and precisely on that account the less dangerous forms of this rule.'

[18] I consider this an advantage of the marxist analytical framework. It does not fetishize into absolutes characteristics that are historically relative. We need not expect that a democratic form is uniformly democratic in all its parts or over time.

[19] Marx 1975: 409.

this system does not extend much beyond the middle classes, especially in the countryside. Within these limits, the laws of accommodation, tolerance, and of not taking conflicts to a rupture, all apply.

Conversely, there are clear limits to the tolerance of the system. The borders of this placid state within a state are marked in blood. Those who operate the system, specially at the grassroots, see and respect these limits. This is reflected in the helplessness of the Block Development Officer (BDO) in the face of feudal authoritarianism. Young bureaucrats are quickly persuaded out of their idealism. They not only gradually accept these terms, they also begin rationalizing them. This is a specific result of the feudal-bourgeois compromise. This dual system operates at its best during elections, when politicians, journalists, and even political scientists come to the village from the democratic world. It works at its worst when local people start taking their rights seriously, and expect the state to enforce them and disobey traditional tyrannies. In such cases the usual reminder about the limits of tolerance takes the form of a Kilavenmani or Belchhi. An event of this kind is followed by an advertised hunt for the major accused, followed by a quiet commutation of sentences and speedy rehabilitation.[20]

Bargaining is not for everyone. Only certain types of interest groups can participate in it. Business interests have institutionalized channels

[20] The normal sequence can be as follows: an event, its denial by officials; its use by unprincipled opposition (Congress people disconsolate over Belchhi; Janata people similarly over Andhra repression or the Rajan case—hence opportunistic); a thickening trickle of news gathered by persevering newsmen; admission by government that the event had taken place, though of course blown out of proportion by the press; newspaper leads and ceremonial elegies; letters by intellectuals (important names and forty others—undemocratic to the smallest detail); if excessively provoked, a public meeting and resolutions followed by a satisfied retreat into untroubled daily life; elsewhere, the return of the criminals to their villages; the dropping of cases for lack of evidence or mediation, a quick return of the momentarily famous village to the solid structures of repressive relations—if anything, with greater arrogance ftom the criminals because they have shown that they can 'get away with it'; occasionally, a grant of a few hundred rupees to the widows of the victim—which does greater service to the minister's public image than to the family's budget. And, of course, total silence by All India Radio over such crimes in both its shackled and its free incarnations.

for bargaining with government agencies. Businessmen, farmers, and provincial and linguistic troublemakers are as a rule heard with patience. One can in fact establish a certain hierarchy of governmental response—from tenderness and understanding to irritation to offence—as one moves down the scale from organized business through 'kisans' to lowly government employees. With still lower interests, like railway workers, the answer is what happened in 1951,[21] or 1974,[22] or Pantnagar.[23] Movements making undemocratic and unpluralist demands are as a rule tolerated, their demands conceded, or their leaders purchased off by other means. These movements can be accommodated because what they demand is the redistribution of surplus and privilege among the ruling elements. If these sacred boundaries are transgressed, even a government dominated by aged vegetarians can find enough reserves of violence to suppress them. Both the Janata and the Congress have fought heroically against undemocratic demands, such as a higher pay for workers or an agricultural wage.

Finally, Professor Kothari shows a symmetry between India's past and its present. He believes that we have been able to create a tolerable form of democracy precisely because we have been fortunate with

[21] 1951 is for the benefit of those who argue that 'Nehru would not have done this.' By the early 1950s he had sufficiently recovered from his youthful fabianism to order exemplary punishment for railway workers. By the late 1950s he had sufficiently recovered from an idealist parliamentarianism to dislodge the Kerala government by nonelectoral means. The JP movement used against Mrs Gandhi a weapon that she had used against Namboodiripad. She therefore had little grounds for complaining. You cannot expect people not to do to you what you have done to others. Between these, of course, democratic norms are weakened.

[22] The massive violence against railway workers was occasioned by their unreasonable claim that the government must honour a prior pledge about wages.

[23] Pantnagar is for the benefit of those who would assure us, after Janata's assumption of office, that we are going to live happily ever after in automatic democracy. Janata's record in its short rule is no less distinguished. An Aligarh for a Turkman Gate; a Pantnagar for a Muzaffarnagar. Typically, top government leaders—who are vegetarians for fear of causing pain to living things—did not care to visit the place. On unofficial reckoning, the number of casualties exceeded a hundred.

a proto-democratic culture earlier, because we have been trained in tolerance, as it were, for ages. Only it was tolerance in a different field. It has only to be transferred to the field of politics.

I too believe that there is a symmetry. But it is a symmetry between our earlier hierarchies, pervaded by a one-way violence of the ruling class, and our present democracy with its tensions and tolerated violence. It exists, I think, precisely because of our earlier political culture—because we have been trained to take intolerance for granted. Our political culture was repressive. It still is. In that sense, tradition has been modernized.

VI

Despite these fundamental disagreements I think Professor Kothari raises a serious question. It is a question that is raised both by the marxist and behavioural problematiques, though, naturally, they would formulate it quite differently. Modern Western political theory accepts that colonialism and uninterrupted capitalist growth were necessary conditions for the growth of early democratic states in Europe. None of these conditions are present in third world states. Most Western observers therefore despair of the prospects of democracy in these states. However, they quickly overcame this despair because the West was able and willing to supply these conditions artificially, in the form of aid. It was not really a question of protecting a free world, but of creating one. This is particularly ironic. Western analysts usually accuse communists of exporting revolution. But the typical precondition for communism—widespread poverty and degradation—are indigenously produced. However, the preconditions for bourgeois democratic politics—consistent secular growth and uninterrupted prosperity—cannot be indigenously produced. They have to be supplied from outside. The Western theory of democracy in the third world, or what they hopefully called 'political development', amounted to an export of bourgeois politics by first exporting its preconditions.

This shows a certain originality in Professor Kothari's position. Unfortunately, this also brings out its intrinsic utopianism. He has a complex relation with functionalism and theories of political development. Epistemologically, he is within the functionalist tradition. He uses the same epistemic assumptions, the same rules of closure, the same framework of concepts and general theory. Still, there is a difference in the way he uses it. He uses it to develop an argument that is significantly different from the ethnocentric, ahistorical, patronizing tradition–modernity theories. In these theories the complexity of historical transition takes on a fairytale black-and-white character. It becomes a misleading replication of the development in Europe over the 17th–19th centuries. Against this simple theory, Kothari has argued for a more complex and continuous relationship. Traditional factors, in his view, support and sustain modern democratic norms. It is essentially a theory of an alternative base for democratic superstructures.

The analytic problem is to explain how a democratic system can function even when what are considered to be its preconditions are absent. Kothari tries to rescue the functionalist-behaviouralist theory from this difficulty. Even if we find his arguments unsatisfactory, the problem remains with us.

VII

Since marxists are accused of indulging in rhetoric, I shall try to live up to this reputation. My disagreement with Professor Kothari is not at the level of analysis alone. I do not accept the way he looks at facts. Because we take different methodological paths, we formulate our questions differently. What do we make of events like the repression in Telangana in 1949–50, the handling of the 1951 railway strike, repression of the food movements in the 1960s, the 1962 Emergency that was reserved especially for communists, the Emergency of 1975, and the repressions of the Janata period? For Professor Kothari these are cases in which our political culture failed. For me, they were the result of the imperfect institutions of our democracy.

There is a deep contradiction in Indian political life between the traditional logic of repression and the democratic logic of participation, between the idea of differential rights for various classes and the idea of 'equality before law'. Professor Kothari puts this contradiction in very low relief. The historic question is how this contradiction is going to be resolved. Will the logic of traditional society prevail over the new political form? Or will the political form transform society? There is a third, more complex and untidy, possibility. There can be a long coexistence of partial democracy and its negation through the non-aggression pact earlier mentioned. In cities, the logic of democracy aided by industrialization may transform feudal practices, or send them into hiding. But in the vast rural sector the reverse process seems to operate. Through the modalities of what Professor Kothari has called vote banks based on traditional loyalties, feudal power relations have forced democratic forms to come to terms with it, to express its logic in a different idiom, to dilute the effectiveness of participatory rights, and render them purely formal.

Professor Kothari's argument contains a double romaticicization: a symmetry between a romanticized past and a romanticized present, a past that never was flowing into a present, that does not exist. Our past cannot fit his description, unless we define the term pluralism the way he does. Our present is not the way he describes it either. A political system that is wide open, based on perfect competition, unlimited bargaining, with its leaders eager to reach an unqualified consensus, would leave little room for discontent. The reality is different. Every time the economy is under strain, this consensus is destroyed. The regularity of our political crises can hardly be missed—1957–8, 1967, 1974–5, and once again in 1977. These were managed with varying degrees of success. The Emergency brought out one interesting feature of the political system—the ease with which our democratic structures can be dismantled. Authoritarianism was overthrown by its own mistake, it collapsed because it gave the indignant peasantry a chance to use the electoral weapon. It was the last peasant revolt in North India. It showed all its characteristics—the suddenness of the explosion when everything seemed still; the shock, the abruptness, the finality of the peasant strike; 1977 was historic. But it shared the usual fate of peasant revolts. Other sections of society ran away with the benefits of political change. It did not change village life in rural India. The electoral process helps in converting private dissent into formal assent. The system is rejected in such a way that it is further strengthened. This is why massive mandates are brittle, for they are votes *against* not *for* something.

On ethical grounds, I have no disagreement with him. I prefer the condition he has described to the one I have. I think his reading of our politics is wrong. I wish he were right.

References

Kothari, Rajni. 1970. *Politics in India*. New Delhi: Orient Longman.

———. 1976. *The Democratic Polity and Social Change in India*. New Delhi: Allied.

———. 1978. Political Culture in Post-Independent India. Lead Paper, Panel II, Indian Political Science Association Conference, Patiala.

Lerner, Max. 1958. The Supreme Court and American Capitalism. In Robert McCloskey, ed. *Essays in Constitutional History*. New York: Alfred Knopf.

Marx, Karl. (1852) 1975. Eighteenth Brumaire of Louis Napoleon. In *Marx, Selected Works, Volume I*. Moscow.

Sen, Mohit. 1978. *Documents of the History of the CPI*. Delhi: People's Publishing House, vol. 8.

Sundarayya, P. 1972. *The Telengana People's Armed Struggle and its Lessons*. Calcutta: National Book Agency.

4

The Passive Revolution and India: A Critique

The story of Indian politics can be told in two quite different ways, through two alternative but mutually reinforcing constructions. The task of a proper Marxist analysis of Indian politics is to construct internally consistent accounts of our political history in these two ways, and to then provide a more theoretical enterprise which involves making these consistent with each other. One of these two narratives would tell the story of structures (if structures are things about which stories can be told).[1] This would be a story of the rise of capitalism, the specificities of transition, the formation and maturation of classes, the internal balance and architecture of the social form, the making and breaking of class coalitions, etc. Such things take long periods to happen, and occur through slow glacial movements. The second story would have to be constructed in terms of actual political actors, suspending the question of more fundamental causalities for the time being; it must be told in terms of governments, parties, tactics, leaders, political movements, and similar contingent but irreplaceable elements of political narratives. This second story—the narrative of the Indian state—would be related to the successes (in its own terms) of Indian capitalism and its failures, but would not be entirely

First presented at the Indo-Soviet seminar on 'The Indian Revolution' in Leningrad, 14–17 August 1987.

[1] There is a theory which holds that structures are constructs of such a kind that they deflect and obstruct historical reflection. On this untenable idea there is an impressive body of literature, the most well known and long-winded being E.P. Thompson 1978.

reducible to them. For, in the growth of a late capitalism like the Indian one, the social form of capitalism itself realizes that the state is a historical precondition for much of its economic endeavours and for its political security. Paradoxically, this state, which seemed remarkably stable and legitimate when Indian capitalism was relatively weak, has come into an increasingly serious crisis with the greater entrenchment of the social form.[2]

Attempted critiques of the Indian polity, to be convincing, must attempt to do the three things I mentioned earlier: they must try to plot the simple narrative line of this crisis, i.e. provide a structure to the simple flow of political events. This is to be taken seriously as a *narrative*. Stories told of the same thing by various reporters differ: similarly, different types of narratives would differ as to where the ruptures lie, where the continuities, how much significance to accord to which incident, etc.[3] This kind of thing could be called an event-to-event line of causality. But this simpler narrative account must also reveal a deeper causal profile related to a structural causal field:[4] it must show fundamental structural incompatibilities which have expressed themselves through these upheavals. This could be called a structure-to-event causal line. In this essay I try to show the kind of political model that might work in the structural analysis of Indian politics; but also that it is inadequate in two ways. First, the model itself is sketchy; and second, I have not worked out how the narrative can be fitted on to the workings of the model adequately. I believe optimistically that such a model has better chances of success than the earlier, more wooden ones generally in use.

[2] Some modernization theorists do note this paradox, but they would give it a bland historical solution by asserting that in the earlier stages the state had to cope with much lower levels of political 'demand'. Present difficulties of the state arise from the fact that these demands have multiplied through greater mobilization but the state's resources for coping with them—its 'supports'—have remained static. This indefensibly marginalizes the question of economic development, and is indifferent to the enormous growth of state resources and its deliberate creation of a network of advantage distribution.

[3] In the periodization of Indian politics, Rajni Kothari, for instance, saw the break with the Nehruvian system as coming in 1975. On my reading, this rupture is a much more slow-moving affair, and begins much earlier.

[4] J.L. Mackie 1975.

Long-term structural compulsions on Indian politics, the choices of both the ruling bloc of propertied classes and the unorchestrated subaltern classes, arise in several well-known ways: (i) inclusion of the Indian economy in the capitalist international market and its division of labour; (ii) the received structure of colonial economic retardation; and (iii) the fundamental choice exercised by the leadership of the new Indian state in favour of a capitalist strategy of economic growth through a set of basic legal and institutional forms, e.g. the format of legal rights in the constitution, the set of ordinary laws ruling economic and corporate behaviour, the enactment of industrial policy and other similar initiatives. This was, in a historical sense, a choice which obviously structures all other choices. These structures and their internal evolution have received a great deal of analytic attention from Marxist economists. For an analysis of the state, we have to assume some well-known Marxist propositions on the nature of India's capitalist development. The social formation in India is generally characterized as a late, backward, post-colonial capitalism,[5] which functionally uses various enclaves of pre-capitalist productive forms.[6] Politically, however, it would be wrong to assimilate the Indian capitalist experience into either the model of late-backward European capitalism of the Russian kind,[7] or into a lower late-backward form in which the imminent collapse of an immature capitalism makes the possibility of a socialist revolution realistic.[8] Although much of the Indian countryside still shows the persistence of semi-feudal forms of exploitation, one can make a case for a characterization of the social form as capitalism, for the judgement involved in such things is not a matter of a simple statistical or spatial predominance. Marx had, in a famous passage in *Grundrisse*, provided a methodological injunction about how to characterize such transitional economies through a

[5] However, I do not find the theoretical positions worked out by Hamza Alavi about the post-colonial state persuasive in the Indian case.

[6] This is contrary to the traditional linear belief that pre-capitalism is *in general* (in this case, taken to mean in every instance) dysfunctional to capitalist growth and would be liquidated historically.

[7] Of the kind analysed by Lenin in his theory of the Russian revolution. Such differences are clearly marked in Lenin's discussions of the colonial question.

[8] Of the type exemplified by China in the Comintern debates from the fourth to the sixth Congresses.

complex, historically inclined, identification.[9] To translate his colourful metaphor is not altogether easy—what does the simile of a predominant light mean in precise economic terms?—but it would be generally accepted that the capitalist form predominates in terms of controlling the economic trends of the totality of the social form. Capitalist logic dominates and gives the general title to the economy through its ability to reproduce itself on an expanded scale, set the tone and the targets for the economy as a whole, and therefore to determine the historical logic of the totality of the social formation. Although there are obviously other sectors and types of production in the Indian economy, their reproduction has been subsumed, both economically and politically, under the logic of reproduction of capital. It is the second part of this nexus which ought to be of special attention in an analysis of the Indian state.

In countries like India the process of reproduction of capital depends crucially on the state. Although the state–capital connection has been extensively studied in empirical economic terms, surprisingly little theoretical use has been made of this in the study of the Indian state. Still, some minimal generalizations can be made as starting points of a *political* enquiry. The state in India is a *bourgeois* state in at least three, mutually supportive, senses. (1) When we say that a state is 'bourgeois' this refers, in some way (though this particular *way* can be very different in various historically concrete cases),[10] to a state of dominance enjoyed by the capitalist class, or a coalition of classes dominated by the bourgeoisie. (2) The state form is bourgeois in the sense in which we speak of the parliamentary democratic form as being historically a bourgeois form of government. This is not just a matter of registering that such forms historically arose during the period of rising capitalism in Europe and spread out through a process of cultural diffusion. Rather, the Marxist view would posit a stronger, structural connection between bourgeois hegemony (or domination) and this form of the state.[11] It arranges a disbursing of advantages in a particular way; and the democratic mechanism works as a usefully sensitive

[9] Karl Marx 1973: 106–7.

[10] For instance, the different political trajectories analysed by Gramsci in the *Prison Notebooks*, especially discussions of the passive revolution.

[11] The sense in which Marx said that it is the democratic form which suits the capitalist mode most properly.

political index as to when the distribution of disadvantages, which is bound to happen and intensify in a capitalist economy, is becoming politically insupportable. This is the best construction of Marx's idea that democracy was the most appropriate political form for the capitalist mode of production. A more Lukacsian view would see this as a homology between a Marxist economy and a market-like political mechanism. Besides, it also lays down norms of management of interest conflicts in a way that, even though political grievances accumulate, their political articulation does not assume a pitch and form which makes the minimal stability required for capitalist production unobtainable. (3) The state expresses and ensures the domination of the bourgeoisie and helps in capitalist reproduction and a subordinate reproduction of other types of economic relations by imposing on the economy a deliberate order of capitalist planning. Those directive functions that capital cannot perform through the market (either because the market is imperfect or not powerful enough, or because such tasks cannot be performed by market pressures) the bourgeois state performs through the legitimized directive mechanisms of the state. The analysis of politics offered below takes such a minimal political economy argument on trust from Marxist economists. But what I offer here, in itself, is not a political economy argument; because I do not subscribe to the view that Marxists trying to understand politics too do the same enquiry as the economists, i.e. their cognitive object is the same. In my view, political scientists should not merely collect the political corollaries of the arguments of Marxist economists; their *object* is different. They study the 'other', the political side.

India has then a bourgeois state, but a state that is bourgeois in three different senses. The last two features are less problematic than the first. A bourgeois format of the state, or the bourgeois character of its legal system, property structure, and institutions of governance are clearly and undeniably evident.[12] These are revealed in the Indian constitution—in its central business of laying down some limits and prohibitions through the rights of property, etc., although this serious and

[12] Detailed analyses could be found in the work of S.K. Chaube and S. Dattagupta on the constituent assembly and the judicial processes, respectively. A more philosophically inclined discussion has been presented in Chhatrapati Singh 1985.

decisive core is surrounded by looser reformistic advisory clauses, and based on some necessary illusions of bourgeois power, such as its extreme constructivism: the myth, seriously believed by the early ruling elite, that patterns of laws can direct social relations rather than reflect them, an illusion which made the framers carry the constitutional document to an unreadable and agonizing length.[13] However, the original constitution reflected the accepted social plan or design of the ruling elite at the time of Independence, unlike the subsequent disingenuous insertions of ceremonial socialistic principles.[14]

A second institutional frame was provided by the adoption of the objectives and increasingly proliferating institutions of planning, which explicitly acknowledged the role of the state in the reproduction of capital and in setting economic targets in a way compatible with bourgeois developmental perspectives.

Clearly, however, of the three reasons for calling our state 'bourgeois' the last two are rather external. They depend, in any case, on the first condition of this characterization, and it is the first condition which is theoretically most problematic. It is a straightforward case of bourgeois dominance if the state is 'bourgeois' because it reflects a state of bourgeois dominance over society, if the bourgeoisie's political predominance is symmetrical with its directive power over the productive processes in the economy and its moral-cultural hegemony. In addition to economic control and directive power, states in advanced capitalist countries in the West employ what Poulantzas calls its 'institutional materiality' to reinforce, extend, and elaborate their dominance.[15] Our third condition can also be expressed in a Gramscian form: one of the crucial legal-formal principles of the capitalist state is the investiture on the state of the title of universality, a legitimate title to speak on behalf of the society 'in general'; this includes an implicit admission that other interests, at least in their raw, economic form constitute a 'civil society' representing the rule of a particularity of

[13] This is not merely a petty and querulous point. Constitutional documents must be read and understood by the people. The Indian constitution is a lawyer's document—a document of the lawyers, for the lawyers, by the lawyers.

[14] Particularly objectionable is the insertion of the term 'socialist' by recent amendment.

[15] Poulantzas 1978.

interests. Clearly, in the Indian case, though it would be wrong to underestimate the survival of democracy for forty years, the Gramscian hegemony model of the capitalist state does not apply in any simple, unproblematic form.[16] It is suggested here that the Indian capitalist class exercises its control over society neither through a moral–cultural hegemony of the Gramscian type, nor a simple coercive strategy on the lines of satellite states of the Third World. It does so by a coalitional strategy carried out partly through the state-directed process of economic growth, and partly through the allocational necessities indicated by the bourgeois democratic political system. Politically, too, as in the field of economic relations, the Indian bourgeoisie cannot be accorded an unproblematic primacy, because of the undeniable prevalence of pre-capitalist political forms in our *governance*; also because the vulgarly precapitalist form in the political life of rural India must be given appropriate analytic weight. Attributing political dominance to the capitalist class in a society in which the capitalist form of production is still not entirely predominant thus raises some theoretical problems.

Coalitional Relations of Classes

Marxists in India have commonly sought to solve this theoretical difficulty by offering a coalitional theory of class power.[17] Formerly, Communist Party literature asserted that power in India was exercised by an alliance of two dominant classes, the bourgeoisie (in some cases the monopoly stratum of the bourgeoisie, in others all fractions of the bourgeoisie as a whole), and landlords who still enjoyed precapitalist privileges and control. This picture did not standardly include the bureaucratic-managerial-intellectual elite as a distinct and separate element of the ruling coalition. In my judgement this was a flaw in the original model,[18] and stemmed from the tendency to underestimate

[16] I have tried to present an argument of this kind elsewhere: see Kaviraj 1987.

[17] Since Independence, almost all programmes by almost all communist groups assert that state power in India is controlled by an alliance of classes, although they differ about which classes, and their relative political weight.

[18] This was a flaw primarily because, though in economic life the public sector and state control on the economy were seen to be important, it appeared these had no political consequences or effects on class formation and class behaviour.

the significance of the political functions of the state and to view the state as merely an *expression* of class relations rather than a *terrain*, sometimes an independent actor in the power process. In earlier Marxist analysis of the 1950s or 1960s the historical necessity of a coalition of power was derived from the inability of the bourgeoisie to seriously pursue, let alone complete, a bourgeois democratic revolution.

The theory of a ruling 'coalition' highlights another essential point about the nature of class power in Indian society: that capital is not independently dominant in Indian society and state; and, for a series of other historical and sociological reasons, single-handed and unaided dominance in society is also ruled out for the other propertied classes. It is a political, long-term coalition which ensures their joint dominance over the state. So the coalition is not an effect or an accidental attribute of a dominance which is otherwise adequate; it is its *condition*. There are several reasons why, despite its weakness, capital exercises the directive function in the coalition. By its nature, it is the only truly universalizing element in the ruling bloc.[19] For, among the ruling groups, the bourgeoisie alone can develop a coherent, internally flexible development doctrine. Pre-capitalist elements have not had an alternative coherent programme to offer; their efforts have been restricted mainly to slowing down capitalist transition and ensuring comfortable survival plans for their own class. They have contented themselves by operating not as an alternative leading group, but as a relatively reactionary pressure group within the ruling combine trying to shift or readjust the balance of policies in a retrograde direction.

In class terms, the ruling bloc in India contained three distinct social groups and the strata internal to or organically associated with them: the bourgeoisie, particularly its aggressive and expanding monopoly stratum; the landed elites (which underwent significant internal changes due to the processes of agrarian transformation since Independence); and last, but not least, the bureaucratic managerial elite.[20]

[19] Although this is not the place for long or detailed theoretical discussions, I find Poulantzas's concept of a ruling bloc suggestive but inadequately clear.

[20] Though I advocate the inclusion of this group into the ruling bloc of classes, it is important to define the boundaries of this social group with precision. To include the entire administration in the ruling bloc would be absurd, but I would include the high bureaucratic elite and industrial management groups.

It must not be forgotten that the policies followed by the ruling bloc often had consequences for its own structure and internal formation. For instance, as a result of policies pursued over the long term, the structure of the classes themselves, especially of the latter two classes, underwent transformation. Although the redistributive aims of the land reforms were frustrated, they had some long-term effects on the class structure of agrarian society, particularly its upper social strata. Over the longer term, as a result of the decline of feudal landlords, a newer segment of rich farmers came to replace them in areas where the green revolution took place—a class of capitalist farmers. This has had serious consequences for Indian politics. Similarly, the third element has also undergone a remarkable expansion in its size, areas of control, and power in step with the development of the state-directed apparatus of economic growth.

Traditional Marxist accounts of the ruling coalition suffered, in my view, because they saw the bureaucratic elite as being too straightforwardly subordinate to the power of the bourgeoisie, and saw what was basically a *coalitional* and bargaining relation as a purely *instrumental* one. Actually, this third group was a crucial element in the ruling coalition of classes. Although not bourgeois in a direct productive sense, culturally and ideologically it was strongly affiliated to the bourgeois order. This class was, even before Independence, as some historical works show, the repository of the bourgeoisie's 'political intelligence', working out a 'theory' of development for Indian capitalism, often 'correcting' more intensely selfish objectives of the monopoly elements by giving them a more reformist and universal form.[21] With the constant growth of the large public sector, some genuine points of conflict between this bureaucratic elite in government and bourgeois entrepreneurial classes began to develop. Most significantly, however, they perform a distinct and irreducible function in the ruling bloc and its sprawling governmental apparatus. It is not only true that they mediate between the ruling coalition and the other classes, they also mediate crucially between the classes *within* the ruling coalition itself. They also provide the theory and the institutional drive for bourgeois rule.

[21] See Bipan Chandra 1979, in which G.D. Birla's behaviour is more startling than Nehru's.

Finally, a coalition is always based on an explicit or implicit protocol, a network of policies, rights, immunities derived from both constitutional and ordinary law which sets out, over a long period, the terms of this coalition and its manner of distribution of advantages. Changes in the structure, economic success and political weight of individual classes give rise naturally to demands for changes in its internal hierarchy and a renegotiation of the terms of the protocol; and discontented social groups use options over the entire range of 'exit, voice and loyalty'.[22] To understand the centrality of the third element, and also how the logic of politics intersects with the logic of the economy, I suggest a further distinction between what is generally known as *dominance* in Marxist theory and a different operation or terrain of what could be called *governance*. Domination is the consequence of a longer-term disposition of interests and control over production arrangements; and in this sort of calculation the dominant classes in Indian society would be the bourgeoisie, especially its higher strata and the rich farmers. This is clearly distinct from governance, which refers to the process of actual policy decisions within the apparatuses of the state. Surely the stable structure of class dominance constrains and structures the process of governance, but it is quite different from the first. This could be extended to suggest that the movement of public policies would be captured by a different concept which refers to configurations of vertical clientilist *benefit coalitions* that these policies create among the subordinate classes. Concessions to agricultural lobbies may create an affinity of interests among the large and the small farmers, or, say, among all those who sell agricultural produce on the market. Such benefit configurations are real and influence policy-makers' calculations of short-term political advantages accruing from policies. These also ensure that actual political configurations do not become symmetrical to class divisions in society. Evidently, this does not turn the small peasant into a part of the ruling bloc. But while it would be nonsensical to see him as a part of the ruling classes, it would be seriously unhelpful for political analysis to ignore such short-term nexuses of interest built up by directions of policy, since what are generally known as welfare programmes are explicitly used in this way. We can account for some crucial shifts in political alliances in

[22] See A. Hirschman 1970.

terms of such deliberate changes in benefit coalitions produced by public policy.

The coalitional nature of the ruling group has another serious implication for political analysis. The groups that are included in the coalition do not share equal power: power within the ruling bloc is evidently hierarchical. But if any of these classes is seriously dissatisfied and leaves the ruling bloc, that not only alters the structure of the coalition but threatens it with political disaster. Theoretically, it follows, any serious political move for each class or its representatives within the coalition is two-valued. These moves are of course in a general sense directed against the classes outside the bloc, but the choices of these moves have real effects on the internal politics of the ruling bloc. If a common objective, say, in industrial policy, can be achieved by three differently worked out policy options, x, y, z, their preference for these options would be often differently ranked by different components of the ruling bloc. These would result in different states of distribution of long-term and short-term benefits, and among these benefits very often figures the purely political strategic advantage of having a favourable format of procedure of decisions. This sort of a coalition theory may help us understand concrete moves and decisions of political life and link these with configurations of class interests, rather than standard academic coalition theories which use individuals as their standard political actors and plot coalition movements in reference to a formal minimality norm.[23]

III

I have suggested elsewhere that the story of Indian politics since 1947 ought to be seen in terms of a crucial initial stage of political realignments, followed by four fairly commonsensically divided periods in our political life.[24]

Realignments 1946–1950

In politics, beginnings often—despite their contingent character—take on the nature of fundamental constraining structures over the

[23] Cf. W.H. Riker's well-known discussion on the size principle in Riker, 1970 (1962): 71–6.

[24] See Kaviraj 1982.

long term. No state is able to erase its beginnings completely: initiatives taken in formative years of the state tend to acquire foundational and determining character simply because of their historical priority. Political scientists have, in my view, been inattentive towards the significance of this period of fast and crucial historical change;[25] and consequently, discussions on Indian politics suffer from a myth of exaggerated continuity between the late years of colonial rule and the early years of independent power.

The Congress which assumed power in 1947 was not in many respects the Congress that won Independence. The post-war years, after it was generally known that Independence was coming in the immediate future, naturally saw a series of quick political changes. Besides, the formal constitutional structure that was adopted set the framework of the moves of different social classes and political actors for quite a long time, until constitutional and formal language fell into sudden disuse after 1969–71.[26] Clearly, this period formed a crucial stage in the history of the Indian national movement. Earlier, the objective of the movement was the rather abstract one of making Independence possible; now the objective of every political group within the broad national movement changed into struggling for determination of the structure of power of the independent state—not an abstract end of

[25] Recently, after the archives have been opened for these years, there has been considerable interest among historians about this formative period; however, not much historical research is yet available.

[26] Ordinarily, the period of large-scale disregard for constitutional rules is set at 1975. But it ought to be noted that many of the initial moves against bour-geois democratic legal norms were begun and legitimized in the immediately preceding period of the 'left turn'. The judiciary, for instance, was attacked as conservative and opposed to the parliamentary tendency towards progressive legislation. This was an argument taken from British political arguments of the 1930s. Of course, it is possible to make a case that the courts generally incline to be conservative, but Indira Gandhi used this to loosen bourgeois constraints over her government, not to strain towards socialism. Unfortunately, leftists willingly surrendered their arguments to her, in return for small favours. These were used systematically to justify precapitalist irresponsibility in governance. Much of the present wrecking of bourgeois democratic institutional norms was done with the help of a disingenuous use of radical rhetoric.

sovereignty, but a far more concrete question of the form of the society and material allocation of advantages. Different political groups showed their common appreciation of this historical fact in their differing ways. Muslim separatism became more strident in demanding a separate state. Communists registered the same urgency by intensifying their struggles for peasant rights. Congress groups responded to this climate of approaching power by a greater ideological polarization and crystallization of political factions. And Gandhi, most interestingly and unpredictably of all, responded by suggesting that the Congress, bearing the imprint of an earlier age, ought to be disbanded in a typically theatrical convergence of the symbols of fulfilment and denouement.

Alongside these secessions from the earlier ambiguous unity of a single nationalist movement there were significant internal realignments within the Congress. Congress's paradox of continuity began from its very early days. It is not only that Indira Gandhi's Congress was very different from Nehru's, although claiming continuity; Nehru's Congress itself was different from the organization it inherited. Within the apparent hegemony of the Congress over the national movement, these two years saw serious political realignments; and, what is more, many of these tended to nullify earlier historical shifts in the Congress organization in a relatively radical direction. After 1942, socialists and their assorted allies came to occupy an important position in the Congress in the Hindi belt, an area that has been since the mid 1960s the despair of radical groups. Popular mobilization of a spontaneous form became widespread and began erupting outside the formal structure of the Congress. In the years just before Independence, the Congress was rising as a paradoxical mass wave, a wave which made its coming to power irresistible, but also a wave that the Congress leadership wished to see controlled rather than encouraged. For it may have meant, if it continued indefinitely, the crystallization of an early radical popular challenge to its new government.

When the Congress assumed power, since questions of social design and distribution of advantages through the legal form had become central, polarization within the party naturally became more intense. Thus the tussle between Nehru and Patel should be seen as a serious conflict of strategy within the ruling coalition, the outcome of which would have seriously affected the fate of the state, the nature of the economy, and the even purely social formation of these classes themselves. This was not, as sometimes claimed, a struggle between a bourgeois and a radical petty bourgeois programme of development of the nation; but equally certainly, it was no mere personal tussle for power between individual factions. It was a conflict between two quite different strategic perspectives within the general direction of capitalist development. And a victory of the more reactionary segment within the Congress could have meant great differences in public policy regarding the public sector, the extent of state control, the play of market forces, the nature of planning and foreign policy. Strategic differences assumed a sharp form between an old style, liberal laissez faire form of capitalist programme, and a reformistic state-centred strategy advocated by Nehru supporters within the party. Eventually, the historical outcome of this strategy conflict turned out to be deeply paradoxical. Through a combination of economic reasonableness and fortuitous events (like Patel's sudden death) the comparative reformists around Nehru won the strategic debate within the Congress, though their complete dominance in policy-making had to wait till the Second Plan.

But something else, less newsworthy and noticeable, also happened at the same time within the Congress Party. This highly spectacular victory of the reformists concealed a more fundamental weakening of their forces. Through a series of political squabbles, socialists who were within the Congress gradually left the party—to form most of the time relatively ineffective and regionally limited opposition groups. Subsequently, socialist groups in North India followed suicidal moves common among political parties suffering the pressure of declining mass support. Under Lohia's influence they went in for slogans and motifs which they thought would stop the erosion of their base and turn North India into a socialist fortress. Actually, this eventually turned into a prison. The adoption of a parochial agenda saved their base temporarily in the North, but ensured that it could not extend its appeal or mass base in other parts of India. It was a heavy price to pay for an advantage which eventually did not last. Besides, the strong anti-communism of the socialists also precluded any collaboration between the two major left parties outside the Congress; though, had they worked together as a joint political pressure group for radicalization of social policies and their implementation, it could possibly have counteracted the disingenuousness of Congress land reforms.

However, the paradox was that the Congress was formally wedded to what we now describe as the Nehruvian reformist programme at a time when the radicals inside the Congress became woefully weak, and when whatever little striking power they had was mainly concentrated at the centre. From the early years of the government, because of the federal distribution of powers, practically all measures adopted towards any reform of the agrarian structure were effectively countermanded by its own recalcitrant and more conservative state and local units. The Nehru government, thus, began its career by playing false to its own adopted programmes. And the quick decline of socialist influence in the states of Bihar and UP, where there had been strong peasant mobilizations in the not too distant past, remains among the large uninterrogated phenomena of recent Indian politics. The departure of the reformist elements from the Congress led to a feeling among the small elite around Nehru of being encircled within their own party organization. It provided the initial condition for, and pressure towards, a 'passive revolution' strategy.

Experimentation 1950–1956

Out of this historical situation arose the enormous programme of a capitalist 'passive revolution' that the Congress adopted in the Nehru period.[27] First, of course, the programme of serious bourgeois land reforms was abandoned through a combination of feudal resistance, judicial conservatism, and connivance of state Congress leaderships.[28] Legal arrangement of property institutions, sanctioned by the constitution, reinforced such opposition and gave it juridical teeth. Thus the only way in which agrarian transformation could take place was through a conservative, gradualist, and 'molecular' process.[29] Feudal and other conservative resistance could, in principle, be broken down if the Congress encouraged the mobilization of the masses and was

[27] For the idea of 'passive revolution', see Gramsci 1971.

[28] For a detailed account of this process, see Frankel 1978.

[29] Gramsci 1971.

willing to use the already achieved mobilizational levels for radical purposes consistent with its own programmes. But one of the central decisions of the Nehru government was on this question: even though it sometimes did not abrogate its reformistic programmes, it decided to give them a *bureaucratic* rather than a *mobilizational* form. For the Congress leadership, clearly, the political task after assuming power was to demobilize its own movement, not to radicalize it further. It also discreetly renounced promises of distributive justice which had come to constitute part of its informal programme in the last stages of the national movement. The basic contradiction of Congress politics in these early years has been analysed in detail in the academic literature: the needs of long-term economic strategy and ideological legitimation in a poor country made an abstractly redistributive programme imperative; but the ends of mobilizing the effective levers of power in the countryside during ordinary times made a dependence on rural magnates equally unavoidable.[30] No party can, after all, expropriate its own power (as opposed to electoral) base.

Although the Congress was content to accept the continuance of semi-feudal rural power, elsewhere in the economy it adopted massive plans for capitalist development. But such plans can assume quite different institutional forms and political trajectories. Evidently, the Indian elite decisively rejected a trajectory of satellite growth, a common destiny which befell most other newly independent Third World states. Consistent with this general objective, the ruling elite adopted a plan for heavy industrialization and institutional control of capital goods industries through the state sector, a largely untried experiment at the time in underdeveloped countries. Economic plans led to some serious shifts in the internal power distribution of society, though primarily within the elements of the ruling bloc itself. Political mistrust of foreign capital and, to a lesser extent, of the potential power of private capital in India, led to much of this new, crucial, and politically privileged segment of the economy being given over to a new and fast-growing public sector, in the face of strong political opposition from internal conservatives.[31]

[30] Frankel 1978.

[31] The *politics* of planning and the public sector, alas, remains a seriously under-researched area.

The larger theory and the economic projections for this huge state-controlled sector, which, in turn, controlled some crucial parts of the larger economy by financial mechanisms, came from a new bureaucracy of economic and technical personnel who entered the earlier, more limited format of the colonial law and order bureaucracy, and changed its structure and practices. Planning assisted and ideologically justified an enormous expansion of a 'welfare bureaucracy' which set in motion some internal conflicts in the administrative apparatus of the state, e.g. the debate about the relative decisional weight of technocrats and bureaucrats, and, more crucially, the division of their respective domains of control.

At the general level, however, they had some common interests. They gratefully accepted the chance of a quick proliferation of bureaucratic occupations and a consequent tendency to bring under bureaucratic administration any new field of social activity. And since the decision about how much the bureaucracy should expand was made by the bureaucracy itself—though occasionally under some thinly assumed disguises of committees and commissions—it is not surprising that this sector spread rapidly in size and increased its strategic control at the expense of more traditional controllers of productive resources. This led in the long run to the growth of a large non-market mechanism of allocation of resources, a process which was originally justified by 'socialist' arguments of controlling private capitalist power, but shown by later events to be increasingly prone to arbitrary distribution of economic patronage by politicians. Originally, this social group had enthusiastically supported the spread of an intricate regime of controls through licences, permits, and government sanctions, which they saw slipping out of their grasp and being put to retrograde uses. Eventually, this entire state-directed economic regime could be singled out for criticism for its political arbitrariness and inefficiency, although actually the public sector is criticized by using examples that travesty its functioning.[32] Anyway, politically this allowed the bureaucracy to gain control over other people's time frames, if not actual decisions.

[32] The ways of the Congress Party are truly inscrutable. It expels leading members for being too vocal about economic scandals and kickbacks, but allows its minister for culture, Vasant Sathe, an equally important member, to launch frontal attacks on the public sector, presumably an important part of

The more Nehru was politically weakened inside the party organization, the greater the resistance at the state level to his reformist policies, the more he was forced into the passive revolution logic of bureaucratization, which saw the people not as subjects but as simple objects of the development process. The theoretical understanding behind this development strategy was also in several ways excessively rationalistic: it falsely believed that external 'experts' naturally knew more about people's problems and how to solve them than those who suffered these problems themselves. By the mid 1950s such an over-rationalistic doctrine became a settled part of the ideology of planning and therefore of the Indian state. 'The state', or whoever could usurp this title for the time being, rather than the people themselves, was to be the initiator and, more dangerously, the evaluator of the development process. A partly superstitious reverence for natural science, undeservingly extended to economists, sociologists, and similar other pretenders to absolute truth,[33] justified a theory which saw popular criticisms of state-controlled growth as 'civic disorders'.

Every advance of this rhetoricized bureaucracy in the control of social life was celebrated as a further step towards a mystical socialistic pattern of society in which, although 'socialists' controlled state power, economic and distributive inequality of other sorts rapidly increased. Although it is important to undermine its unfounded and arrogant socialistic claims, it would be unrealistic not to see that this state, under this particular balance of its ruling bloc, worked out a fairly elaborate theory of import-substituting industrialization and ran a limited, in the sense of unevenly spread, system of parliamentary democracy. Two points, however, have to be mentioned about the

---

its own economic programmes. Evidently, the Congress follows a special logic in defining consistency and programmatic loyalty.

[33] This group of course emphatically includes political scientists who had convinced themselves that the truisms they uttered about Indian politics were different from popular wisdom by the important fact that theirs were produced by the application of *the* scientific method. I have omitted them from the list because the spirit of the age has not been in their favour, and they were given much less advisory importance than their colleagues in the dismal science. Although their labours in the spread of a degenerate form of positivism was second to none, they never made it to the high advisory councils.

internal balance of the regime. Successful functioning of this regime depended on, first, the existence of a strong constitutional–legal system, which enforced legal responsibility; and second, it worked successfully in the early years because the relation between the bourgeoisie and the new bureaucracy was relatively antagonistic rather than collusive. Bourgeois political interests attempted to fight it out frontally, in an ideological battle, trying to argue through political doctrine that a more market-oriented approach would be better for economic growth than allowing a ceremonial programme to stay and buy surreptitious reprieve from its rigours through large-scale corruption. Both these conditions were reversed in later years.

Consolidation 1956–1964

To emphasize these features of the political economy of the Nehru years is not to deny that modern India is still held together by a partially infringed frame which is a legacy of his period, despite the best efforts of the party he had once led to break down its structural principles during the rule of his political successors.[34] Unfortunately, Indira Gandhi and Rajiv Gandhi can be seen only as his filial, not his political, inheritors. If his policy frame has not been entirely destroyed, it is certainly not from any want of effort from his party or those who followed him into power. Nehru's historical importance is signalled by the fact that any programme of bourgeois reconstruction still speaks of a return to his 'system' as opposed to the later Congress performance in the political and economic fields.

It is false to claim, as Nehru's official admirers often do, that Nehru was a political theorist who had worked out a prior strategy for 'independent capitalist development' which he slowly unfolded when in power. In fact, he was no theorist; but he had an overwhelming sense that political programmes in countries like India must be set in the frame of objectives in the historical long term, so that, for him, political ideology meant an interpretation of historical possibilities rather than populist gimmicks. Nehru's regime thought seriously that reduction of poverty would necessarily be slower in a state in which legal bourgeois rights to property exist; Indira Gandhi's regime cheerfully

[34] I have tried to deal with this in Kaviraj 1984.

promised its abstract eradication in the elections of 1971, though none of the conditions which forced Nehru's hesitation had changed. Although no theorist, Nehru certainly had a statesmanly nose for reading 'the dialectic of the concrete', and he picked up the elements of a fairly coherent social and political design as he went along, mainly reading the logic of colligation between one basic policy and the next. The use of political power by a ruling elite involves serious recursive calculations about the effects of earlier policies, and ensuring conditions for the success of one policy by means of others. If the bloc in power survives over a long enough time, this makes it likely that a coherent policy design will gradually emerge. But here again a prior political condition is that the elite must feel securely in power and work on a certain short-term dissociation between the political objectives of continuance, economic distribution, and creation of resources. It is this which can allow tying up resources in investments with longer periods of gestation, against the temptation to use resources in the form of direct subsidies to volatile sections. Since Nehru's regime never had serious doubts about its electoral future, it could embark on programmes like the Second Five Year Plan; for later governments, similar uses of economic resources under government control became politically unfeasible.

Although Nehru did not enter office with a fully worked-out programme, he did eventually create a distinct policy design. In its final form, its elements were internally coherent. Political stability and the realization of independence of decision-making required an improvement in the food situation, since American food aid, from early on, was used by the USA to exert political pressure on basic policy issues. This meant that in foreign policy India should seek alternative sources of international support. Parallel considerations—of protecting the political sovereignty of developmental decisions—led to the major thrust of the Second Plan towards primary sector industrialization. Gathering the results of these policies depended to a large extent on keeping these sectors of the economy under direct control of the state. Driven by political-economic calculations of this kind, the Indian state opened up its diplomatic relations with the USSR. Of course, a whole range of external circumstances helped this process of a surprising connection between the leading socialist state and the country in the Third World in which capitalism had a somewhat greater chance of success. This was greatly helped by the fact that the USSR pursued in its foreign policy minimal objectives as opposed to the unpractically maximalist ones of the USA.[35] This mutual need was the ground for early friendship between the two countries, rather than an Indian attempt to build a version of socialism, or Soviet assistance to a regime trying to build a 'non-capitalist form' of society.[36]

However, there were two ways in which the Nehru model was subverted by later political initiatives: much of it was an inversion 'from inside', as it were, as in the case of bureaucratic control over the economy—turning the power of overriding market mechanisms by the state over to the service of an arbitrary granting of favours to pliable corporate houses, companies, and individuals. On some questions, however, there was a more explicit reversal of formal government policy about the generation of growth and managing its distributive effects. One significant element of the Nehruvian growth model, discussed at length during the finalization of the Second Plan, was the connection between industrial and agrarian strategies, a doctrine decisively rejected during Indira Gandhi's regime. A strong push towards industrialization in the heavy industrial sector was supposed to be related to a parallel drive for land reforms through a large programme for cooperativization. This involved pressing reluctant and procrastinating state governments to enact more serious land reform legislation. Government doctrine asserted that the requirements of raising surplus resources for massive industrialization, increasing agricultural productivity, and preventing a fast cost-push inflation could be served by change and redistribution of control over land and resources in the rural sector in a more egalitarian direction. The Nehru regime, with its finer sensitivity to legal propriety, had felt legally handicapped

[35] A simple definition of minimal and maximal objectives in international politics would be as follows. When state A wishes state B to do what it wants it to do, that could be called a maximal target; a minimal objective is one when A wants B to do something different from what its rival C wishes B to do.

[36] See the famous controversy in communist circles about the article by Modeste Rubinstein arguing that the Nehru government was proposing to follow a non-capitalist path. Ajoy Ghosh wrote a remarkably scathing reply to this article.

because land came under the state list in the constitutional division of powers.[37]

Indeed, the federal division of powers could be seen in terms of our model as a coalitional proposal directed at the regional bourgeoisie and dominant agricultural interests, giving them relative autonomy in their own regions. The insistent requirements of capitalist development now threatened to infringe that agreement within the protocol. Besides, the decline of the zamindars and direct feudal landholders left the field free for the accumulation of power in the hands of a stratum of richer farmers who wished to inherit political immunities implicit in the initial protocol. This introduced a conflict of interests within the structure of the ruling coalition in India, the effects of which were significant in the long run. Nehru's policy initiatives in the late 1950s and early 1960s led to a double process of polarization in politics. Government initiatives in three interrelated areas—creation of heavy industries in the public sector, increasing reliance on Soviet assistance in their construction, and pressure from the planning element in government for changes in the agrarian sector towards cooperativization—led to sharp criticism of the Congress. Individual capitalists, sometimes even the entire class, have to be pardoned for occasionally failing to see what was to be beneficial to the system as a whole. These Nehruvian policies, celebrated now as a triumphant design for the successful construction of retarded capitalism, came under strong fire from a panicking combine of representatives of proprietary classes. The Congress's industrial policies were interpreted as the thin end of the socialist stick; land reform proposals, shamefully mild and solidly bourgeois, appeared to them as the programme of an agrarian revolution from above; the public sector, intended merely to displace the centre of control towards the state, was seen as an attack on private enterprise. For the first time, a large right-wing coalition of conservatives inside and outside the ruling party seemed to be emerging.

[37] It is interesting to note that Indira Gandhi's regime increasingly freed itself of these legal encumbrances, leading to a general decline of the institutional system. Initial arguments in favour of this softening of bourgeois legal norms were made by using 'socialist' ideas; but, remarkably, the room for manoeuvre created by this has never been utilized for radical reforms.

The political consequences of such misreadings of Congress policy were considerable. Two trends of political realignments began soon after the adoption of the Second Plan package of policies. Grievances against industrial policy and related issues led to the formation of the Swatantra Party; but more significant changes happened in the rural political scene. Congress pressure for cooperativization came just at the time when the beneficiaries of the agrarian changes were enjoying the first impulse of their power. This led to serious shifts within the ruling bloc. Although, in terms of the distribution of unequal benefits, the rural elite must be considered to have been part of the ruling coalition, they constituted undoubtedly its most quiescent part. There were imaginary threats of disadvantage;[38] but, more concretely, grievance against the fact that they were not getting a larger share of advantages, and that their rising economic power was insufficiently translated into political authority because they thought the rulers of the parliamentary game constantly wrongfooted them, made them increasingly restive.[39]

The farmers' groups, in other words, demanded a more equal share of the fruits of inequality. There was large-scale exodus of farmer support from the Congress and the formation of regional farmers' groupings. This should be seen in my judgement as a move by these two subordinate and quiescent groups to set up relations across the boundary of the coalition with other dispossessed groups.[40] All over India, but particularly in the more agriculturally successful states, peasant parties sprang up and became part of the growing opposition blocs in the fourth general elections. Their typical leaders were Charan Singh and Rao Birendra Singh—the latter more typical than the former, because he later rejoined the Congress. Because his self-respect was not plastic enough, Charan Singh could not do that. Some of these

[38] There is always a hypothetical calculation of possible benefits made by classes and groups quite apart from threats of disadvantage.

[39] Most of these demands are spelt out clearly in Charan Singh 1978.

[40] If the whole society is made up of the letters of the alphabet, and abc are in that order wielders of power, if c is disgruntled, it can establish alliances across the boundaries of the ruling coalition with d e f . . . This would bring instability to the coalition where a + b + c was a *condition* for their being in power. But c's leaving the a b c coalition would not be read properly if we do not see this leav-ing itself as an offer to return to an a c b coalition.

disgruntled elements retained their loyalty to the protocol by announcing that they would retain their Congress labels with suitable adjectival modification.[41]

The fates of the two critical realignments were eventually very different. The relative success of the policy of heavy industrialization and the Second Plan was soon generally accepted by even the recalcitrant bourgeois groups; and the Swatantra Party consequently sank into political irrelevance. But the secession of the farmers' lobbies over much of northern India, led first to a political debacle of the Congress, then to internal changes in Congress policies. Their withdrawal of support from the Congress weakened it seriously in both class and party terms; and the Congress leadership saw it as a double-valued move: an exercise of the *exit* option, which concealed a proposal to return if the protocol was restructured in their favour. In coalitional politics, every threat is an offer. Changes in Congress policy in agriculture towards a 'technical' solution of the food problem, through heavy government investment in 'advanced' sectors—which was known to be likely to result in an accentuation of rural inequality—showed that the Congress had read this move correctly and was prepared to make alterations in its policies to accommodate the ambitions of regional farmers' groups.[42]

Foreign policy issues so heavily dominated the last years of the Nehru period that some of the long-term consequences of his programme of passive revolution took longer than normal to surface. The imbalances left behind by Nehru's government affected the policies of successor regimes. Such imbalances threatened to rupture the coalitional

[41] The country was full of non-national Congresses of all kinds—Bangla Congress, Kerala Congress, and so on—asserting the reassuring concreteness of regional identity as opposed to the greater abstractness of the national one.

[42] Surprisingly, the farmer lobbies were proper examples of the theory that there are unmarked, but very significant frontiers of regional consciousness. Thus, a potential national combine of such groups—which would have been formidable, if not simply overwhelming—has not really come into existence. Peasant lobbies seem incomprehensibly trapped within frontiers of regional consciousness; for some reason, they cannot recognize an entirely abstract we, linked entirely by modern economic interests, unsupported by any directly available form of historical self-conceptualization like Jat, or Kamma, or such cultural identity. If they describe themselves as inhabitants of UP, this would indicate a more abstract consciousness of territoriality.

unity of the ruling bloc by creating a rift of interest between the bourgeois, bureaucratic, urban segment, and regional bourgeois interests and agrarian propertied classes.[43]

This picture of the Nehru period should not be taken as unhistorically one-sided and pessimistic. Although all Third World societies with ambitions of capitalist growth have failed, I do not deny that Indian society has failed much better than others.[44] There are undoubted advantages to the Indian case over other competing models, like Pakistan, or now, more fashionably, South Korea. India is quite obviously better than the tinpot but nonetheless vicious dictatorships in Latin America and also some unproductively austere regimes in Africa that were given a prematurely lyrical reception by radicals in the 1960s. Such successes of the Nehru regime are accepted, but remain unstated here because I primarily intend to draw something of a causal line from what we consider our 'best' period to our worst.

Instability 1965–1975

Contradictions in the policies of the Nehru period surfaced after the somewhat artificial national unity of the mid 1960s disappeared. Nationalist hysteria naturally created a temporary alliance of sentiment which brought together political forces from the hard right to the mild left into an easy patriotic combination that isolated the communists, especially the CPI(M). But the artificiality of this was shown by the fact that, within three years of Nehru's death, left forces could regroup sufficiently to form coalition governments in states.

India passed through a deep political crisis in the immediate years after Nehru's death, a crisis that, in policy terms, was fraught with the most serious retrograde possibilities. An orchestration of pressures—from both internal and external reaction—created a situation in which

[43] For an economic pursuit of this phenomenon, see Ashok Mitra 1977.

[44] Nothing illustrates this more clearly than the abandonment in the 1970s of the argument popular with Western bourgeois theorists that India and Pakistan were two opposed models of development for Third World societies. Although the attachment of large Western democracies to an oppressive and economically unsuccessful tyranny like Pakistan was always difficult to explain, now Pakistan has become too obvious an ideological liability and is defended by purely security arguments.

the Nehruvian plan for a reformist capitalism, with its policies of public sector, state control over resources, planning, and a relatively anti-imperialist foreign policy could all be renegotiated.[45] Indira Gandhi's government initially gave in to some of these pressures, its most celebrated collapse being acceptance of the devaluation of the rupee. In the fourth general elections, Congress fortunes declined alarmingly, and it was evident that to get out of the deepening politico-economic crisis, the party needed some drastic measures. The initiatives taken by Indira Gandhi in the years after 1967 showed that in her view the Congress was facing a crisis of legitimacy. Unlike the years after Independence, it was not seen as a force of redistributive change, but a conservative party underwriting social inequality. Legitimacy could be renewed by restating the objectives of distributive justice with dramatic splendour. Some changes in economic policy were evident to the earlier policy on agriculture, with an implicit acceptance of the iniquitous social consequences of the new line and the gradual decline of emphasis on planning,[46] and the policy of large investments.[47]

The politics of the Indian state and the Congress Party entered a different historical stage by the fourth general elections. Earlier, electoral survival of the Congress, and the simple control over state governments which was a precondition for making and shaping policies, was never in question, although Nehru's electoral majorities were never dramatic.

[45] I have sketched this out more fully in Kaviraj 1986.

[46] Planning had become too much of a slogan for the Congress to be dropped altogether, and the concept carried pleasant reminders of Nehru. Although the thing could not be dropped entirely, its substance could be hollowed out and thrown overboard. Economists who are critical of government policy have concentrated too much on the technical economics of the plans rather than their larger ideological concept. To an untechnical eye, whatever its mathematical triumphs in recent years, planning seems to have degenerated increasingly into an accounting and housekeeping operation rather than a directive mechanism for the productive forces of the economy. Planning was a blessing for the self-reproducing bureaucracy. Every claim for creating the post of an unproductive, and possibly corrupt, bureaucrat could be said to be in the general interest of the country's economic progress. Thus, although we have much less planning, we have, happily, a much larger commission.

[47] Several Marxist economists have forcefully stressed this point. Cf. Bardhan 1985.

Going by purely electoral statistics, Nehru would appear retrospectively to have been permanently insecure, enjoying unspectacularly simple majorities in parliament. By contrast, Indira Gandhi and Rajiv Gandhi would appear unassailably secure, riding great waves of popular affection. This only shows, in the face of much political science in the last twenty years, that electoral 'behaviour' is a rather poor indicator of what a people politically do to themselves. Actually, there was a displacement of the question at the heart of these elections. Formerly, the major question was not whether the Congress would remain in power. It was assumed that it would; the debate was about its policies. After 1967, every time, except in the last elections, the question was whether it would remain in power or not. Thus pre-1967 politics revolved around real ideological issues—what should be the path of national development, what would be the distributive character of economic growth? After 1967, the attention of Congress politicians went entirely into electoral issues and the matter of staying in power. In my view, contrary to what is often said, Indira Gandhi's politics became decidedly less ideological.[48]

By a populist move Indira Gandhi solved this electoral crisis of her party.[49] But the long-term effects of her policies have created a crisis of a different kind. Congress politics was marked by a paradox of continuity. No one would normally claim that Indira Gandhi wished to take the country on a very different line of development or diverge sharply from the policy design left behind by Nehru; yet probably no one would claim either that she left this design unaltered, or deny that her initiatives or interpretations have had serious negative consequences for the Nehruvian model.[50]

[48] For the contrary view, cf. Ulyanovsky 1974.

[49] I have suggested that this has altered the significance of elections and turned them into plebiscites: Kaviraj 1986.

[50] Some criticisms of the argument of this essay at the seminar where it was presented touched on this point. Several critics thought that the line was too heavily 'structuralist' in the sense that it did not recognize the possibility that politics of indubitably bad consequences could have originated in 'innocent', defensible, and entirely understandable intentions. Structuralism need not deny the necessary untidiness of political life and the complex, asymmetric relation between intentions and consequences. It is simply required, in the face of such criticism, to state a sufficiently complex theory of intentionality and accept

It is not necessary to retell the melancholy narrative of how quick but indecisive victories contributed to a long-term crisis of the state, and how the state structure was centralized to such an extent that the political difficulties of the leader or the government party became generalized into a crisis of the entire state.[51] We shall simply mention the political shifts introduced by her 'pragmatic' translation of Nehru's political strategy.[52]

In one sense, Indira Gandhi faced a situation similar to the one Nehru had encountered, with the difference that she obviously, in the mid 1960s, lacked Nehru's irreplaceability within the party. Thus, by the logic of the situation she had to intensify the passive revolution features of the Nehru period, often however to a point where these tended to subvert their own original purpose. Control over government initially, because of the parliamentary format of political power, depended on her control over the party. Since after Nehru effective power within the Congress had shifted to the state bosses, and they could and did mount an offensive against her leadership position, she set about systematically undermining state Congress caucuses. This had two types of effects: first, party posts and patronage at the state levels

---

a weak truth in these objections. Surely, Indira Gandhi did not wish to wreck the Indian state, but equally certainly, she nearly did. Part of the problem lies in our ambiguous use of the verb phrase 'Indira Gandhi did x', which is underdetermined between 'intended to do x' and 'effected x'. Even unacademic observers of politics would admit, I suppose, that between two lists—the first of which showed what Indira Gandhi wished to but failed to do, and another which showed what she perhaps did not deliberately intend but nonetheless caused—the second would be the analytically more serious one. A structural argument need not entirely erase intentions, only de-emphasize them. It has no quarrel with the reporting of intentions as long as that does not displace the causal line. For instance, as long as intentional arguments do not go into rationalizing forms saying 'Indira Gandhi intended to eradicate poverty, but unfortunately, *unimportantly*, she could not', they are not seriously harmful. It is in this sense that S. Gopal's book tells half the story of the Nehru era and gives an account of Nehru's intentions. To use our argument a trifle lightheartedly, it requires a complement which would state more fully Nehru's consequences.

[51] Kaviraj 1984.

[52] Ibid.

shifted towards less effective leaders, to people who had no political base in their states. Though on some occasions the process of replacement of older Congress leaders by the new type was accompanied by ideological rhetoric—for instance, the new leaders being dedicated removers of poverty—this was not taken seriously by the public, nor was the pretence kept up for too long. No one suspected the new leaders of harbouring ideology. In the event, most of them proved themselves to be men of astonishing doctrinal suppleness. In the days of the socialist forum they thought only socialism could end Indian people's sufferings; but during the Emergency they were quick to appreciate the advantage of the Brazilian path; and some, the subtlest of all, declared in the days of the Shah Commission how they had nothing to do with the Emergency regime but helplessly enjoyed its benefits.

Second, after the fall of the earlier, older generation of state leaders, Indira Gandhi's Congress did not allow electoral processes to be revived, and these organizations, nominated from the centre, remained completely ineffective. The resultant ineffectiveness of the state Congress machinery made it inevitable that power would be shifted even more towards the bureaucracy.[53] And this was a bureaucracy that would soon declare itself 'committed' to unspecified ideals.[54] Mine should not be seen as an argument that prettifies the older state leadership of the Congress. Earlier leaders of the Congress, like Atulya Ghosh,

[53] As the internal linkages in the party turned increasingly one-way, governance required some two-way flow, and it shifted to the only alternative—a degenerat-ing bureaucracy.

[54] A committed bureaucracy was an odd idea. And it was not consistent with the professed purposes for which this idea was advanced. If this meant that the bureaucracy would remain committed to the elected government, the idea was redundant, because it was meant to be so anyway. If it meant commitment to a party irrespective of its electoral fate, this was blasphemous, because it went right against the principle of democracy. If it meant a commitment to socialism, it was the most paradoxical of all, because socialism is a matter of policies; and either before or after the bureaucracy's commitment to the government, the government failed to commit itself to socialism. If it meant a coded appeal to leaders for preferment to a small coterie of politicians and bureaucrats for their commitment to socialism in some mistily distant past, this was understandable and part of a solid tradition of sycophancy stretching into medieval times.

S.K. Patil, and Nijalingappa, never enjoyed great moral stature and dealt in quite a malodorous form of patronage politics—and thus Congress did not have much moral eminence to lose. But the new leaders were not even products of local factional conflicts; they were simply imposed on state parties externally. They were not even significantly hated, they were merely unspeakable non-entities.

In such circumstances, it was hardly surprising that although securely in power as long as they enjoyed the confidence of the central leadership, these leaders lacked the ability to resolve state problems or serious regional conflicts, and tended to send up all local issues for a central settlement. The advisers of the Gandhi regime read the shirking of responsibility by the new vassals as a touching mark of their loyalty. Although this certainly showed loyalty to the centre and kept the minions gainfully underemployed, it tended to overload the centre in terms of the sheer number of decisions it had to make. In effect, this also shifted the power of decision-making from those who knew state politics well to those who knew it less, and accounts perhaps for the wildly fluctuating pragmatism of Congress rule in the states after 1971.[55] The new state leaders lacked the ability to hold political equilibria in the states by the creation and manipulation of interest coalitions and factional politics—an unpleasant but efficacious art that Congress leaders had perfected in the earlier period of condominium with a more distant, non-interfering centre.

The destruction of state-level Congress organizations was not accidental, for it happened not only at the time Indira Gandhi was under pressure but continued way beyond 1971, when she was in uncontested control of the party and the state, and the Congress went on in unembarrassed cheerfulness with nominated state committees, reducing state leaders to mere clients rather than supporters of the

[55] Congress pragmatism was fluctuating in the following sense: various social lobbies—ordinarily caste and regional groupings—perpetually contended for control within the Congress Party. Access to high government positions made it possible to restructure governmental benefits in their favour. Often, one interest lobby of this kind would be replaced by another, and immediately restructure benefit legislations to the utter detriment of consistency in government policy. In recent years, this has happened most frequently through caste-related reservation legislations, for example in Gujarat in the very recent past.

central authority.[56] Thus, Indira Gandhi changed the Congress into a highly centralized and undemocratic party organization, from the earlier federal, democratic and ideological formation that Nehru had led. It should be a minor issue of Indian politics that the party which vowed to defend democracy in India could not retain it within its own fold. Also, the earlier unstated doctrine was that a strong centre could be based only on powerful states; in her regime, the power of the state governments and of the centre began to be interpreted in entirely zero-sum terms, irrespective of whether states were controlled by the Congress or opposition parties.[57] Eventually, we witness a further paradox of power. The Indira Gandhi regime's answer to a general sense of gathering crisis was an obsessive centralization that defeated its own purpose. She was arguably a more powerful prime minister than Nehru in terms of control over the party and the state. But she presided over a system which, though more centralized, had actually become far weaker.

Gradually, the redundancy of state parties also extended to the centre, and effective power shifted entirely to governmental echelons. Ceremonial leadership of the Congress Party became a redundant function: either Indira Gandhi herself was the leader but derived her legitimacy from being the premier; or when it was someone else, his position was purely decorative. This development implied the destruction of one of the checks within the Nehruvian structure: the party could often balance the governmental wing. Except in times of elections, Indira Gandhi ran what could ironically be called a partyless government, in which, symbolically, some of her minor office functionaries assumed more importance in terms of access, timing, and powers of facilitating and delaying decisions, than senior party leaders.

But this decline of the party could not have happened had not Indira Gandhi changed the entire nature of politics. This new, populist

[56] Tendencies of this kind towards atrophy of the party mechanism have been studied for quite some time, not surprisingly more often by liberal academics than by Marxists.

[57] The central Congress leadership appears as suspicious of an H.N. Bahuguna as of a Jyoti Basu, an extraordinary attitude if one took party divisions seriously.

politics turned political ideology—a serious disputation about the social design during the Nehru era—into a mere electoral discourse. Her use of vacuous slogans were not meant to be translated into government policies. The shift of Congress to populist politics quickly set up a new structure of political communication in which Indira Gandhi could appeal directly to the electorate over the heads of party organizations. The relation between the party and its leader was turned around: instead of the organization carrying her to power, she carried them. Naturally, the Congress became a less serious political mechanism because both of its significant functions were slowly taken away: elections were won by Indira Gandhi's ability to directly appeal to the masses; daily governance was slowly given over to the official government machinery and an increasingly politicized administration. During its great electoral victories in the early 1970s, amidst the celebrations the Congress Party as a political organization died a quiet death.

A natural correlate to this was the gradual shift of political (as opposed to administrative) tasks to the higher echelons of the bureaucracy, which became increasingly more powerful at the cost of becoming more politicized.[58] As the logic of modern bureaucracies is centralist, this aided the tendency towards a mindless centralization of increasingly irresponsible power. Countervailing institutions gave way, through a simultaneous decline of parliament and the court—though the first was less remarked because much of its humiliation and ineffectiveness was self-inflicted. Majorities became so large as to make their tending and discipline unnecessary, leading eventually to the comic situation of the present Congress Party worrying about the attendance of its members in crucial debates in parliament.[59] Although shortsighted bureaucrats may have initially rejoiced at this accession to power, often misreading this as an instrument of reformist policies, it was gradually

[58] 'Politicization' here does not mean the bureaucracy's devotion to social programmes on ideological lines, but to a personal leadership of the state. Ironically, it became so devoted that it lost all capacity for self-defence when the high coterie fell for the seductions of the 'Brazilian path'.

[59] The Congress Party had to issue a particularly stern admonition to its members to respect the whip. There was an alarming tendency among parliamentarians of the ruling party to take their massive majority for granted and pursue other interests when parliament was in session.

realized that bureaucrats could not always perform the tasks of political leaders, and the decline of procedural civilities of capitalist democracy could be eventually used to the detriment of all elements. Particularly fatal was the loan that the CPI lobbies made to the Congress of its own slogans, symbols, argument, and language—to their own detriment, as it turned out in 1976.

A remarkable feature of the new politics was the quickening of the political cycle. Indira Gandhi had carried her party to power in 1971 on promises which were more radical and proportionately more unrealistic than earlier programmes. Factors which obstructed the realization of milder promises still remained and equally prevented any realization of the stronger promise, if of course this was taken literally. Governments had to pay the price of such populism sooner than expected. Under Nehru, the electoral majorities of Congress had never been comparably large; yet none of those administrations had difficulty in seeing through their appointed constitutional terms. Remarkably, after Indira Gandhi's victory in 1971, no government has actually lasted its term. By 1973, Indira Gandhi's large parliamentary majority notwithstanding, she was in deep political crisis. The Janata government, with a large majority, lasted barely three years. Indira Gandhi, in her second term in power, was politically in trouble at the time of her death.

This calls for some explanation. In fact, the textbook translation of electoral majorities into administrative capability to rule was failing to take place. Indeed, it seems that the larger the majority of the government, the more difficult it finds the general business of orderly governance. I have claimed elsewhere that this is due to a change in the nature of elections—which was initiated by the government party, but later used by the electorate to register its protest against the current political dispensation.

Elections have turned increasingly into populist referendums, in which a highly emotive, rhetorical issue is placed before the electorate immediately before the polls, screening off from view the mixed record of an incumbent regime. This has given these governments exaggerated electoral majorities without clear mandates; but, more significantly, it has destroyed the effectiveness of the electoral mechanism as a register of popular dissatisfaction. Thus, governments which a few months earlier achieved massive mandates, could face equally massive popular movements, as happened in Gujarat in 1974. Popular criticism of governmental performance was deprived of its legitimate channel in elections because of populism spilling out on to the streets. Indira Gandhi's answer to previous electoral instability under opposition rule in the states was not much better than the earlier situation. Instability was not reduced, but internalized. Instead of unstable opposition coalitions following one upon the other, now equally unstable Congress coalitions followed in quick succession; and since Congress did not have a clear programme in terms of policies they could follow widely divergent trajectories in distributing benefits to social groups.

The evolution of the Congress in the years of Indira Gandhi ought not to be seen in purely party or governmental terms. I have suggested that the Congress debacle in the late 1960s was related to a threatened secession of rich agrarian groups from the ruling coalition. But, as every threat is an offer, it represented their willingness to return to the fold with the terms of the protocol renegotiated in their favour. Under the pressure of the Emergency, and partly through the systematic concessions given to the agrarian rich, the Congress gradually got them back into its fold. Congress organizational positions were laid open to these politicians, who were sometimes unused to the subtleties of bourgeois democracy. The agricultural policy of the government showed reluctance to either tax or impose other levies on the major beneficiaries of the green revolution.

The Emergency, of course, overshadowed all other political questions for some time. Although initially defended by seemingly economic arguments, the Emergency regime soon ran out of arguments of justification in redistributive terms. Politically, however, it showed an extreme point of centralization. It showed literally how a personal crisis of the leader could be turned into a political crisis of the state. It showed how, through a combination of centralization and the suspension of normal constitutional procedures of responsible government, actual power could shift to extra-constitutional caucuses. In a country with such a rich and varied culture of past tyranny, this revealed a particularly dangerous trend. It also showed, finally, how an excessively authoritarian regime blocked off its own channels of communication to the extent of believing that it could win elections after the Emergency. Historically, however, the experience of the Emergency demonstrated that a solution to India's political ills should not be sought in an authoritarian alternative. Democracy had lumbered on untidily for thirty years; authori-tarianism took less than two years to make the country ungovernable for itself.

Crisis 1975–1987

Though the period after the death of Nehru was one of political instability, the character of political turmoil and the sense of pessimism associated with it were of a different character from the present gloom. What declined then was a government *party* and not the institutional structure of the *state*. Slowly, such distinctions have become obliterated, and the general tone of thinking in India has become perceptibly darker, moving from political disquiet to a deeper historical pessimism. And this sense of apprehension about the fragility of Indian democracy, and pessimism about the tasks which the young state had once hopefully set itself, is naturally deeply associated with the dark experience of the Emergency years.

There has been a great deal of debate about the significance of the Emergency period: whether it was inevitably caused by a crisis of capitalism or simply a generalization of a personal crisis in an excessively centralized state; whether it was an aberration or showed a more insistent long-term tendency towards authoritarianism. Although the form in which the political crisis erupted during the Emergency has gone into the past, I think it can be argued that the period marked the beginning of a quite different kind of difficulty for the political order in India. This is a process in which a crisis-laden ruling group is drawing the party, the governmental system, eventually the state itself, into crisis. Empirically the assertion that the period since 1975 has been one of almost uninterrupted political disorder hardly needs demonstration. Occasionally, the crisis has changed form, terrain, expression, nodal points—in structuralist language, its site, and its bearers. But a sense of a historical crisis—a sense of increasing vulnerability and exhaustion of the state in face of self-produced disorders—has scarcely ever disappeared in the last ten years. The way the Emergency ended showed that authoritarianism blocks off its own channels of political communication and response, and makes a violent retribution highly likely. The Emergency did not improve either the state's economic performance or administrative functioning, and appeared a gratuitous exchange of bourgeois authoritarianism for bourgeois democracy. But it made some earlier detractors of 'bourgeois' democracy see its limited advantages—something that had not appeared clearly to some radical groups in the thirty years when rights were available became clear in the nineteen months when these were denied. An ironic 'gain' of the Emergency years has been a greater appreciation of the value and vulnerability of bourgeois democracy when no higher form seems to be in sight.

The end of the Emergency, however, did not see an alteration of this crisis politics. The Janata regime failed its mandate in all possible ways. First, it wrongly translated a matter of principle into a question of personal vendetta, which invited the nation to read the principles and issues involved in the experience in a wholly misleading way. Second, it entirely misjudged a negative vote against the Emergency into a positive vote for its more conservative policy inclinations. To put it rhetorically, its leaders first thought this was a vote of no-confidence by the nation against the Nehru model of policies; while, in fact, it was a vote calling for a return from the Emergency rule of Indira Gandhi to the policies of Nehru, a vote for the past Congress against the present one. In any case, it did not have a long enough term to clearly work out its policies on major politico-economic questions; so that its supporters and critics can carry on an infructuous debate, maintaining that if it had been in power for a long term this would have been, respectively, for better or for worse for India than under the Congress regime. Its internal factional squabbles, its inability to set its own terms of policy, its acceptance of the terms that an out-of-power Indira Gandhi set to it, converged to bring about an ignominious departure from ineffective power into abusive exile. But its greatest failure was in not being able to restore politics to policies and principles of bourgeois democratic government. In fact, its attacks on Indira Gandhi actually increased the indistinctness of persons and institutions. The joyous enthusiasm with which the liberal intelligentsia joined these personal debates and debased questions of principle into a ledger of personal qualities contributed to this denouement. As a result, what could have been turned into an occasion for restating an agenda of political principles went waste.

As the Janata Party failed to pose questions of principle, Indira Gandhi's return to power in 1980 did not involve any serious critical self-reflection on the part of the Congress. Consequently, several tendencies opposed to bourgeois principles of democratic governance, introduced during the Emergency, came back with her restoration to power. The equation of the fate of a nation with that of the Nehru family, the open support for hereditary succession to power, and the total suspension of electoral forms within the Congress remained entirely unchecked and uncriticized within the ruling party, due mainly to the ineptness of the Janata Party in posing a principled challenge. These were simply the more dramatic instances of a reintroduction of retrograde, nearly feudal, forms of irresponsible power in the bourgeois state apparatus itself. And since the state occupied such a large space in modern Indian society and was, in a true sense, the educator of educators, appointer of appointers, and patron of patrons, these deformations travelled rapidly down the system into a quick subversion of principles and formats of equality of opportunity and merit at every level of institutional life. It helped do away with bourgeois principles of recruitment and advance, and replaced them with a system of patronage in the huge network of public institutions, starting from the planning mechanism to the socially irrelevant universities.[60]

The dominant patronage groups in such a system changed rapidly, along with bewilderingly quick changes of policy orientation—an abject indecisiveness rationalized in the name of pragmatism. The 'correct' ideology in the early 1970s was a vague espousal of socialism uninsistent on its policy realization. Those who attained eminence from this political group were replaced during the Emergency by politicians who favoured the 'Brazilian path' and forced sterilization as solutions to the country's economic problems, and confused improvement of society with the beautification of its capital cities. Subsequently, even these leaders made way for a newer group

[60] Indeed, the kind of decline the universities have undergone, their pitiful collective inability to ensure the imparting of skills which their degrees certify, could have been tolerated by society only because they were in a large measure irrelevant. Had it been otherwise, there would have been strong counterpressures from interested groups like the entrepreneurial class and the middle classes to make them deliver the goods.

of 'modernist' politicians, believers in the powers of modern advertising and a judicious combination of religious and electronic superstition. What was remarkable about Indira Gandhi's leadership was the equal tolerance she extended to such diverse 'ideological' groups and the equal willingness to unsentimentally distance herself from them when the occasion arose.

Indira Gandhi's rule, notwithstanding its rhetoric, resulted in a decline of political ideology, a delinking of power from ideological and social programmes. This has led to a general debasement of political ideology in the popular mind (except obviously in states ruled by left parties which treat ideology as serious business), to which the opportunism and personalism of her opposition made a distinguished contribution. Eventually, her last years came to be dominated by two regional movements which, though superficially antithetic, were actually linked to each other by internal relations of a structural sort. These were related because they show two poles of the intensification of regional inequality due to unrestricted and unreflective capitalist development. At the time of her tragic death, Indira Gandhi faced, for the third time in her eventual political career, a threat of encirclement by difficulties and insurmountable problems. And even if she had fought the elections it is likely that she would have won with a far reduced and insecure majority. Her career illustrated the deeper crisis of Indian polity: that even dramatic electoral victories were indecisive and could turn dramatically quickly into their opposite.

Indira Gandhi's period in power, underneath the misleading formal continuity of the Congress system, revised some of the fundamental premises of the Nehru model. These are not accidental or style differences, but of principles of structuring the political order. The Nehru elite tried to take a historical view of the possibilities of social change and came to the conclusion, written into its social theory, that the construction of a modern, relatively independent capitalism required a reformist and statist bourgeois programme. Indira Gandhi's successor regime gradually abandoned the element of historical thinking as a matter of dispensable luxury and went for what it rationalized to itself as a more pragmatic programme. It reduced even the planning apparatus, entrusted by Nehru with the task of serious long-term developmental reflection, to more short-term accounting, though depending on its statistical ability to turn the poverty of the people into the wealth of the nation. Its pragmatism led it to abandon some of the points of the Second Plan kind of strategy.[61] Gradually, the government allowed a massive campaign to gain momentum for the privatization of industry and other economic activities, reducing public investment, and altering the nature of the investment where it still existed. Its successor regime also started plans for extending this policy of liberalization towards greater foreign collaboration in order to obtain more sophisticated technology. Politicians within the cabinet began to launch open attacks on the public sector on the grounds of its inefficiency, though much of the inefficiency is due to the interference and wasteful exploitation of its facilities by the government bureaucracy and politicians. It abandoned the earlier strategy of institutional changes for agricultural growth in favour of a green revolution strategy unaccompanied by any redistributive controls.

Political changes were equally vital. The Congress government under Indira Gandhi gradually allowed a profitable breakdown of bourgeois frameworks of formal propriety since they were occasionally inconvenient encumbrances in its path. In bourgeois political systems, there must be a reliable relation between the structure of classes and the format of parties.[62] The abandonment of ideological politics by the ruling party and cheerful retaliatory imitation by opposition groups causes this relation to break down through defection, the bending of constitutional norms, etc. This can destroy popular faith in democratic institutions. Besides, the breakdown of ground rules of political behaviour tends to make the political world unfamiliar and unrecognizable to the political actors themselves, encouraging behaviour that is blind, wild, and anomic.

The Congress under Indira Gandhi, in effect, renegotiated some of the fundamental definitions of Indian political life. Two of these crucial principles were those of 'the national' and 'the secular'. Some amount of regional political articulation was unavoidable in

[61] There is a fairly large and incisive literature in Marxist economics about this turn in the nature of government economic policies and the consequent retrogressive trends in planning.

[62] This does not mean, however, that a single class would be represented by a single party. It simply means that for social pressures to work through the party system, there must be some reliability in party programmes.

the aftermath of Independence. Capitalist development increased the economic power of two regionally conscious groups, the rich farmers and the regional bourgeois interests. In face of the first wave of regional movements in the 1950s, the Nehru government had made a relatively clear distinction between cultural and economic questions, and had conceded the first kind of demand. Demands for linguistic states or the use of vernaculars in state administration, occasionally even negative sensibilities, such as opposition to the introduction of Hindi, were accepted through a generally consultative process. Strikingly, acknowledgement of such demands did not weaken the process of centralization of planning decisions about the economy. Decisions regarding development investments were left, partly due to the political quiescence of these groups, to the central planning machinery.

Under Indira Gandhi, the situation changed drastically. Increasing pressures were now mounted for regional allocation of heavy industries and other such symbols of regional prestige. It is misleading to believe the vulgar theory that opposition parties alone pressed for economically unjustifiable regional demands. Indeed, many of these regionalisms were first articulated within the ruling party itself, Congress often having absorbed them.[63] Indira Gandhi's state increasingly gave way to such internal regionalisms. Often, it would have been better to describe the Congress as the only party which was hospitable to regionalisms of all areas, with a thin crust of the central leadership and, naturally, the central bureaucracy providing a failing counterweight. Worse, occasionally the regime played one regionalism against another, as it also did with religious communities, hoping to benefit electorally from their double insecurity. Surely, these were clever manoeuvres in the short run; in the long run they undermined the bases of nationalism. In fact, the region of the national capital came to develop a pampered regionalism of its own.

Evidently, similar things happen with regard to communalism too. Concessions given to religious communities as communities undermined the theory of a common individual citizenship and created

[63] The two clear examples of Congress hospitality to regionalism in recent times are the handling of the Andhra agitations of a decade ago, and the early encouragement to breakaway groups from the Akalis in the hope of splitting the Akali vote in Punjab.

the grounds for a rapid increase of majority communalism. Telling Muslims or other minority communities that their fate was secure only with the ruling party kept such insecurities alive. Most seriously, the government allowed a subversion of secular principles of the state by increasingly invoking the religious principle of *sarvadharmasamanvaya*, entirely incompatible with democratic secularism. The Indian state today declares itself to be multireligious, a complete reversal of the Nehruvian principle that there was an equality of all religions to be practised as the private affair of individuals. Finally, the inability of the Congress government to clearly denounce the communal riots after Indira Gandhi's death provided a significant encouragement to the forces of Hindu communalism.

The state curiously believes even today that the best way of controlling religious fanaticism is to lend the government-controlled media to religious leaders, and give the greatest coverage on TV to routine religious practices. During the Nehru period, Dussera, Diwali, Id, and Christmas, celebrated presumably with customary enthusiasm, passed off unnoticed by radio, in contrast with the present coverage by secular television. A state armed with such suicidal weapons does not need communal parties for its destabilization. Remarkably, the subversion of the definition of secularism was not done by communal forces and political parties but accomplished by the state.

The lack of historical self-analysis by the state and its supporting intelligentsia and its conversion to a doctrine of pragmatism meant, in effect, that even normal rational procedures of reflection on effects of earlier policies have been abandoned in favour of an exclusive search for electoral power. Its correlate, pointed out by economists, is a tendency to channel resources increasingly into 'dole' programmes rather than the creation of productive resources, which have longer gestation periods and cannot be adapted to the eventful electoral calendar.

Politicians of the Nehru era would have been surprised if told that, forty years after Independence, the state they had set up would be riven by conflicts over two retrograde forces—regionalism and communalism. And the regionalism that threatens to engulf the polity today is quite clearly a consequence of the inequities of the capitalist growth process. Governments have been consistently inattentive to regional economic inequality inherited from the colonial period. Capitalist development has further intensified these imbalances. Nowhere is this revealed more than in the internal incompatibility between regional demands. Regionalism in Punjab is essentially an anti-redistributive agitation which insists on retaining and extending the economic advantage of the state, particularly of farmers, over other states, regions, and classes. The Assam agitation presses what are, in essence, redistributive demands on the central government; and the two kinds of demands are incompatible.[64] The centre also sometimes plays up regional demands with incredible shortsightedness. At present, it is mildly encouraging the causes in Gorkhaland and fighting the consequences in Punjab, a subtlety of approach truly worthy of the present Indian elite.[65]

A crisis can be called structural, not conjunctural, if it arises from inside the basic laws of movement of a system, rather than from externalities. Several aspects of the present crisis of the Indian state need to be noted. It is not a simple crisis of the economy translated deterministically into political disorder. Some of the cultural processes of crisis have hardly anything to do, directly at least, with the logic of economic development. No deep economic logic made it destroy elementary definitions of secularism. The cheerful indifference with which it has allowed the education system to decline is certainly not induced by economic necessity. This has given the state a great choice of weapons with which to deal self-inflicted wounds on its own structure. Interestingly, these trends have appeared not because capitalism has not been able to develop adequately but precisely because of the

[64] It is remarkable how the logic of regional demands of the 1950s and the 1970s differs. The demand for a linguistic state, once conceded in one case strengthened the case of other, similarly placed areas. In the case of the demand for economic resources, the game is principally zero-sum, with the share of one state cutting against the share of all others.

[65] Since the writing of this essay, the state has brought about a truce in the hill areas of West Bengal. But how far and how long it holds is to be seen. The few years of Rajiv Gandhi's rule have been strewn with the debris of pacts and accords. He has made more pacts than Metternich; and the fact that internal conflicts in the Indian state are attended to in a style of diplomacy says something about the processes of national integration that the Congress has set in motion.

manner of its growth. So, with greater growth of capitalism, these incompatibilities are likely to intensify and not ease off.

The idea that capitalism is a social form implies that to expand or to simply carry on, its economic structures require some political-institutional complements. There are certain types of political-institutional forms which constitute preconditions for a purely economic reproduction of capitalist society. Indian capitalism is in a state of serious *political* crisis. Conservative economists would argue, though I think unconvincingly, that the Indian economy has done reasonably well, if you ignore the distributive performance of the system; no political analyst can, however, claim that the Indian state has done reasonably well in quite the same sense. It is reacting defensively, and adopting undemocratic and precapitalist responses on vital issues. Most alarmingly, it is increasingly proving incapable of providing the most vital precondition for bourgeois development—the provision of political stability.

The state's difficulties should be seen as a structural crisis. Political crisis may break out through the mismanagement of political options by rulers, or sub-optimal decisions by the ruling bloc. A crisis is *structural* if it arises out of self-related difficulties, because it emerges not out of the failure of the social form, but its successes. It is not a condition of 'abnormality' which could be expected to disappear with a change of leaders or parties. It is coming to be a condition of stressful, violent normalcy of this late, backward, increasingly unreformist, capitalist order. It is different even from a standard Gramscian case; because here even a passive revolution has not succeeded, but is lapsing into failure. Those who would see present difficulties as 'failures' of Indian capitalism would find this difficult to explain. It is the 'successes' of Indian capitalism that have caused them. So, if it becomes more 'successful' in the ways it has pursued over the last twenty years, these problems will not go away, but perhaps intensify. The tragic thing is that the crisis of ruling-class politics plunges not only the ruling bloc, which has ruptured its protocol, into serious disorder, but the whole country. An exhaustion of the politics of the ruling bloc does not automatically prefigure a radical alternative. It is a particularly sad chapter of a story which had begun with the promise of something like an 'Indian revolution', an understandably unpractical and sentimental beginning which promised to 'wipe every tear from every eye'. Even if we consider only the socially relevant tears, the promise is as distant today as at the romantic time when it was made.

References

Bardhan, Pranab. 1985. *Political Economy of Development in India*. New Delhi: Oxford University Press.

Chandra, Bipan. 1979. Jawaharlal Nehru and the Indian Capitalist Class. In idem, *Nationalism and Colonialism in Modern India*. New Delhi: Vikas.

Frankel, Francine. 1978. *India's Political Economy*. Princeton: Princeton University Press.

Gramsci, Antonio. 1971. *Selections from the Prison Notebooks*. Trans. and ed. Q Hoare and G. Nowell-Smith. London: Lawrence and Wishart.

Hirschman, A. 1970. *Exit, Voice and Loyalty*. Cambridge, Mass.: Harvard University Press.

Kaviraj, S. 1982. Economic Development and the Political System. Paper for a colloquium on Indian Economic Development, October 1982, University of Economics, Vienna.

———. 1984. On the Crisis of Political Institutions in India. *Contributions to Indian Sociology*, no. 2.

———. 1986. Indira Gandhi and Indian Politics. *Economic and Political Weekly*. September.

Kaviraj, S. 1987. Gramsci and Different Kinds of Difference. Seminar on Gramsci and South Asia in July 1987, Centre for Studies in Social Sciences, Kolkata.

Mackie, J. 1975. Causes and Conditions. In E. Sosa, ed., *Causation and Conditionals*. London: Oxford University Press.

Marx, K. 1973. *Grundrisse*. Harmondsworth: Penguin.

Mitra, Ashok. 1977. *Terms of Trade and Class Relations*. London: Frank Cass.

Poulantzas, Nicos. 1978. *State, Power, Socialism*. London: New Left Books.

Riker, W.H. 1970 (1962). *The Theory of Political Coalitions*. New Delhi: Oxford and IBH.

Singh, Charan. 1978. *India's Economic Policy*. New Delhi: Vikas.

Singh, Chhatrapati. 1985. *Law between Anarchy and Utopia*. Delhi: Oxford University Press.

Thompson, E.P. 1978. *The Poverty of Theory and Other Essays*. London: Merlin.

Ulyanovsky. R. 1974. *Socialism and the Newly Independent Nations*. Moscow: Progress Publishers.

5

On the Crisis of Political Institutions in India

Historical puzzles appear to be generally of two types. Some are about facts—those arising out of our not knowing what had been the case. There is a second kind of historical puzzle in which the difficulty is that we know the facts but not what to do with them. Puzzles about contemporary history are often of the second kind. These problems elicit different kinds of response—in the first, empirical solutions, in the second, solutions of an interpretive kind. This essay is an attempt at interpretation, putting together the possible causes, patterns, and consequences of a crisis of political institutions in an intelligible design.[1]

Because the way something is explained depends logically on what is first shown as being in need of an explanation, and given that later explanatory moves always have some collusion with prior descriptive ones, it is necessary to set out the frame in which my questions are posed and sought to be answered. I take my frame to be marxian political theory; but the way I see it may be controversial. I think much of the space in marxian political theory is underdetermined by its general theoretical propositions; and these can be filled in by different explanatory styles (Kaviraj 1984: *passim*). The argument here is presented in four parts. In the first, I briefly set out the theoretical frame in which I have tried to work my explanation. In the second, I examine some theories about the historical derivation of political institutions in India, especially some optimistic ones. The third part gives an

First published in *Contributions to Indian Sociology*, no. 2, 1984.

[1] For recent exercises with very similar objectives but of entirely different theoretical provenance, see Sheth 1982 and Kothari 1984b.

account of the attempts at institution-making in the first period of Indian politics—its patterns and premises; in the last, I try to analyse why these quasi-institutions have come under increasing pressure.

I

Unlike other traditions of social theory, marxists use fairly strong conceptions of a social totality. In recent years, however, there has been a distinct move in the marxian concept of a totality from an expressivist notion around a mode of production, to a more authentically complex concept of an overdetermined structure (Althusser 1969; Althusser and Balibar 1970). Traditionally, marxists were quite content with the use of a single ordering category of a mode of production which helped them make their two elementary principles of ordering. It provided them with a structural map of the social form; and usually with the structural map went a recognized stock of historical inferences. They could infer, for instance, what its most likely points of stress would be, what types of conflict were likely to arise, and their probable course. But in the entire history of marxism there was a parallel tendency towards a more complex picture of the totality. In Marx's own works, after 1848–9, there is an explicit distinction between 'first way' and 'second way', or classical and belated capitalism.

Apart from significant economic differences, one major difference between the two paths was a dislocation between two types of structures, or their transformation in differential rhythms. In classical cases, the capitalist transformation of the structures of production was accompanied by antecedent, consequent, or in any case functionally related transformation of other, non-economic structures also, particularly the structures of the political and cultural levels. In late capitalism, as in Germany, the relation between these two processes seems to be sundered, and becomes increasingly asymmetric.[2] This seems to provide a conceptual point that can be used as a point of departure for the study of Indian political reality. A society, on this view, does not have an essentialist centre in its economy, such that economic change would bring its corollaries inevitably. Its centre was in fact an 'overdetermined' centre. The 'structuralism' of Marx included this

[2] The *locus classicus* for this argument is of course Marx 1848.

element of historical contingency in the logic of the structure itself.[3] What is crucial for our analysis here is the way it renders the concept of a social design complex—a social design, this implies, consists not only of a map of primary economic relations; it includes an at least equally significant map of institutional power. And the exact structure of a society would depend, consequently, on what this institutional map did to the economic one. By corollary, what can be called the 'logic of the society' would have a structure identical to Althusser's outline of 'historical time' (Althusser and Balibar 1970: ch. 4). It would be the result of what the logic of these different structures did to each other, and to the social whole.

This conceptual logic has been carried forward in the modern argument about the conceptual relation between modes of production and social formation.[4] As a result, marxists now work with more complex initial presuppositions, and also regard the principles of ordering as more complex and plural. Briefly, one can now suggest a method of using social abstractions stretched over three levels: (i) a mode of production orders (ii) something which is itself an abstraction—the functional concomitance between the economic and other structures, now called a social form—which is checked against (iii) the historical evidence of concrete societies. In my view, a marxian analysis should enquire about modes of production, domination, and consciousness in a lexical order.[5] If we use the common distinction between the economic and non-economic, then this means that the basic ground plan of the social design could be worked out by running the production map through the society's institutional matrix.

Finally, the transition to capitalism which India is undergoing should be characterized as a form of the second way, or what Gramsci calls a 'passive revolution' (Gramsci 1971: 105ff.). For, the central feature of this is the relative weakness of the bourgeoisie, a social force that

[3] I have tried to show this in logical terms elsewhere (Kaviraj 1984).

[4] For a brief account of the issues involved in this debate, see Hindess and Hirst 1977, particularly ch. 3.

[5] It is I think quite wrong to believe that any moves of this kind lead to a collapse of marxism into explanatory pluralism, for the obvious reason that pluralists would deny the existence of such ordering principles (which they regard as dubiously transcendental), while this line of thought retains the idea of an ordering principle, but makes it internally complex.

has been strong enough to prevent a collapse of bourgeois industrialization (unlike in other parts of the third world) but weak enough to leave institutional structures largely untransformed despite initial efforts. In the concept of a 'passive revolution' Gramsci condensed three related processes, all of which occur in India. First, the relative weakness of the bourgeoisie leads to a state of affairs in which agricultural production remains backward and unaffected by capitalist relations, marked in social terms by an absence of agrarian reforms. Secondly, a passive revolution has some political features: it is not a revolution led by a hegemonic class like the French or English bourgeoisie. It is not a class, a force of civil society which accomplishes the capitalist revolution through exercising a moral-political function of 'leadership'. Because of its weakness, relative political isolation, and lack of cultural leadership, it abdicates its tasks to a state bureaucratic agency which accomplishes social transformation through a function of 'domination'.[6] In historical terms, the state is a poor surrogate for the class, for the transformations by the class are worked through the institutions of civil society, through a politics of discourse, by a slow but certain change in the structure of common sense, a process that is democratic. A state bureaucracy does it by fiats, through a non-discursive politics of commands. In the first case, people are talked to and can talk back—which eventually structures the new moral order. In the second, the state seeks to regulate and control by commands, with the attendent danger of violent reactions. Third, in a passive revolution the common sense of society is not restructured around principles of rationality. So the society that emerges from a passive revolution lacks internal coherence between the logics governing its economic, political, and cultural instances. Thus, it is a 'revolution without a revolution'; for the term revolution has two connotations in marxian theory. It signifies a deep social transformation; but it also means a transformation through a mass movement. Late capitalism mostly produces a revolution in the first sense unaccompanied by the second.[7]

[6] Several Indian marxists have seen the possibilities in the concept of a passive revolution. One of the first to do so was Sen 1976; Chatterjee 1984 is another attempt in the same direction.

[7] There is another count on which Gramsci's model fits our conceptual needs. It is part of the argument condensed in the model that 'second way'

II

The historical experience of Indian society after Independence has been of a transition to capitalism, but evidently one that fits Gramsci's model. But, as in the European cases of late capitalism, it was initially widely believed that a transition to something less fragmented and internally contradictory was possible. In any case, there were contending theories about whether institutions of bourgeois democracy could be established in post-colonial India. There were, it seems, three strands of pessimism, which shared no premises but arrived by different routes at a similar conclusion. Classical colonialists saw these institutions from a European essentialist perspective—i.e. they were so linked to the peculiarities of European history that they were not replicable elsewhere, and this view often recommended a political form of 'intermediate technology' instead of exaggerated ambitions of working a parliamentary democracy.[8] There was a mirror image of this among chauvinists arguing from a reverse essentialism. Marxists too expressed a similar pessimism, though differently grounded.[9] Interestingly, what has happened in the years after Independence does not bear any of these out.

To understand why political institutions have not taken root, one must contend with arguments which were optimistic that they would. This optimism was not entirely gratuitous. Apart from the general utopianism about decolonization in the 1950s, they rested on three—now it seems oversimplified—readings of political history. Even nationalist textbooks often asserted a curious continuity between

---

capitalism produces greater regional imbalance, which Gramsci analysed in his articles on the 'Southern Question'. Cf. Gramsci 1978 for an elucidation of the idea of passive revolution and Buci-Glucksmann 1979, 1980: 54–63.

[8] It is not uncommon to find vestiges of this attitude to this day, advancing an 'intermediate technology' argument in politics and expressing relief that most third world countries have adopted forms of authoritarian politics rather than the more delicate mechanisms of representative democracy.

[9] Democratic institutions, so the argument runs, were successful only in situations of colonial capitalist expansion in Europe; as these conditions are unrepeatable, to expect democratic institutions to take root is an optimistic fallacy.

colonialism and the post-colonial state, by stating unproblematically that British rule sought to build rationalist institutions with the usual list—the common law, the bureaucracy, the judiciary. Obviously, there was a certain negative effect in being subject to a single set of iniquities, administered by a common set of rules under the control of outsiders, from which it was more difficult to purchase reprieve by the traditional routes of corruption and influence. But the institutional instinct of British imperialism was hardly coherent. Spells of evangelical utilitarianism were tempered by an ingenuous regard for traditional eminence. Many of these colossal structures of colonial 'rationalism' had feet of vernacular clay.[10] At the most general level, they lacked a crucial precondition of institutions: on both the Durkheimian and the Gramscian views, these have to be part of an unforced common sense. Rules of behaviour, to become institutions, require 'moral' legitimacy,[11] a sanction by the Durkheimian 'common consciousness'. A colonial order lacks this element by definition; its method of directing society is anything except hegemonic.

True, the British exerted themselves to ensure a sort of surrogate rationality for the upper order of the bureaucracy by gradually training up a small stratum of bi-cultural bureaucrats through the ICS instead of the initial policy of dependence on simply bilingual subalterns. But to see this as a plan for a rationalization of the social order is to misjudge their crucial and limited instrumental intent. With greater integration of the colony in politico-economic terms, this became a necessary requirement for a purely administrative 'meshing' of the upper bureaucracy in India with the rest of the administrative structure in metropolitan Britain.[12] A minimal order had to be created simply to ensure that the Indian administration functioned in a social

[10] Most of the so-called rationalistic institutions were bywords in petty corruption—including the blindfolded sword-bearing figure of justice. As social novels often point out, she could only understand English, and often her rationalistic deliberations were controlled by the translating, less highly principled babu. The law was often shockingly exploited by crucially placed bilingual scoundrels.

[11] A term which, oddly, Durkheim and Gramsci use in exactly the same sense.

[12] The famous trials of some of the successful colonialists probably had something to do with this. Those who came to know the ropes in the Indian

language that the colonial office understood. Such attempts at rationalization were anyway hedged in by exemptions for the lower bureaucracy, the enormous administrative underworld too vast and too insignificant to be transformed. British administration followed a policy of studied non-interference in the social institutions of the colony. In the princely states, and in other spheres of political life, the British underwrote the existing styles of pre-capitalist authority. The institutional legacy of colonialism was indeed extremely mixed.

Attempts at introducing modern institutions also led to some paradoxes. Practically, it was false to believe that institutions of Western provenance could not be worked by Indians. Economic structures like handling companies or stock exchanges were soon mastered by eligible Indians. Marwari businessmen on the Calcutta jute market were getting the better of their English or Scottish counterparts, though wholly unassisted by the Protestant ethic (Goswami 1982). For political institutions, however, there were some difficulties in a simple extension of this argument. Certainly, the early development of the Congress as primarily a lawyers' institution had parallels of a sort; and the preconditionality of a knowledge and use of British law for the work of breaking it continued in subtle ways, ironically, into the Gandhian period of mass mobilization. The legal preconditions of Gandhi's strategy are, I think, inadequately emphasized: only one who knew British law exceedingly well could know how to defy it so perfectly.[13] But the fact that these institutions were of British provenance created ideological obstacles to their easy absorption. Politics, after all, was the theatre on which the everyday defeat of the Indian was enacted. This made it possible for some to adopt an attitude of retrograde relativism which perceived these structures as 'alien' and therefore to be rejected once independence was achieved (Austin 1966:

---

system and handled them well to the advantage of the Company found them untranslatable into the norms of administrative behaviour in Britain.

[13] Of Gandhi's many personalities the most neglected is that of the lawyer. Apart from his role as a mystic, politician, etc., his ambidexterity with both British and Indian codes of behaviour and rationality must have constituted a crucial element in his success. It is his familiarity with the British legal system that enabled him to feel his way to its centre, and to pose it questions which often it could not answer very well.

ch. 2). In the culture of colonialism there was thus a peculiar convergence of opposites—colonialists who thought that Asiatics could not work these with chauvinists who regarded these as alien constructs.

Historians with a more nationalist inclination have sometimes taken a second line of argument about the possibility of bourgeois democratic institutions. Oppositional movements can escape absorption by a superior power only if their internal rules of governance are different in principle from those of the society they wish to subvert. Colonial rule could not be hegemonic; but there were the makings of a counter-hegemony in the national movement (Bhattacharyya 1979). Institutions of democratic decision-making, and traditions of secular, national (as opposed to regional) policy, it is said, emerged through the activity and experience of Congress nationalism. It was therefore a simple transfer of rules which had governed the internal functioning of the Congress into general rules governing the politics of the whole society. The trouble with this argument is that in its extreme form it rests on a highly idealized portrait of what the national movement was like. It exaggerates the homogeneity of the movement and the connection between the elite and the masses; and it discounts the play of local and personal interests and of the regional fractures within the Congress set-up. Modern trends in historical research have undermined these nationalist myths.[14] The labours of the Cambridge historians on the unlovely side of the Congress machine have shown that it was internally more contradictory than is commonly believed. It is possible now to see underlying continuities in political attitudes and actions between the pre-Independence and post-Independence periods of its history.

The attitudes of Congressmen towards institutions were deeply schizophrenic. Institutions signify, in terms of choice theory, a kind of pre-commitment.[15] Such precommitment can have two types of sources—first, in a calculation of interest: through the conviction that if one sticks to certain norms, even though this is constraining in an immediate way, it creates reciprocal constraints on other players. Without these, uncertainty and the attendant risks become too high.

[14] Researchers of the so-called 'Cambridge school' and, more recently, *Subaltern Studies* have done this in opposite ways. Cf. Seal 1968, Gallagher, Johnson, Seal 1973, Baker, Johnson, and Seal 1981, and Guha 1982, 1983.

[15] Elster 1978 provides an interesting account in these terms.

A second source could be a moral commitment to a rational social order, which had to be supported, if European experience is any guide, with an intellectual tradition that analysed, in a kind of slow replay, the historical experience of each round of social conflict. That Indian society has lacked this is perhaps best reflected in the absence of a tradition of social or political theory.[16]

On none of these counts was Congress opinion entirely undivided. Internal cohesion of an organization as diverse as Congress required some pre-commitment, but of an imperfect sort. But there was hardly any common enthusiasm for a rationalistic institutional order. It was too easy to damn these as Eurocentric visions. Congress bodies (sometimes even top leaders) obeyed these rules halfheartedly, as the incident of the Tripuri Congress presidency showed clearly. Congress, however, certainly wanted some pre-commitment to rules of the game on the part of the British. To ask the British to stick to some rules was one thing, to act oneself by them was quite another. The internal practices of Congress showed a coexistence of varying styles, and an ad hoc manner of resolving differences between them. Crises were resolved provisionally, without much attention to the question of a design, and by intervention of great men, who could, as Gandhi did at Tripuri, take up stances of an endearing unreasonableness.[17]

Unlike some other revolutionary organizations, Congress did not raise the question of social design—of the kind Lenin did when he said that it would be easier to make a revolution in Russia but more difficult to build socialism; in Germany it would be the other way round. Congress had little clarity about the social design it espoused, or the positive tasks of the political order against traditional society, once power was transferred. This was reflected in the peculiar ecumenism of its social programme: its equally cheerful acceptance both of hard

[16] What is odd in this is that philosophical skills were not lacking; what was lacking was the crucial hypothesis that they could, if applied to a replay of history, lead to a more rational and controlled pursuit of political business.

[17] A third line of optimistic reasoning held, somewhat unconvincingly in my opinion, that the 'pluralism' internal to Hindu religion could be transferred to the political level, and this could provide an alternative base for a pluralist political regime (Kothari 1970: ch. 7). I think this conflates two different senses of the term 'plural' and underestimates the repressive aspect of traditional Hindu social structure (Kaviraj 1983).

socialist programmes and of hard bourgeois ones for a future social design. This was less a sign of belief that these could be mixed into a workable synthesis than of a lack of seriousness about the question itself. Thus, on any count, the institutional 'legacy' that the new Congress regime carried with it at the time of Independence was inconsiderable.

If these arguments are right, and we are not romantic about either colonialism or the Congress or the pluralism implicit in traditional society, then it will be seen that the task of the founding elite was extremely complex. There were no tender institutions which they brought with them; these had to be built, not with the assistance of traditional social structures but against their logic. Particularly, the tolerance of the British for pre-capitalist forms ensured that structures of irresponsible power existed. To build institutions was to circumscribe these with limits, rules, and accountability.

III

Parliamentary institutions were introduced in India in conditions radically different from Europe. In Europe, there was a slow growth of a stratum of institutions through the church, the emergence of a legal order, and the rivalries between the church and the absolutist state which eventually specified the limits of jurisdiction for both. On top of these institutions, democratic polities were constructed from the seventeenth to the nineteenth century. These limits, rules, and conditions of political conduct were imposed on the elite from the outside, by repeated waves of popular movements. In India, these limits on the elite's power had to be self-imposed. Besides, it is a popular fallacy that the Congress sought to impose these limits; a segment of it did—against hard resistance from another group. Earlier differences of attitude towards these 'Western' institutions were hardly composed after assumption of office; these were exacerbated. The conflict between factions around Patel and Nehru was so significant precisely because a whole series of conflicts found a dramatic condensation in it. Essentially, it was a conflict about social design, and the relation the political order would bear to the logic of traditional society; whether it would simply express that logic, or try to curb and transform it. It was hardly accidental that these two elite groups had structurally different bases of support, and that the major drive towards institution-building came from the modernists.

Although perhaps in pure social weight the traditional opinion may not have been weaker, Nehru's victory in the factional conflict symbolized the triumph of the modernist forces, starting the most long-drawn attrition in Indian politics. But the efforts of this elite were marked by what *faute de mieux* can be called a historical evolutionism—a complex of beliefs that governed much early constitutional experiment in the third world. It regarded history not only as a succession of social forms, but also treated this sequence as a rational order. The underlying premise was that if two types of social organizations are placed side by side, the less rational or less advanced would decline inevitably, collapse almost out of embarrassment. Social change is seen as a teleology of transition; not a clash of opposing forces, in which each short-run outcome is uncertain, however final the long-term transition may be.

Evolutionism is, in this sense, the direct opposite of a mobilizational picture of a social revolution. These evolutionist beliefs provided the fundamental ideology of the passive revolution. Transformation of the society, it was believed, was not to be achieved through a mass movement; it could be safely left to a large bureaucracy to supervise.[18] The logical obverse of this bureaucratization of the problem of development was the demobilization of the Congress from its earlier militant political form into ordinary ministerialism. The mixed character of the Congress, an invaluable asset in the struggle against imperialism and a considerable instrument for winning elections, made it an inappropriate agency for directed, decisive social change. For the opposition to these changes came not only from without, but also from within. In its ruling coalition the bourgeoisie enjoys a partly gratuitous ascendancy, for it is won more by default than by serious leadership.

Classical bourgeois revolutions achieved the transformation of what I have called the institutional map through a politics of discourse

[18] Of course, it now appears from researches by marxist historians that the picture of the 'classical' revolution implicit in Marx and Gramsci was perhaps overdrawn. The state had much more to do with the development of capitalism in France than was initially presumed. Thus, the distinction between the first and the second way has been chipped away to some extent. But the distinction holds good if it is read in a double sense, as I have suggested: if the criterion is not the internal structure of the economy, but the balance between the economy and the other instances of the social formation.

(unlike others in Italy and Germany, where it was left to the state). In Europe the critical institutions emerged through a long social debate, which provided an opportunity for a kind of experimentalism which perfected their function, increased their coherence, and won acceptability for them. Through political revolutions, the entire society was present as it were at the spectacle in which the boundaries of powers and institutions were slowly interrogated. In India, the opposite happened. Nehru's isolation in the political machine made him depend increasingly on the bureaucracy. But a bureaucracy is unsuited to do these jobs in a double sense. First, the revolutionary classes in Europe had a greater homogeneity of interests. Secondly, the bourgeoisie had a strong ideological cement, a Calvinist sense of purpose, a political programme. Where the agents of change in Europe saw a mission to transform the world, the bureaucracy sees a tiring daily chore. In the formation of institutions and the transformation of social relations in India, this was the central paradox. The modernist elite was doubly encircled: first, by the opposition of a faction of the Congress; second, by the intended instrument of bureaucracy.

There was not one bureaucracy, but two. Under the thin crust of a Europeanized elite, the British had tolerated the untroubled continuance of large expanses of vernacular graft. The only good thing about the latter was its limitedness. It was an arm of an essentially negative state, limited to the task of maintaining law and order. Traditional legacies interfered with even well-intentioned legislation. For each decision there was the internal distance in this large and ill-regulated machine, as it journeyed from adumbration as a policy, through its transmission, decimation, and eventual ironical 'implementation', often in unrecognizable forms.[19] Secondly, across the massive structure of this bureaucracy (which became steadily larger with more welfare and accounting functions) fell the shadows of class and culture.

Bureaucratic functioning was deeply afflicted by the two cultures in Indian politics. The modernist decision-maker at the level of ministries shared no common language with the village clerk whose ideas of social reasonableness were radically different. Certainly, deliberate evasion and non-implementation did occur on issues in which interests were directly involved. But, on other issues, a complex order, originating in

[19] Perhaps the best example of this would be land reforms. See Frankel 1978: ch. 4.

one culture and in its perception of the social world, had to negotiate the boundaries with another in its course down the administrative structures. All efforts at rationalization and democratization had to contend with this subtle but irresistible attack of interpretation. Rationalistic and democratic ideas very often lost the battle against this attrition of administrative hermeneutics. The division between two sectors of the polity was no less marked than the economic. Policies from the metropolitan, central sector faced an invincible coalition at the rural and state levels—between the traditional Congress elite controlling the state organizations, and the lower bureaucracy; especially because the lower orders of administration, unlike the IAS, were locally recruited, and were vulnerable to local pressures. The Nehru years saw a continuous struggle between these two alphabets of social action.

A further reason for the difficulty in social transformation could be the nature of the social totality itself. It has been forcefully argued by some (Kothari 1970; Nandy 1980; Sheth 1982) that a crucial feature of traditional Indian society was its ability to marginalize the political order. It developed a complex determination of its structure such that the logic of political change remained isolated from the logic of social order. This could be done only if the state, in its resplendent majesty, could be kept a relative stranger which did not interfere in the locally struck balances between local interests.[20] The country had two histories, as it were—the fast-moving history of the theatrical world of high politics, but its height also rendered it marginal; and the quiet history of the everyday with extraordinarily long rhythms of change.[21]

But by any account the advances made during the Nehru period, despite late anxieties, were considerable. These two theatres of existence—of politics and society—were being brought into one single whole. More significantly, the early elite posed the question of

[20] This is an idea of extremely eminent but also extremely complex ancestry, flowing from European orientologists, to British ethnographers, to Marx to modern functionalists.

[21] One way of contrasting European with Indian history has been to contrast their obviously differential rhythms; but this view goes further by linking this differential rhythm with a contrast in the principles organizing the social totalities.

the making of institutions correctly: as an imposition of the logic of democracy through the political order on the pre-capitalist logic of society—against the normalcy of caste, community, regionalism, and other cellular pressures. It had also been able to induce a quantum leap in industrialization, and a considerable urban constellation. This was followed by a period of political changes that seemed unimportant in the short run but which appear, over a somewhat longer perspective, to have restructured political relations in a retrograde direction, a process that began, like many significant historical processes, unspectacularly.

IV

After Nehru's death the adaptation of the political system to these changes was itself a test of institutionalization. It was to show how much of his authority had been charismatic, and how much part of a 'rational' constitutional order. The Congress immediately faced at least three types of difficulties. First, the two rounds of selection of individuals for leadership put the internal machinery of the Congress to great strain. Secondly, the relation between the Congress as the central party and the political world around it went through a dramatic transformation—reflected in its disastrous electoral performance in 1967. Finally, it soon faced a crisis of legitimacy (Sheth 1982).[22] In combination, these led to a reversal of the most fundamental relation in Indian politics; between the state on the one side, and the social structure and structures of traditional ideology on the other. The state lost its superordinate position between the two instances of the social totality; and the relationships which constituted the 'historic bloc' were renegotiated. Driven by the need for survival, the state elite began to seek alliances with pre-capitalist forces on a larger scale, and lost its ability to dictate to them, to a large extent. Instead it began to register passively the trace of the resurgent forces in the social order.

Three types of changes seem to have set in as a result of the alterations in the late 1960s. The overwhelming preponderance of the

[22] Sheth argues that Nehru's Congress enjoyed legitimacy, which the Congress has lacked later on; but one construction of his own evidence can be that the earlier Congress did not have to pass a test of legitimacy.

Congress in the political system as a whole became a decisive factor; because although, in a technical sense, some of these were changes in the structure and balance of the Congress Party, as the Congress occupied so much of the political space, the rest of the political order could not isolate itself from the effects of these occurrences. First, institutions sometimes came in the way of political survival of the high elite; and they thought, implausibly, that an occasional defiance of norms for self-defence was permissible; after the situation normalized, norms could be called back in. This misunderstood the reciprocal nature of institutional norms, a point that Western political thinkers have sought to underline by the metaphor of a contract. Transgressions of norms make the implicit contractual pre-commitment collapse.

Second, the limitedness of the reforms of the Nehru era took its revenge, as it were. With the weakening of the political centre, and the gradual alteration of politico-economic balances in the rural areas, social groups that had earlier been weak partners in the ruling coalition began to renegotiate its terms and surface at the national and state levels.[23] Their unfamiliarity with, and intolerance of, limits, rules, and principles of accountability began to tell on the upper levels of the polity. The circumstantial weakness of the new leadership forced them to alter their policy of trying to change the logics of society into one of accepting them, and reflecting and registering them in policy-making—causing long-drawn, subtle, graduated but nevertheless definite redefinitions of political ideals like secularism, nationalism, etc.

Finally, subtle but significant alterations took place in the structure of legitimacy. Legitimacy of institutional power was increasingly giving place to a legitimacy of individuals; and perhaps still more significant, the new rhetoric of socialism, indiscriminately used by nearly all political forces, signified something often fatally misunderstood. Socialist rhetoric often gave a respectable cover for the re-emergence of an essentially pre-capitalist alphabet of social action. It looked upon impersonal rules and application of rationalistic norms with derision, as forms of 'bourgeois' fastidiousness.

[23] I have argued elsewhere (Kaviraj 1982) about the nature of this coalition, and the modifications in its structure in the late 1960s and early 1970s.

All these contributed to a weakening of institutional drives; and lack of concern about the fundamental social design was rationalized as a policy of pragmatism. The changes around 1967 were often welcomed by political scientists as a shift forward from a monopolistic to a competitive structure (Morris Jones 1978: 144–59); actually, it was a watershed of a different kind. The relation between the political level and the social structures of traditionalism were reversed in those years of political instability. Political structures lost the capacity of reordering social relations; these latter, on the contrary, reasserted themselves over, and soon through, the political system. The political elite abandoned the practice of reckoning in historical terms, preferring a pragmatic reckoning of their own record, reflected perhaps in the vastly different attitude towards planning. Short-term solutions and concessions on questions of religion and regionalism were to embarrass the elite subsequently. But it is not easy to avoid the consequences while courting the causes. Besides, the beauty of pragmatism as a political doctrine is that it reckons everything, even historic things, in measures of the everyday, and reconciles people to a collapse of structures because it comes in easy instalments. As democratic institutions in India were largely a question of self-invigilation of the powers of the elite, without strong democratic popular movements to keep them from transgressing institutional limits, changes of attitude among the rulers had signal consequences.

To say that institutions which had been set up in the Nehru era collapsed during the period of Indira Gandhi, as is often done (e.g. Shourie 1978) is to overstate the case. It ignores the frailty of the structures in the earlier epoch: the Nehru period provided the Indian polity not with sturdily functioning institutions but with an institutional design. It confuses, plausibly, political stability with institutional strength. But it also misjudges the time scales in which alone the question of the rise and decline of institutions can be asked. Fifteen years or thirty is not the span in which institutions can get either built or destroyed. Nonetheless, there was a definite shift in the career of this design; and politics in India has come to assume a pattern vastly different from what it had in the 1950s and 1960s,[24] though this must

[24] For three recent accounts of these, see Sheth 1982, Manor 1983, and Kothari 1984b.

imply the mild paradox that randomness and contradiction are themselves ingredients of a pattern.

There is a double logic in the politics of crisis after the 1960s: first, there is a logic of crises fanning outwards from a political centre—the crisis of a leader becoming the crisis of a party, and that turning into a crisis of the system. In reverse, there is also a logic of condensation of political crises—from the periphery to the centre, from the larger system to its central institutions, to the party, to the elite.

Institutions represent a form of pre-commitment in making political decisions,[25] but there are some preconditions of a pre-commitment strategy. Pre-commitment techniques can figure only in strategies of the long run. Actors who agree to a strategy of pre-commitment must possess a fair knowledge of the kinds of crises or problems that are likely—in other words, a historical foresight. Moreover, the knowledge of possible dangers has to include not merely the dangers from outside or from others, but also those from the self; an understanding not only of external threats but also of those arising from the disposition of the actors themselves; for it is largely a strategy against one's own failures. Constitutionalism, as a version of pre-commitment, is therefore related to an ability not to take courses of action which might offer immediate relief but are fraught with dangers of long-term calamity.

Even in Nehru's time, this kind of self-invigilation by the Congress was imperfect. In case of constitutional crises in states (especially in the 1959 incident about the communist ministry in Kerala), the Congress disregarded constitutional norms. Secondly, despite the formal principles of the system, caste sympathies and solidarity were enlisted for electoral purposes. In situations of crisis, both these trends intensified: indiscriminate use of president's rule under thin subterfuges undermined the federal system and led to the far more explosive regional contradictions of the 1970s and 1980s. Electoral necessity often tempted political parties of both government and opposition to enlist other primordial identities besides caste, particularly religious and regional mobilization.

[25] The Ulysses myth brings out clearly the preconditions of a pre-commitment strategy: a fair knowledge about what might come, which is based on a knowledge of the self, and of adversaries and environment (Elster 1978).

Thus, the meanings of secularism and nationalism (as an antonym for regionalism) have been largely renegotiated through accumulating concessions, altering very largely the rationalistic ground plan of the constitutional system. Secularism means a process in which religious considerations gradually become irrelevant to public decisions; instead, it has come to mean an equal right of religious elements to meddle in public decisions—a not unnatural development in view of the policy of concessions so structured as to sensitize people to their community identities rather than to forget them. In a crucial throwback, secularism itself has come to be defined in religious terms. A national perspective, similarly, often means a simple contingent average of regional pressures. The principle of bargaining, sometimes celebrated as a central principle of the democratic system in India, had retrograde effects because it became often a case of bargaining between non-secular or sub-national identities.

This is not to say that such identities did not surface in earlier phases of politics. They did—but with a kind of shamefacedness, looking for masks of different slogans. But after 1971 even the ideological environment of Indian politics has changed. Manor has recently talked about a depreciation of the language of politics (Manor 1983: 727). This came about through the Congress attempt to use a language of socialism in its support, an irresponsible introduction of ideology. But it led, in a way familiar in Indian politics, to its use by all other political contenders, and an eventual collapse of the essential tools of political identification. As ideological divisions declined, it became easier for primordial forces to reappear without masks.

Forms of constitutional behaviour in the Congress were related, in the 1950s and 1960s, not only to cultural accomplishments of the upper political elite; its decline afterwards was also not purely because of the absence of such training. For institutions get developed and accepted not through the personal cultivation of elites, but because these serve functional necessities in the system. It has something to do with the collective self-interest of all political actors in keeping the terrain of their conflict recognizable, and the returns for actions predictable. Perhaps the most potent cause for constitutionalism is the realization that political risks are reciprocal. What a party in power administers to its opponents is exactly what it can expect to get when others are in power. The rise of constitutionalism had surely as much to do with such universalization of risks as with the rational power of Lockean theory.

In the Nehru era, although the Congress was too electorally predominant to be concerned about such risks, its internal structure did call for such rules. The Congress was inhabited by such discordant ideological tendencies and social interests that its internal politics required some minimal trust, which could be secured by an implicit adherence to norms. The heterogeneity of the Congress made it necessary to work by some abstract, general, impersonal principles. For example, the principle of the majority decision usually went in favour of the modernist elite at the central levels of the Congress organization; but equally frequently it went in favour of landed elites in the provinces/states. In these circumstances, the Congress functioned by a miraculous balance of forces; social or class divisions were reflected with almost linear directness in its spatial and structural characteristics. In these circumstances, a functioning by fiat from the top, very largely the rule since the early 1970s, would have been insupportable. The majority rule, thus, was accepted as a shared institutional practice not because of its overwhelming Lockean rationality, but because it randomized victory well enough to be acceptable to both factions or both sets of interests.

Often, this was also the functional necessity behind the resurrection of the supposedly traditional Indian method of consensual politics. Although it made resultant decisions inevitably fuzzy, it gave something to everybody, and therefore an incentive to all parties to the consensus to rationalize what every side conveniently thought had been decided. It was a sort of proportional representation of interests in every single decision, once more a practice which had more to do with the heterogeneity of interests and their cellularity, rather than an improbable resurrection of a morally compelling tradition.

In any case, in both instances—of majoritarian institutions or their informal shift to consensualism—these political forms were based on institutional pre-commitments, and these forms performed a function which was seen as being important by all players in the political arena. To the marginal groups, they ensured some minimal consideration in the decision-making process, which in their absence these groups were unlikely to achieve. For weightier interests, they provided a possibility of containing, often pre-empting, opposition. Most of these institutions can therefore be traced to their fit, however transient, with some configuration of interests and perceptions. But there was always, in the structure of this politics, a real possibility of a fundamentally different kind of solution—a tendency which has surfaced recurrently after the Nehru period, as Congress became increasingly unmindful of questions of social design: the danger of a 'Bonapartist' solution, a style of functioning that combines the ad hoc with the arbitrary in mediating between conflicting interests, a solution which gives the political elite more power but weakens the political order against other instances of the social form.

After Nehru's death, there was certainly no change of course by the Congress Party. If anything, the new elite paid great attention to preserving continuity with its objectives. But this masked an alteration in the principal fact of the political world—the new leadership around Mrs Gandhi had a different relationship with the political universe. Its considerations of survival led it into conflict with some established institutions within the Congress, and later with the constitutional system. Continuance of Nehru's policies was bought at the cost of some of the institutions he had helped to fashion. As initial challenges to authority came from state-level leaders of the Congress, state organizations were systematically undermined. As a means of keeping control over the state organizations, the Congress largely dispensed with internal elections, and substituted these with nominations from above. This severed state leaderships from the flows of local politics, prevented the training of new leaders, and attenuated the political effectiveness of the lower orders of the Congress organization—leading to greater reliance on Mrs Gandhi's charismatic authority. Instead of a system of gradients, the Congress became a curious amalgam of two increasingly distanced processes—at the centre and at the local levels.

It has been widely noted that the Congress that emerged from the turmoil of the 1960s was quite different from the earlier Congress. Nehru presided over a strong centre which rested on strong states. Mrs Gandhi's regime increasingly saw their relation as zero-sum and worked on an implied policy that the weaker the states, the stronger the centre. Partly, this was due to the rise of non-Congress state governments after 1967, making it claim that the strength of the nation depended on weakening such recalcitrant governments. But paradoxically the Indira Gandhi regime faced far more intense regionalist pressures than the Nehru regime did, after the initial problems about the reorganization of states. The reasons were a combination of regional inequalities produced by the growth of capitalism, and the hardening of central policies. As the informal federalism within the Congress broke down, more states went to non-Congress parties, the central government faced demands of great obduracy and stridency, and more significantly, ones which, under the abstract classification as 'regional' claims, were mutually incompatible.[26] Often, inattention to regional problems early enough let them grow into proportions in which the only responses could be concession or massive repression. The first would immediately set off similar demands from elsewhere, the second a downward spiral of attrition, both in the last analysis weakening the state. Concessions are unwise because ungeneralizable; and the use of repressive measures is ineffective unless the forces have been politically isolated in advance. What is remarkable in regional difficulties of the regime is their 'structural' nature. For several of the regional articulations were nursed in their more tractable adolescence by Congress governments.

In the case of both the government and the opposition one can apply a model in which the 'rationality' of the agents (individual or collective) undermined the rationality of the system. Actors, in maximizing their utilities, have made demands which would disrupt the system, which is a precondition for their own existence. In doing this both the regime and the opposition have increasingly played beyond the institutional map. Mrs Gandhi's regime did this in one way at the time of the Emergency, and by the constant drive for centralization. Opposition parties have done this by increasingly articulating non-ideological, regional demands. It is a significant mark of the change in Indian politics that Nehru's opposition was primarily ideological: Communists, Socialists, or Swatantra contested the design of society but concurred in regarding this question as fundamental, while Mrs Gandhi's opposition has been increasingly regionalist.

[26] The Assam and Punjab agitations, though these are both regional demands against the centre, have economic demands that are diametrically opposed and incompatible.

Several other changes in politics are related to the decline of these institutions. Institutions provided a lit stage on which conflicts between political interests were fought out. It was a public spectacle, while now there is an increasing trend towards settling disputes outside them. Politicians who earlier used to enact this spectacle regarded themselves as representatives of large social interests or recognizable ideological positions. The new politicians now have little legitimacy, and the institutions which could have trained them have collapsed. The skills of diplomacy between interests have therefore been in short supply. Defections from one party to another, and the generosity of parties in opening their never very strait gates to them, leads to long-term results. Defection is not only morally execrable; it also introduces a functional disability in the system. In a highly diverse society like the one in India, the political process needs to have some kind of stable, intelligible relationship with social cleavages. This is a precondition for political self-recognition of groups, as much as for political self-expression. Interests need not always find satisfaction within the dominant government party. It is equally possible, and indeed important, that groups which feel that their interests are not really looked after by the government (as regional bourgeoisie and rich farmers felt in the 1960s) support oppositional parties, to exert their negative, restraining, critical influence on policy-making. Defection on a large scale disrupts this map of political relations, for it undermines the reliance on the party system as a reliable register of political attitudes.

It is not a government, or a party, that is undermined by this, but the state. Recently, political observers have persistently reported two kinds of developments. First, there is a growth, in my view somewhat overestimated, of grassroots movements which seek 'non-state' solutions to political questions (Sheth 1982, 1984; Kothari 1984a).[27] This in itself is fraught with potential dangers. For problems which are of local origins are not necessarily of localizable consequences. Therefore, even initially workable solutions at the local level may, as time passes, lead to difficulties of composition. Secondly, there is a marked tendency for social tensions to break out into violence (Kothari 1984b). Caste conflicts in eastern and central India, particularly, appear to be of this

[27] I find their understanding of the causes of these developments plausible, but of their possible consequences unconvincing.

kind—in which the combatants deliberately move the theatre of violence outside the normal markings of legal authority. And thus some of the most fundamental conflicts of rural society tend to happen, paradoxically, neither against, nor in favour of, but bypassing the state. This threat to the state is no less portentous than the direct onslaughts on it. For even an attack on the power of the state recognizes its centrality to social experience. Occasions of violence which happen without reference to the state, in which the arms of the law act, if they act, *ex post*—such occasions question even its claims and capacity for this sort of centrality.

The state has answered these difficulties through two strategies. The first is one of isolating what are seen as core areas. Institutional structures have been informally disaggregated to defend the 'core sector' to the detriment of its periphery. This has happened in sectors as diverse as education, transport, and politics, so that it can be plausibly seen as the logic of a strategy of pragmatism. Skills which such core sectors require or provide will be defended, it is occasionally announced, 'at any cost'.[28] Such policies heighten the contradictions in two ways. First, of course, there is an immediate rush to get into these sectors or institutions, so designated into an unfortunate eminence, so that these are threatened by severe overloading. Besides, it misjudges what is isolable within structures of modern society. Efforts at preserving excellence in particular educational institutions have failed simply because these are fed by other parts of the structure which are allowed to decay. In general, the main fallacy in this strategic argument is that elite institutions are fed by the non-elite ones; and therefore this kind of segregation does not protect the high institutions from the logic of decay; it merely inserts a lag. The logic of decline does catch up with the high institutions too, but with a lag; and because of the inevitable relativity of all comparisons, these can still be mistaken for centres of an insecure excellence. In India, in nearly all sectors, one can find examples of such a downwardly mobile excellence.

[28] Examples could be found from all important sectors of social life: elite educational institutions like IITs and the central universities; in the railways the trains which run between metropolises and cater to the upper middle class: the frequent establishment of elite groups in the police and administration all seem to exhibit the same optimism about a small part along with a pessimism about the whole.

A second response by the state has been through a form of frenetic centralization.[29] But centralization arguably is a wrong answer to the basic problem; it misreads what was involved in institutionalization itself. For the question of institutionalization was of effectivity of the political order against the logic of pre-capitalist social relations. Centralization means simply a reordering of relationships within the political order itself, rather than reordering the relationship between the society and the state.[30] If, as I have argued earlier, traditional forces or the logic of their operation find a sanctuary within the political order itself, it can hardly carry on the task of reworking the map of the older social relations. Centralization, if anything, shows the decay of institutions rather than their revival. For these, if they are working, assign conflicts to pertinent levels and roles, instead of sending them all up for what can only be hasty solutions. But the gathering crisis is not simply political. The development of a large modern industrial structure in India has continued unabated. Despite its inherent iniquities, it is the economic expansion that has continued. But running a large-scale economy of this kind requires commensurate, concomitant, social and cultural skills. This is the central idea behind the notion of a logic of a social form. For economic growth—achieved largely through imported technologies and organizational models—has no magical powers of working all other institutions around to mesh with its own logic. This is why the role of the state is critical in providing capitalism with the conditions of reproduction of its production relations. It is not merely contradictions within the economy, but the further contradiction between it and other instances of the social form which is precipitating the social crisis in India.

[29] Although I think the usual policy of centralization has been misconceived, I do not wish to suggest that decentralization is either an effective solution or a morally justifiable alternative under all circumstances.

[30] Kothari 1984b offers a similar argument. However, there are important points of difference with my argument, especially at the theoretical level. I do not accept his thesis that the state is always autonomous of class interests in a democratic polity; marxists, when talking about relative autonomy of the state, mean something quite different. Secondly, he uses the term civil society as opposed to state to mean simply society, rather than in the precise Gramscian connotation used here or in Sen 1976 or Chatterjee 1984. My contention is that many of the deformities of capitalist development in India arise precisely because of a lack of development of what Gramsci calls a 'civil society'.

Institutional pre-commitment restricts the options available to political actors, but yet these constitute a groundmap of relationships necessary for political behaviour. Political actors in India have often been tempted to destroy this map in search of means that will heighten the insecurity of their adversaries. Playing beyond the rules is a way of wrongfooting others, upsetting calculations, and creating a surprise that gives an ineradicable advantage; but there is a paradox in playing beyond the institutionally marked space. This absolves other players of all kinds—parties, primordial communities, social forces—of pre-commitment in equal measure. This creates a more fundamental disorientation. Ironically, it destroys the markings on political space, destroying the set of recognitions and identifications which makes the game of constitutional politics possible. This makes the world of politics unrecognizable—affecting the stronger as much as the weaker contenders; for politics requires an initial reliability of identifications, a common register. A loss of these would lead to false identifications, to unreliable perceptions, and so to responses exaggerated or insufficient. The contradiction between the two rationalities—of the agent and the system—has a limit to its elasticity. In Indian politics there are clear indications of a growing alienation—a feeling of loss of direction and control, a feeling of a surprisingly familiar world growing increasingly strange and intractable.

Traditionally, there have been two conditions which eased the dealing with political crises. The first was the relative isolation of the political order from the social structures, so that political upheavals affected the social structure relatively little. The growth of capitalism under state aegis has ruled that out; for one of the most remarkable transformations in society was the reduction of these barriers and distances, and the permeation of society by the instruments and effects of politics. It ended, to use a counter-marxist phrase, the relative autonomy of the society from the political. Another traditional condition was that of dispersal, or the isolation of the crisis field, so that disturbances would remain localized. But that required governance that was looser, more decentralized—an option ruled out by the logic of centralization. All power becoming central extracts a price in its logical obverse: all problems become central too. The centralization of power has led to a centralization of political difficulties.

The story of Indian politics shows with particular clarity an important historical proposition. In transitional societies, the question of social design is not a dispensable consideration, to be taken up only if politicians feel philosophically disposed. It permeates all other questions. The long-term problem of social design and the short-run one of political utilities are inextricable from each other. Pragmatism may make politicians collectively turn their backs towards the former; but it does not go away. It merely intensifies the paradox of political pragmatism. Each of its short-term solutions comes eventually to add to its long-term problems.

References

Althusser, Louis. 1969. *For Marx*. London: Allen Lane.

———, and Etienne Balibar. 1970. *Reading Capital*. London: NLB.

Austin, Granville. 1966. *The Indian Constitution: Cornerstone of a Nation*. Oxford: Clarendon Press.

Baker, C.J., G. Johnson, and A. Seal, eds. 1981. *Power, Profit and Politics*. Cambridge: Cambridge University Press.

Bhattacharyya, Sabyasachi. 1979. Notes on the Role of the Intelligentsia in a Colonial Society: India from Mid-nineteenth Century. *Studies in History* 1: 89–104.

Buci-Glucksmann, Christine. 1979. State, Transition and Passive Revolution. In Chantal Mouffe 1979: 207–36.

——. 1980. *Gramsci and the State*. London: Lawrence and Wishart.

Chatterjee, Partha. 1984. The Analysis of Nationalist Discourse. Paper for Second Conference of the Study Group on Analytical Political Philosophy of the International Political Science Association, Baroda. 19–22 March 1984.

Elster, Jon. 1978. *Ulysses and the Sirens*. Cambridge: Cambridge University Press.

Frankel, Francine. 1978. *India's Political Economy, 1947–1977*. Princeton: Princeton University Press.

Gallagher, J., G. Johnson and A. Seal, eds. 1973. *Locality, Province, and Nation*. Cambridge: Cambridge University Press.

Goswami, Omkar. 1982. 'The Jute Economy of Bengal, 1931–1947'. Unpublished PhD thesis. Oxford University.

Gramsci, A. 1971. *Selections from the Prison Notebooks*. London: Lawrence and Wishart.

——. 1978. *Selections from Political Writings, 1921–26*. London: Lawrence and Wishart.

Guha, Ranajit, ed. 1982. *Subaltern Studies I*. Delhi: Oxford University Press.

——. 1983. *Subaltern Studies II*. Delhi: Oxford University Press.

Hindess, Barry and Paul Hirst. 1977. *Modes of Production and Social Formation.* London: Macmillan.

Kaviraj, Sudipta. 1982. Economic Development and the Political System. Paper for Vienna Colloquium on Contemporary India, Vienna. October 1982.

——. 1983. Political Culture in Contemporary India. *Teaching Politics* 3–4: 1–22.

——. 1984. On Political Explanation in Marxism. Paper for seminar on Marx, Schumpeter and Keynes. Indian Council for Social Science Research, Delhi. January 1984.

Kothari, Rajni. 1970. *Politics in India.* Boston: Little Brown and Co.

——. 1984a. The Non-Party Political Process. *Economic and Political Weekly* 5, 4 February: 216–24.

——. 1984b. Will the State Wither Away? *Illustrated Weekly of India* 8 July: 8–14.

Manor, James. 1983. Anomie in Indian Politics. *Economic and Political Weekly.* Annual Number 18: 725–34.

Marx, K. (1848) 1972. The Bourgeoisie and the Counterrevolution. In Marx and Engels. *Articles from the Neue Rhenische Zeitung.* Moscow: Progress Publishers.

Morris Jones, W.M. 1978. *Politics Mainly Indian.* New Delhi: Orient Longman.

Mouffe, Chantal, ed. 1979. *Gramsci and Marxist Theory.* London: Routledge and Kegan Paul.

Nandy, Ashis. 1980. *At the Edge of Psychology.* Delhi: Oxford University Press.

Seal, Anil. 1968. *The Emergence of Indian Nationalism.* Cambridge: Cambridge University Press.

Sen, Asok. 1976. Bureaucracy and Social Hegemony. In *Essays presented to Professor S.C. Sarkar,* New Delhi: People's Publishing House.

Sheth, D.L. 1982. Social Basis of the Political Crisis. *Seminar* 1, 1–9 January.

——. 1983. Grassroots Stirrings and the Future of Politics. *Alternatives* 1, 1–24 March.

——. 1984. Grassroots Initiatives in India. *Economic and Political Weekly* 6, 11 February: 259–62.

Shourie, Arun. 1978. *Symptoms of Fascism.* New Delhi: Vikas.

6

Indira Gandhi and Indian Politics

This essay tries to see Indira Gandhi's period in Indian politics historically. It does not try to give a detailed historical account of its events, but to make sense of what happened. Do the events, beyond their quotidian diversity, show some pattern? Did Indira Gandhi's actions weaken, retard, rework, redirect the scheme of national reconstruction laid down by the earlier regime? What are their likely long-term consequences? I try here to ask some of these questions through a division of her term into four fairly obvious periods: 1966 to 1971, 1971 to 1975, 1975 to 1980, and from 1980 to her death.

I

Nothing was less inevitable in modern Indian politics than Indira Gandhi's rise to power. Yet, as often happens in history, once it happened, nothing was more decisive. It was modern Indian history's most crucial and indelible accident; for, once this accident took place, other political necessities were restructured according to the logic of this single fact. Her coming to power was not dynastic, though subsequently it came misleadingly to appear that way. She was not prepared for premiership of India by Nehru for the simple reason that even if he could have foreseen his own death, he could not have foreseen Shastri's. Even after Shastri's death Indira Gandhi's election to power did not lie in the logic of history in any sense, it was not made to happen by the logic of either political support, control over party machinery, personal

First published in *Economic and Political Weekly*, 20–27 September 1986.

charisma, or personal intrigues. She was elevated to the leadership of the Congress Party through a negative decision, in one of the most difficult periods of the party's history, in the middle of a serious crisis of the Indian state. Two rather contrary reasons contributed to this—an impression of her weakness and ideological indistinctness, and an ability to metonymically extend the charisma of Jawaharlal Nehru.

Indira Gandhi came to power because she appeared to have a set of paradoxical political qualifications, most significantly of indistinctness and ambiguity. To read the quality of personal decisiveness of her later years into her beginnings would be entirely wrong, because it would ironically destroy the means of knowing the process by which she became what she was. Evidently, the greatest qualification of Indira Gandhi at the time of her accession was her weakness, and the fact that she was not too strongly associated with any policy line to give offence to any of the groups which dominated the polycentric structure of the Congress Party after Nehru's death.[1] Obviously, members of the group which supported her candidacy feared the decisiveness and dogmatism of Morarji Desai; but they were too jealous of each other to accept the dominance of any one among themselves. They therefore chose Indira Gandhi because she did not represent anything too decisively. At that moment, she was the symbol of a stalemate; and this group had visions of enjoyment of that rarest form of political power through remote control—which would have given them privileges of decision without its responsibilities.

It was also possible for interest groups associated with the ruling elite to believe that she would make way after some time for someone with clearer policy preferences, or, if she survived, she could be encouraged, pressured, or cajoled into line. Sometimes Indira Gandhi's regime is analysed by observers in terms of a 'caesarist' model from Gramsci;[2] but the initial conditions of her rule were anything but caesarist. Hers was not a classically Bonapartist position in terms of Marxist theory, for the caesarist elite is dominant over class and group interests when these contending groups are too closely balanced.

[1] Frankel 1978 gives a detailed account of the developments in the Congress at the time of Nehru's death. Cf. chs 6, 7.

[2] Gramsci 1971: 106ff. Buci-Glucksmann 1980 draws, in my judgement, too strong a connection between passive revolution, caesarism, and fascism, making it difficult to apply it to more mixed cases.

Indeed, her position was a kind of caesarism in reverse, because her government seemed to be equally vulnerable to diverse forms of pressure. Even the mildest radical associations would have been fatal for her fortuitous rise to power. Such associations disqualified people like Krishna Menon from any importance in the post-Nehru Congress. To the Congress bosses she was a good candidate precisely because her symbolism of Nehru was in a sense false; she could, in their eyes, benefit from her connection with Nehru without any inheritance of his reformism.[3] Purely politically, she had come into a situation of an even balance of political and group interests in which she was very weak; naturally, she wished to see a situation of even balance in which she held the balance. Thus her initial moves were unrelated to clear policy or strategic issues; they were simply devoted to working out a logic of political survival. In this respect, it is inappropriate to see parallels between Nehru and Indira Gandhi. To follow policies of any kind at all, even to follow the policies of her father, she had to survive. Initially, this logic of survival made her act pragmatically, but eventually these ad hoc and individual initiatives altered the basic structure of Indian politics. We must however briefly turn to see what these structures were.

Indian politics in the Nehru period was coalitional in two senses.[4] It was coalitional in a class sense, as Marxists claim, although there are differences among them about which classes or groups constitute the dominant coalition. It appears that the most interesting and explanatorily successful model of this ruling group would see it as a combination of the bourgeoisie and the landed interests, which meant after land reforms the rich peasantry, the major beneficiaries of this slow, disingenuous, and uneven legal transformation, and the professional elites.[5] To include professional groups in the dominant coalition seems

[3] This was also largely the initial leftist picture of her, because of her role in toppling the Communist ministry in Kerala.

[4] The idea that state power in India was coalitional was quite common among Marxists from the mid 1960s. In Communist Party literature this is expressed in terms of the more conventional terminology of an alliance of classes. For a more academic argument using the idea of a dominant coalition, cf. Bardhan 1984: chs 6, 7 and 9.

[5] Conventionally, the professional elites were not considered part of the ruling class coalition.

essential for several reasons. Coalitional politics is hardly ever 'spontaneous', arising from an unmediated coalescence of brute interest between dominant classes; it requires political mediation which is often provided by intellectual groups, which are, in this sense, conditions for the existence of the coalition. They are the major mediators between the state and the people, they perform an increasingly large role in the state sector after the bureaucratic translation of the concept of development (as opposed to a possible concept of development as a movement), and must be, in purely economic terms, one of the largest unequal beneficiaries of social transformation under Congress rule. It is also this group, or rather its directly political and bureaucratic segments, which constantly arranges the mediation between the elements of the coalition itself.

This element of the coalition has a direct interest in the large bureaucratic control over resources. That gives them the power of internal allocation of resources through their connection with and control of the bureaucracy. Planning, licensing, fiscal controls—this entire apparatus, so crucial to India's political economy, should be seen in double terms—both as strategies of economic development and strategies within the political coalition. It is in the interest of nearly every section in the ruling coalition (though not to an equal degree) to have large common funds in the form of state-controlled resources, because they are politically negotiable resources on which a political demand may succeed. However, this constantly increases the allocative power of the third, professional element in the ruling bloc.

These roles make them functionally crucial to the dominant coalition, but not its dominant partner. Most modern Marxist theories after Gramsci would make a distinction between domination (which is basically reckoned in terms of distributive arrangements and interests) and governance (which is related to the actual use of legitimate, or even illegitimate, power), and would see the longevity of capitalist democracy as being crucially related to this complex structure of power.[6] While the power of the other groups arises out of their control over processes of production, theirs arises out of strategic control. When

[6] Although this idea comes originally from Gramsci, it could be found, in the modern literature, in Poulantzas 1973, Miliband 1983, Olin Wright 1978, Therborn 1978, and Buci-Glucksmann 1980.

Indira Gandhi came to power this coalition was still in place, although on the brink of serious changes.

It must be seen, however, that this is not a picture of Indian politics in the narrow commonsensical sense, but rather of the 'structure' that constrains its movement. As structure is a term used most commonly and confusingly, let me state what I indicate by this. In politics structures would mean essentially long-term inelasticities, or long-term constraints on choice in policy matters. Structural elements are basic; but when we say something is basic in an explanation, it means that something is latent. This means in turn that these cannot produce explanations by themselves, unaided by another level of explanatory exercise which takes into account more contingent facts; but they must figure in all explanations offered. The structure and slow historical change of classes would form, in this sense, the structural frame of political analysis.[7]

There was, however, a second sense in which Indian politics was coalitional: this was at the level of parties or political formations. Functionalist political scientists worked out an adequate model for this level in the late 1960s through the idea of a one-party dominant system.[8] The predominant fact of this model was the enormous space the ruling party occupied in the political system, reducing other parties to marginality. This made it pointless to try to understand politics according to the standard textbook format of government and opposition. Around a central, disproportionately large party of consensus were arranged much smaller parties of pressure, which imposed a coalitional logic on both government and opposition political groups. The size, regional spread, and ideological diversity of the Congress turned it into a loose organization, with groups ideologically stretched across a spectrum from extreme right to mild radicalism. Opposition groups were so disproportionately small compared to the Congress that their success depended on their functioning more like indirect pressure groups. They could do this precisely because of the

[7] I have tried to state the case for such an explanation elsewhere: Kaviraj 1984.

[8] The most well-known exposition of this party model is in the work of Rajni Kothari. Cf. Kothari 1970. He was also sensitive to the changes worked into it by the Emergency. Cf. Kothari 1976.

heterogeneity of the Congress structure and the consequent severity of its internal ideological conflicts. Often, a political group inside the Congress would have more in common programmatically with a group outside but immediately neighbouring it in the political spectrum than with other Congress groups. On issues like planning, the public sector, and friendly relations with communist states, the Congress left had shared objectives with Communists outside. Similarly, the Congress right wing often shared public policy preferences with conservative parties like the Swatantra. Thus a one-party dominant system imposed a coalitional logic on groups inside the Congress as much as on the opposition. Policies were often decided effectively by cross-party blocs rather than by inner-party voting or a conventional division on lines of government and opposition.

This had a significant implication for the political options of the central elite within the Congress. For this showed that the central leadership of the Congress Party could transfer a decision from the space within the party to the space of the political system as a whole if they were sure of the support of a winning coalition. When hard pressed by the right wing, Nehru came close to adopting such a strategy towards the end of his life, and this is what Indira Gandhi did in the crisis of 1969. Although he does not use an explicit model of this form, Max Zins's study of Congress crises shows that practically every serious conflict within the Congress was solved by a device of this kind.[9] This coalition at the party level of course had to work within the constraints set by the 'structural' coalition mentioned before. To put it another way, the structural coalition had to work through the party model; since classes and their interests are figurated on the political arena by parties and other political formations, the deep impulses of the first coalition had to express itself through the format of the second.

However, the fact that the nature of the class bloc was not basically altered at the time of Indira Gandhi's accession to power does not imply that significant political conflicts could not occur. I have argued elsewhere that serious conflicts within Congress should not be seen as mere power rivalry between personal factions, but as serious differences about development strategy.[10] At the time of Indira Gandhi's accession

[9] Max Zins 1978.

[10] Kaviraj 1980.

the strategy chosen by the Nehru regime was going through its first significant crisis, serious enough for those who were opposed to it to ask for a renegotiation of its structure.

What sort of a crisis was this? Was this crisis really comparable to the foundational conflicts of the 1950s? I think there were close parallels between the crisis of the 1950s and the mid 1960s. The comparison is not only at the level of party; these were comparable in a deeper sense too. The crisis of 1951 was significant not only because it involved the two most powerful leaders of the Congress—Nehru and Patel; there can be personality clashes where serious historical consequences are not involved. But in this case so much else was condensed into the conflict between two individuals, for they represented two ways of running the party organization, two very different stances in foreign policy, and two different strategies of capitalist development. If the struggle had gone the other way, there is no doubt Indian capitalism would have followed a different structure and historical sequence.

At first sight, the late 1960s and early 1950s may not appear comparable periods, and it could be objected that, although there were political crises in both periods, the crises were not of the same kind. During the early 1950s, it could be said the Indian leadership was still untried, and its policy preferences were still indeterminate; in the late 1960s, by contrast, all the canons of Nehruvian ideology were firmly laid out. This however is only superficially true. Developments over some years before Indira Gandhi's accession to power contributed to an unprecedented weakening of the Indian regime. Although Nehru's policy frame received a great deal of retrospective congratulation at the time, it came up against stiff political resistance and considerably polarized opinion about basic policy. After Nehru's death such opposition to his policies and pressure for renegotiation of policy naturally intensified. Foreign affairs contributed to these difficulties. The border war with China not only weakened Nehru personally; more fundamentally, it seemed to call into question the entire foreign policy which constituted such an important constituent of his overall strategy for development. Though the USSR adopted what must appear in retrospect an astonishingly neutral stance in a conflict between a communist and a bourgeois state, its influence and credibility declined. So did the power and credibility of the internal left-wing lobby which supported Nehru's foreign policy. Arms had to be hastily imported from the US, adding a significant and crucial element to the existing dependence on food aid.

The context seemed exactly right for an orchestration of internal and external pressure for a change, not in the accent but the basic design in policy.[11] Pressure from the World Bank made the government accept the Bell report, and, soon after, under the pressure of a foreign exchange crisis, a sharp 36.5 per cent devaluation of the rupee. Internal pressure from business lobbies mounted for a more hospitable policy towards the private sector and Western investment. These problems of dependence and restriction were exacerbated by the fear of crop failures and poor agricultural outputs. As a combination of all these, the government in the early years of Indira Gandhi faced serious constraints on its policy options. Not surprisingly, in subsequent periods her public policy would concentrate on precisely these areas. The military objective was achieved by negotiating supplies from the Soviet Union, and later through a tendency to diversify military and technological supplies by buying from other Western states, like France and England, purchases from whom, one suspects, had not only military but also political reasons. Economically, of course, one of the major fronts of policy effort during Indira Gandhi's regime was raising agricultural output. At the end of her rule, these basic changes altered the structure of the government's field of choice. First, the Indian government became far less restricted in its basic decision-making than at the time of Nehru's death. Secondly, it also broke the direct causal line between food shortages and political crisis; it has as it were broken the phase between the economic and political crises of the state. Political difficulties have not gone away; indeed, they have become more complex, but they are much less direct consequences of crop failures and food shortages. The structure of political crisis has fundamentally altered since the mid 1960s. Thus, whatever Indira Gandhi intended to do, she did not attempt, as was uncharitably alleged in the mid 1960s, abandoning the design for an independent capitalism for the stiffer iniquities of a satellite growth.

Coalitional Politics

As it happened, however, Indira Gandhi headed off this orchestration of pressures by use of the logic of coalitional politics through several

[11] Frankel 1978 gives a detailed account of such pressures.

political crises of the short term. Politicians need crises. But crises can, from their point of view, be of two types: crises which break on them, and those of their own making. Indira Gandhi was able, through a combination of adroitness and good fortune, to move from the first kind of crisis to the second. Sometimes the logic of situation may cut against the logic of structure, allowing politicians to play off this asymmetry to create room for manoeuvre for themselves.[12] Unfortunately for Indira Gandhi, the constraints arising out of the logic of structures and situations were for her grimly symmetrical. And those who brought her into power could always combine to overbalance her if she showed signs of excessive independence. Thus her interest as a politician and those of the group which initially supported her were inversely related.

The way Indira Gandhi broke out of her constraints determined the course of later Indian politics. Her first constraints were her former allies, the state bosses within the Congress; and her first initiative was to play a variation of the strategic struggle Nehru had with Patel, and assert the supremacy of the parliamentary and governmental segment of the party against the organizational wing. Although as leader of government she had formal control over both the party and the government apparatuses, her ascendance over these was clearly asymmetric. Bureaucratic structures were under her direct command by virtue of her being the head of government; control over the party was largely nominal. The power of the Congress state bosses came from the basic structure of Congress politics since Independence—its dependence on the support of local magnates for electoral support. Challenging the power of the state leaders was not just a matter of personality conflict. It could be done by changing the nature of the Congress machine and the structure and nature of electoral support.[13] Earlier forms of aggregation of local influence required two conditions. First, it assumed a low level of popular mobilization, when the lower orders of the electorate voted on the advice of superordinate interests of some kind. Secondly, this also presupposed a loose and largely federal political machine in which negotiation of local support, at local prices, was left to local bosses of the Congress. Indira Gandhi correctly assumed that lower orders of people were becoming less inclined to vote on the basis

[12] Cf. Gramsci 1971.

[13] Frankel 1978: ch. 1.

of primordial controls, and soon the former system, indirect, partly patriarchal, would have to be replaced by something else.

If the dependence of the central leadership on the negotiating ability of the state leaders was to be dispensed with, it could be done only through a radically different electoral strategy, one in which the central government or its leader could set up a direct relation with the electorate. Accordingly, this change led not merely to a new style—of populist rhetoric instead of serious programmatic proposals; the new style had significant political and organizational results.[14] Sometimes, one comes across the apparently plausible argument that Indira Gandhi neglected to build up her party organization, which implies that this was the fault of accident, and she need not have done so. She could, so the argument runs, have undermined and removed the individuals she found obstructive and put more congenial or pliable people in their place. But this appears to me to misjudge the basic nature of the new politics. It seems, in retrospect, that the systematic destruction of the party apparatus was not contingent; it was a necessary part of the populistic transformation of Congress politics. This argument should not be interpreted to mean that the electoral process—which is the basic discursive process linking the rulers with ordinary voters—became more economical. Ironically, centralized systems are often more complex and less economical than more decentralized ones. Congress election campaigns were still massive operations; what changed was not the size of the apparatus or the size of people involved, but their relation with the top leadership.

Gradually, they became utterly heteronomous and substitutable instruments, and although *faute de mieux* designated 'politicians', they lost all contact with the essentially dialogical nature of the political process. Earlier, this enormous retinue came from within the Congress Party. There were politicians who were recruited through a stable and predictable procedure, worked patterned techniques of political negotiations, and had a predictable scale of rewards. Politics, or this kind of discursive practice, requires a long process of acquisition of skills, familiarity of the political terrain, a career that takes long to build up. Mediation by a party made up of functionaries of this kind led to two consequences in the earlier Congress system. First, it made

[14] Kothari 1984 has tried to analyse the consequences of populism.

for decentralization; secondly, it also made the organization sensitive to peculiarities of local and regional politics—a fact which explains at least partly the far more sensitive and sensible handling of regionalism during the Nehru years.

Under the logic of the new dispensation this sort of regional structure was replaced by a new one. People who were pressed into political service were more in the nature of political 'contractors' who were willing to go to any length to dragoon votes, systematically replacing discursive techniques with money and subtle forms of coercion. Thus, out of the logic of the technique Indira Gandhi brought in, Congress started becoming gradually depoliticized. Even earlier, people had regretted that arguments were being replaced by resources as the primary political asset; now the only arguments used were resources. Although Indira Gandhi is often accused of turning Indian politics ideological by conservatives, in fact what she represented was a massive decline of ideology. Ideology did not mean serious disputation of the social programme underlying government policy, a debate about means and ends of national objectives. It came to a devaluation of political speech, a use of discourse for purposes utterly inimical to the purposes of discourse.[15]

Such a fundamental transformation of the relations which constitute our political world could not happen overnight. I also do not wish to suggest that the entire change of design was wholly deliberate, though they were certainly, as I argue, the results of interconnecting rational decisions taken ad hoc, with short-term objectives in mind. It happened through two interconnected processes: first a change in the Congress apparatus, and subsequently a change of the relation between this apparatus and the general field of Indian politics. Indira Gandhi got the first opportunity for political restructuring after the defeat of the Congress in the fourth general elections in many state assemblies, and its less than reassuring victory at the centre. One of the tests of a political leader is the extent to which she can turn a defeat into a victory, to avoid responsibility for a defeat and deflect it on to others. Indira Gandhi did this with remarkable success after the fourth general elections. She turned the consequences of Congress defeat into a condition for her own personal success. Congress defeat in the states, and the

[15] Manor 1983.

depleted majority at the centre imposed a coalitional logic on her and the Congress. Indeed, it intensified this logic to its limit, which prepared the ground for its decisive transformation. Since she was cornered within the party, she used the familiar technique of invoking the wider, national coalition. In trying to fight her internal opposition she inclined towards a strategy of a wider coalition of the near left. In this, fortuitously, the group known as the CSF (Congress Socialist Forum) played a crucial role, enabling her to build a bridge across a longstanding history of suspicion.

As a weaker player inside the Congress she intuitively grasped an aspect of the political situation—that the timetable of her adversaries had to be initially her timetable too. As a weaker player she could not hope to set the terms of the game, she could simply try to win it within terms set for her by others. This was simultaneously true of all adversaries she faced—international forces, political opposition within India, and her especially intimate enemies within the Congress parties. Others could think of choosing their time, of delaying a decision; she, because of her circumstances, could not. She could, however, have a shorter time-frame than others. It was politically rational for her to forestall others by acting quickly. Every time she did this—acting with decisiveness—the consequences fell more benevolently for her than for her enemies. After accepting the time horizon of her tormentors, she decided to act quickly, before others had decided what to do. Thus, within three years after the elections of 1967, she could seize the initiative and impose her terms on others. She provoked a crisis in the Congress when the state bosses thought she would not dare. She declared her left-wing policies with deliberate suddenness and chose the grounds of the conflict. She took up the challenge of the Bangladesh crisis without flinching, and forestalled other pressures by the treaty with the USSR. This way she could always be the giver and not the receiver of surprise.

The results of the 1967 elections had some clear implications—for those who were willing to see them. It confirmed a line of thought that communists had been developing for some time in their party documents. The one-party dominant model offered two planes of self identification for political groups. By the constitutional criterion, they could be seen as government and opposition, but, more significantly, by use of an ideological criterion they could be stretched along a continuum from left to right with the Congress occupying the ambiguous and profitable zone in the rightish middle—which allowed it to shift its centre of gravity conveniently as the situation demanded. From the early 1960s the communists were worried by a different possibility: that this party system might, under the stress of a crisis, get split down the middle, and a wide arc of a right-wing coalition of Jan Sangh, Swatantra, right-wing socialists and Congress conservatives might emerge and revoke much of the reformist nationalist policy structure of Nehru's Congress. This would of course immediately bring into existence a left coalition, and they thought that the future of Indian politics depended on the speed with which either of these possible coalitions could get organized, because the first to appear would have an ineradicable advantage over the other. Indira Gandhi too saw this logic; and, more importantly, she saw that the CPI saw this logic; and she acted on the basis of this political perception when she had to tackle the crisis within her party over the Congress presidency, thus converting a party issue into a national one. If it had been decided simply within party terms, she was likely to have been defeated, but given the strategic form she gave to it, she simply could not have lost.

But the elections of 1967 showed another implication for opposition politics. It revealed an interesting and recurrent paradox of party politics. In a period of economic difficulties and declining legitimacy of the Congress, a wide opposition coalition had a good chance of success, partly of course because it simply offset the usual disadvantages of simple majorities; i.e. a united opposition meant that, to win, the Congress required something close to an absolute majority. The experience of the next few years, however, showed that the coalition technique which worked so wonderfully for the Congress did exactly the opposite in the case of the opposition. Electorally, right and left parties working together widened their electoral support and made winning elections possible. But the same thing made any reasonable administration by the opposition impossible. Coalitions which could win elections could not govern, and coalitions which could run administrations (if they were ideologically more homogeneous, like the CPI(M)-led front in West Bengal) could not win. Consequently, most states which had slipped out of Congress control came to be recaptured within a few years. In all this there was a certain pattern; Indira Gandhi broke out of her political encirclement almost always by a similar move. Through an arrangement of issues in a political crisis of her making she wiped out the record of the earlier period; she forced not only the electorate but also other parties to take vital decisions episodically rather than in a longer-term way, i.e. not allowing them to decide about her regime on its basic record over a long period of time—which would enable rational and less dramatic decisions, rather forcing them, by a break of some kind, to take sides on an all or none sort of choice. No other Indian politician had used to such effect the art of brinkmanship.

After 1967 Indira Gandhi consistently took the initiative in the repeated crises which punctuated her time in power. She forced the issue in the case of the Congress presidency; in the case of the presidential elections, in formally splitting the Congress; in the decisions about the Bangladesh crisis; in the declaration of the Emergency; even, ironically, in the case of the elections of 1977 which led to her defeat. Her ascendancy was so great that the opposition could not even defeat her until she invited them to do it. Till the Emergency, all her initiatives were such that she kept the opposition divided, and deepened and intensified their division. Ironically, Indira Gandhi was initially more successful against her own party than against the opposition. But the way she accomplished her victory foreshadowed a format, a logic of crisis solving which had to be applied repeatedly in her regime. Her call to the Congress members in the presidential elections to vote for a specific candidate showed a disregard for institutional norms which was essentially different from Nehru's. It is false to treat this as a matter of style—as the beneficiaries of such evasions would suggest. It was a failure to appreciate the requirement of formal, impersonal principles, of the theory of a capitalist (or perhaps in her terms a modern) social form.[16] A bourgeois system requires, as both Marxists and Weberians point out, a logic of 'rationalization', greater impersonality and predictability of decisions, and a building of institutions to control modern processes. The initial evasion of institutional controls during Indira Gandhi's rule was highly significant, for they were not always desperate moves to avert crises, but systematic attempts to see their usefulness. In retrospect, it was not only a personal fault of hers. During her rule, an entire political elite emerged which looked at the processes of development through fatal simplifications, reducing institutions,

[16] I have tried to spell out this argument about institutional decline: Kaviraj 1984.

(e.g. education) to merely their material structures and budgets. Typically, such evasions were accompanied by a rhetoric of radicalism—a particularly dangerous combination of a bourgeois leader invoking socialist principles to evade encumbrances of bourgeois constitutionalism.

This was reflected in Indira Gandhi's treatment of other leaders of her own party after the rout of the 'syndicate', her inexplicable sensitivity to people who could never become in any sense serious contenders to her eminence. She seems to have always confused between the political necessity of reducing an individual and the historical folly of reducing the role along with the institutional structure which supports and frames it. As a result, one finds an increasing hiatus between two levels of politics which could be called its surface and deep structures. On the surface, after the decline of opposition coalitions, Congress ministries came to power in most states. Yet at bottom political instability and its effects did not go away, but only changed form. Instead of a highly visible instability in which unstable and constantly fissile coalitions of opposition groups came and went out of power, there was an endless turnover of ministries within the seeming continuity of Congress rule. In an atmosphere in which politics was in any case becoming less ideological, this often meant wild shifts of populist emphasis in policies. At a deeper level, there was an even more fundamental reversal.

Formerly, the legitimacy of a politician depended on some impression of being fair, evenhanded in the handling of interests, however disingenuously; because minimally, politicians glimpsed the bourgeois liberal view that the state was supposed to be the representative of general or universal interests, and the play of particular interests should be left to the field of 'civil society'. Increasingly now, politicians were seen to be legitimized not by their claim or pretence to universalism, but by their evident and aggressively declared affiliation to particular interests. Installation of a middle-caste chief minister, for example, could openly mean imminent advantages for this caste, which, though perhaps culturally understandable, goes against the logic of any viable large-scale operation. Indian society is so heterogeneous that this meant that the building of legitimacy on general principles would become practically impossible.

Such groups and their leaders also became correspondingly dependent on a distant, all-powerful central leadership for concessions and mediation. Essentially, it was an extension of the politics of heightened insecurity of groups, since in India every member of a majority is a member of a minority of some kind. The destruction of the state-level leadership intensified the need for a populist structure of politics where a central leader could appeal successfully to the electorate through a suitably simplified, unmistakably large-grained theme. The earlier ambiguity and complexity of electoral appeal was sacrificed for a clear, if rhetorical, national platform. Earlier processes which acted as filters in recruitment were given up. The party became an anteroom or a waiting room for entirely insignificant aspirants to high office. As a political instrument the party became redundant, illustrated by the fact that even the subtlest of political negotiations were handed over to officials rather than party men. Electorally, of course, Congress did not win the elections for Indira Gandhi; she won them for Congress.

By the time the next round of significant political events came along, the two basic tendencies associated with Indira Gandhi's rule were clearly at work: a revival of the fortunes of the Congress at the surface, and a simultaneous destruction of its party structure at a deeper level. Despite its well-known infirmities, factionalism in the Congress—at the centre at least—had been partly ideological. Increasingly, the programme of the Congress, over which there had been so much ideological bloodshed, came to be replaced by a platform of a different kind—not prepared through a debate over a long period, and in which contending interests fought to shape its idiom and its possible influence over policies. The internal scene in the Congress became close to a situation Marxists call Bonapartism, i.e. because of the stalemate in the strength of organized groups, decisive decisions come to be taken by a group or individuals relatively independent of them. Although in a statistical and sociological sense organized interests are weightier than individuals or coteries, there could be a situation in which such groups, despite their weight, become increasingly dependent and forced into a client relationship with a political leadership. Organized groups require stable structures of representation to translate their preferences into political programmes. With the decline of such institutional spaces and formats, ideology, freed in a sense from the anchoring in interest lobbies within the Congress, became more irresponsible, prone to sudden and baffling shifts of emphasis. During the Emergency, suddenly and inexplicably, fertility and not poverty became the major obstacle to Indian development.

Clearly, this unpredictability was a powerful electoral weapon, for it made Indira Gandhi's ideological moves unpredictable: an emphasis on distributive justice today could suddenly turn into a rhetoric of productive discipline, to the chagrin and detriment of others who suffered from the disadvantages of political consistency. But in terms of deeper concerns for political stability, this was destructive, for it devalued political ideas and disturbed the logical pursuit of a consistently worked-out long-term policy.

II

By a series of measures after her split with the Congress organization, Indira Gandhi relentlessly drove the logic of coalitional politics, constantly increasing her payoffs. The same drive, carried on through the nationalization of banks, and the abolition of privy purses and related measures, won her a double victory, first against her enemies within the party; second, no less decisively, against the opposition. Since the elections saw an extension of the logic of a 'progressive coalition', Congress continued its association with the CPI; but this was less a necessity of political arithmetic, more the production of ideological conviction. It already showed how the success of a strategy made that strategy redundant.

Indira Gandhi dissolved parliament when the trend was strongly in her favour, a bare three months after the initiative to abolish privy purses. In retrospect, the timing of the elections turned out well for her, for she could face the worst international crisis of her career with the elections behind her, not in front, much the safest way politically. Nonetheless, facing the crisis over Bangladesh required other resources and other skills, because assets like a large majority did not translate simply into resources in foreign policy. Perhaps the most dramatic test of her government came at the end of 1970 when the crisis broke out, putting her in a situation of considerable pressure, a situation fraught, as most decisive situations are, with serious contradictory possibilities. The scale of the refugee influx from Bangladesh made its economic costs heavy, but the prospect of a war with Pakistan was in some ways equally forbidding, as India was emerging from a period of threatened isolation. The Soviet attitude towards India had changed considerably after Nehru's death, and their overtures with the Ayub regime sometimes created discernible strains with India. On the American side, the

Nixon administration tilted US policy heavily against India, in an accentuation of the eternal paradox of American foreign policy—its steadfast preference for an avowed dictatorship to a democracy. China too could be expected to favour Pakistan. Risks of isolation were considerable and quite real. A possible war with Pakistan and the creation of a friendly state in the east could, however, alter the strategic balance considerably, and reduce the requirement for military preparedness and related costs—at least so it was believed at the time.

During the Bangladesh crisis Indira Gandhi showed her qualities of decisiveness. The treaty with the Soviet Union was sudden and remarkably effective in counter-balancing American support for Pakistan. The ineffectual brinkmanship of the Nixon government at the height of the war, though calculated to confuse and undermine her government, actually worked to her distinct advantage. After the victory in the Bangladesh war she reached the climax of her leadership and power. However, there is a remarkable fact about this period of glory: it was intense but curisouly brief, which goes to illustrate the sense in which Marxists use the notion of a long-term or a general crisis. Such periodic advantages cannot be converted into stability of the system as a whole. But, for the time, her position seemed literally invincible, because it was based on the combination of radicalism and patriotism: for those who would not support her for the promised removal of poverty could do so for the liberation of Bangladesh; and those who would not support the strength of India would for the eradication of poverty. She had characteristically reduced the opposition to a state of being without any possible slogan: promise of reform outflanked the left just as much as patriotism outflanked the right.

Some aspects of the 1971 elections were extremely significant, because these would become permanent features of her rule. Indira Gandhi broke the normal schedule for elections, calling a mid-term poll. Earlier, the constitutional system created an implicit symmetry between the government and the opposition, which could both prepare equally for elections at a preset time. Elections, from now on, would be set by the ruling party, which meant that the issues on which the elections would be fought could be structured with a degree of deliberation unseen before. Elections under her turned into something very close to referenda. No longer were these formal occasions in which the electorate gave a reasoned verdict about the necessarily complex record of a government's performance over five years. Instead, these became occasions when the electorate was asked to take sides on a highly simplified, dramatic, emotive and misleadingly rhetorical question (i.e. questions to which there could be, barring perversity, only one answer)—such as whether they wished to see poverty removed. Of course this raises some difficult problems of the culture of power in our country. It is astonishing how the Congress could claim ideological advantage by thundering against its own failures. As the government party a substantial part of the blame for our bleak performance in relation to poverty must lie at its door; yet it was able to claim the allegiance of the poor precisely by such appeals. Turning elections into referenda of course made more decisive and dramatic victories possible, by making one single issue take precedence over a complex record. But, ironically, it also made electoral results less reliable as an indicator of real historical trends, or the actual configuration of political forces. For the basic questions of distributive justice did not go away; simply, a curtain was drawn before it at the time of elections. Victory in elections came to reflect less of the real balance of political forces in the country. This is why the textbook translation of electoral majority and power to administer effectively simply breaks down in Indian politics after 1971. The size of the majorities becomes larger; the power of the governments to administer the country becomes distinctly less effective. Nehru never had majorities of the size that Indira Gandhi or Janata enjoyed; yet his governance was far more effective than theirs.

Thus it was possible for a government to be decisively victorious and pitifully vulnerable at the same time. That is why, even at the times of her greatest victories, Indira Gandhi remained so close to defeat. And this is at least one reason why, even after her triumphs, she herself could speak of crisis, encirclement, and disaster. For the politics of electoral populism did not give her organized strength to pursue more radical policies, or act for political stability, or move effectively in the direction of greater distributive justice. This is why, despite the rout of the opposition, her regime remained permanently insecure. Opposition politicians and her critics occasionally argue that this insecurity was a pretence, simply a technique of gathering support by panic, by turning elections into stampedes. But this is not true. By the nature of her politics, Indira Gandhi lived, in quite a literal sense, close to both victory and disaster.

All these trends, in their conjunctions, set in motion a peculiar but increasingly evident disjunction between electoral balance and the deeper balance of political forces, the balance of satisfaction and dissent among social classes. This translation broke down, reflected in the dramatic trend of mortality of governments in their relative infancy. After her spectacular successes at the end of 1971, her government, armed with the same majority in parliament, was in deep trouble by 1973—which meant that such majorities had in some sense become 'misleading', that some crucial translation in the political process was failing to come off. In this phase, because of a form of politics which is similar to Bonapartism, linear expectations were completely falsified. Politics increasingly assumed a volatile and pulsating form, reflected in its electoral or phenomenal form as a 'politics of waves', or of radical negations.

What is remarkable is not the way Indira Gandhi won her legitimacy in these years, but the way she lost it. One of the decisive differences with the Nehru period is precisely the short-tenure nature of this legitimacy: the new politics set up between the electors and the rulers a new relationship, as long at least as the vote remained a register of political sentiment. It meant that support given overwhelmingly could also be withdrawn with dramatic suddenness; the electorate imposed a much more short-term accounting of the results of political support. Electoral figures show this particularly clearly, despite the objection that the percentage of Congress votes remains more or less constant, and therefore the fluctuations are simply the unintended consequence of an insufficiently mastered machinery of simple majorities. But this can be answered by the argument that this format of pluralities is itself part of the format of choice, and therefore results could not be attributed to purely unintended consequences of public choice. For, after all, the way the field is structured is one of the factors taken into account in the electorate's deliberate strategy for voting.

Unprecedented Political Crisis

Within two years of her greatest political ascendancy, Indira Gandhi's government was in deep trouble, facing an unprecedented political crisis. Some of the factors which led to this crisis would be unregistered in long-term statistics.[17] First, of course, there was the inherent danger of radicalized distributive expectations. If electoral promises raise people's expectations, this could lead to a real performative paradox; for even a performance which was roughly equal to earlier periods would appear poorer because of the government's own move to set higher performance criteria. Secondly, economic trends went against the government: some of the circumstances which fuelled the crisis would be difficult to register in long-term statistics; indeed, the use of long-term statistics makes unnecessary and inexplicable mysteries out of the short-term finalities of political life. Sometimes, political resentments which have far-reaching consequences have purely local or regional origin in avoidable inequalities of distribution, or short-term abuse of administrative power. Thus, although official statistics show a relatively minor shortfall in food production in 1972–3 and in per capita availability of foodstuff, shorter-term inelasticities created by defective distribution created serious political turmoil. Similarly, although a long-term rate of inflation in the Indian economy is not high by international standards, what affects political behaviour is precisely what hides and disappears within the average. For ordinary people perceived the period from 1971 to 1974 as being one in which there occurred one of the most serious inflationary rises in the Indian economy. Between these years wholesale prices of rice, wheat, and pulses went up sharply, and although these tapered off later, this happened after its political consequences began and developed an autonomous logic of its own. Food shortages in Gujarat set off political trouble in December 1973, starting a chain of events which led to the most serious rupture in Indian political experience since Independence.

Political trends after the end of 1973 showed some unprecedented moves. Since the mid 1950s, after the strange decline of the socialist base in North India, most mass movements were either regional protests or movements led by radical parties of the left. Regional movements by definition could not lead to a national coalition of threatening proportions. Leftist politics had suffered a setback in the mid 1960s, partly through the nationalist backlash after the war with China and

[17] An analysis of such longer-term statistics can be found in Bardhan 1984; one attractive feature of Bardhan's analysis is precisely his unwillingness to derive or deduce explanations of political events from long-term structural trends.

partly through internal division. Since 1967, however, there was a resurgence of leftist opposition to the government in various forms, through the UF governments and later through Naxalite insurgency. By 1971, however, these challenges were spent—through a combination of containment and repression. Regionally, and culturally, too, these challenges could be more easily marginalized, because left movements were never strong in the central heartland of India, the major area of Congress support. The movement in Gujarat and its spillover into the JP movement in North India was a movement of a different kind. It was the first serious mass movement organized by opposition groups in which some right-wing elements were strongly represented, because there is no doubt that the major organization of the JP movement in the North came from the cadres of the Jan Sangh and parties which would, in August 1974, form the BKD—a combination of right-wing chauvinistic elements and right-wing socialists. This showed a significant alteration of political forces in India in comparison with the Nehru period. Then, despite serious disproportionality of strength, the left constituted the more serious opposition to the Congress. By 1974 it was clear in contrast that the more serious opposition to the Congress was offered by a non-left alliance; and, more significantly, it seemed to confirm the picture of a wide right-wing coalition which might overwhelm the Congress.

In fact, the rapid growth of the JP movement also stemmed from the logic of the new politics which had come into being since the early 1970s; but naturally, with the inability of politicians to see historical trends, Indira Gandhi was incensed when this logic tended to turn against her. It showed the effects of the quickening of the political accounting cycle, the same redundancy of political institutions. In fact, what was remarkable was the similarity between the two sides in the great confrontation: the same resort to populism, the same reluctance to go by institutional norms, the same tendency to substitute a programme by a personality, the same shortsighted eagerness to ride a popular wave of negative indignation, the same confusion between what was a defeat of its opponent and a victory of its own. Indira Gandhi's sense of encirclement was heightened by her own initiatives earlier in destroying left bases. Fortunately for her, ideological considerations stopped the major left groups from joining with the JP movement.

In other ways too the successes of the Gujarat and Bihar agitations were related to the politics of populist referenda. As electoral results were no longer a reliable register of political assessment, people felt, soon after the elections were over, that their longer-term problems had not gone away. Since elections were not due for a long time, this led to pressures for agitations outside the constitutional space, eventually to a demand for a dismissal of these massively supported elected ministries. It would be too simplistic to believe that those who elected these governments and those who agitated for their removal were entirely discrete groups of people. This was a direct result of the changed character of elections, though Congressmen did not see it. They even pretended to find the demand outrageous, although this was a fairly regular occurrence within their own party, or what was left of it.

This hypothesis appears to be confirmed by the swing of political crises after the Gujarat agitation. From Gujarat it spread to other states where Congress had fairly comfortable majorities, and on electoral showing these states should not have been found ungovernable so quickly. The government then faced another serious challenge in the form of the railway strike—one of the largest and longest among industrial demonstrations after the Nehru era. It was put down brutally—the inappropriate parallel being the truckers' strike against the Allende regime in Chile. By the end of August seven opposition parties had formed the BKD with the odd programme of a 'total revolution' coming incongruously from some of the most conservative Indian political groupings. Party politics in India seemed in 1974 to have a particularly dim future, Indira Gandhi having destroyed her party practically, and JP suggesting their abolition formally. The spread of the agitation to the central states in India must have appeared particularly alarming to the regime. On the other side, Indira Gandhi's apparent invincibility in elections must also have rendered the route of anti-government agitations outside the electoral framework attractive to some parties.

The Congress response to the gathering crisis was seriously jeopardized by Indira Gandhi's populism. Her initiatives had systematically shifted functions, initiatives, and decisions from party to government bureaucracy; and the slogan of a 'committed bureaucracy' was explicable in these terms, since the unavailability of party men forced her to demand increasingly explicit political work from high officials. But this worked to a point. Countering a mass agitation politically was something that officials could not perform. A technique which made her electorally invincible made her, when faced with popular agitations, extremely vulnerable. Accordingly, she found herself resourceless in dealing with the political agitation, which required the construction of an alternative political discourse—one which could communicate to people another construction of political reality in line with their own experience. As the government party lacked an effective party machinery—it had long given up a politics using discourse for a politics using resources—the elite around Indira Gandhi had two options: either to borrow a political organization and face the JP movement politically, or to respond by using the massive apparatus of the state.

Initially, the Indira Gandhi regime tried a political answer through its collaboration with the CPI, which had a mass base in Bihar. But since it was too small and proved ineffective, the only recourse left was eventually a repressive and bureaucratic solution. The CPI, particularly, responded to Indira Gandhi's call for support, seeing a danger of fascism arising onesidedly from the JP movement, and reading the situation through allegories of the Weimar republic and Allende's Chile. But even with in a non-analogous reading of the situation, there were deeply disquieting signs. There was something very unconvincing about political groups which had been more concerned about the Hinduization of India, and the spread of Hindi or the demands of rich farmers, and which had never been known for their sympathy with revolutionary causes, being suddenly won over to a revolution of a most immoderate kind—in comparison to which even the communist conception was merely partial. Besides, most of these parties, when in government, had shown a remarkable ability to tolerate corruption. Now, suddenly, they seemed resolved to stamp it out of political life, Undoubtedly, however, the movement under Jayaprakash Narayan's leadership became the most serious challenge to the Congress government in North India, and by the first quarter of 1975 Indira Gandhi faced her most serious crisis. On top of this came the unexpected judicial invalidation of her election on 12 June 1975. Congress, in its new form, was entirely unable to deal with this. Without a clear internal line of command, without strong party institutions, Indira Gandhi eventually decided not to step down from premiership but escalate the problem even more by declaring the

Emergency—seeking a solution beyond the format of democratic government. A party which had grown accustomed to the indispensability of an individual was flung into confusion when this came to clash with the needs of constitutional form.

III

Curiously, although the Emergency represented a deeply significant phase of our political history and showed in different ways both the vulnerability and strength of Indian democracy, it has rarely been seriously analysed. Some amount of purely empirical and journalistic material is of course available, besides the enumeration of events catalogued by the Shah Commission.[18] Still, the question of what happened in the individual instances of abuse of power is quite distinct from the historical question of what something like the Emergency signified. Obviously, one major handicap has been the inapplicability of our well-rehearsed moves of 'the scientific method' of electoral studies on this particular area, which meant that our discipline's entire training in the last fifteen years became simply and heartbreakingly redundant. It also means that scientifically inclined students of politics are perpetually condemned to a state in which we can never have scientific knowledge of the Emergency years. Scientific studies, fortunately, were resuscitated in 1977. But, apart from political science literature, there is little serious study of the Emergency of any kind, probably on account of the cheerful assumption that it was an aberration unlikely to be repeated.

Two radically different explanations are offered for the imposition of the Emergency, both of which are exaggerated forms of what are basically sensible ideas. Sometimes, it is argued that the Emergency lay in the logic of a structural crisis in India's political economy. I am basically in sympathy with this view, although I consider the fatalism

[18] Sometimes, it is argued, using statistics prepared by the Shah Commission, that the number of arrests during the Emergency was 'not very large' considering the size of the country. This is a seriously flawed argument on two counts. No amount of statistics can capture the change in political atmosphere during the Emergency. For, those who were not arrested also decisively altered their political behaviour. There can be statistics of arrests, but not statistics of fear. Secondly, it avoids the moral issues involved in denial of freedom.

and determinism implicit in some forms of this argument unacceptable. But surely there were long-term crisis tendencies in the Indian system, and they came to a head through Indira Gandhi's personal difficulties precisely because of the trends towards centralization and condensation of problems. A second view holds that the crisis leading to the Emergency was purely contingent; its reasons lay in Indira Gandhi's personal unwillingness to give up power—which is true in quite a different sense—that it was after all her difficulties which created the occasion for Emergency rule. There is no deep incompatibility between the two theses if one thinks of long-term structural tendencies as not producing events by themselves, but constraining developments in a particular direction, and waiting on contingent causalities of a secondary kind of causation of particular events and their exact shape.

The imposition of the Emergency came with the excuse that two things were getting out of hand and the central government required exceptional powers to deal with them. The first of course was a threat to the unity and integrity of the country, dubiously equated with the ruling party's dominance. A second and perhaps more popular rationalization of the Emergency was that it was meant also to negotiate the inflationary situation—an immensely popular slogan, understandably, for the middle and lower classes. Actually, as happens with moves which the regime expects to be intensely unpopular, the Emergency promised everything to everybody, setting to itself entirely incompatible objectives. To the bourgeoisie it offered a perfect climate of industrial discipline; to the middle classes lower prices and better administration; to the poor the abolition of poverty; to every citizen the assurance of their country's integrity. More seriously, although this was perhaps not done deliberately, in the rationalizations of the Emergency there was a tendency to turn around all the allegations of the JP movement—its allegations of inefficiency, corruption, inflation. In a piecemeal fashion the government and its supporters made out a case that there was another—the real—set of reasons for these undoubted evils of social life. Commonsensically, all these could be attributed to the government and its manner of functioning—its unresponsiveness to popular demands, its bureaucracy, the cynical wastefulness of its public sector managerial groups, the increasingly less scrupulous behaviour of political leaders. Implicitly, if the unrestricted abusive rhetoric of the Emergency could be euphemistically regarded as an argument, the government paradoxically decided to blame its failures on itself in a specially disingenuous way. After all, the problems of corruption, inefficiency, and to a lesser extent inflation were all related to transactions in which agencies of government were primary actors, and the ordinary citizens were recipients; and such arguments suggested the ungovernability of government rather than of the citizenry. Yet much of the early justification of the Emergency was given in these pragmatic terms, mixed occasionally with the terrifying analogy of fascism.

After the initial months, when the political crisis was over, the Emergency became increasingly pointless, and it became increasingly oppressive while trying to hide its pointlessness. On its own account, the government's showing in economic terms was not much better than in normal times, except for a discernible drop in some consumer prices during the early part of the Emergency. This too was due to unfounded fears among retailers about a sudden and improbable alteration in the moral behaviour of the police and the lower bureaucracy. They found out through experience that structural tendencies were not so easy to countermand, even by an authoritarian government; and the Emergency did not end corruption, it merely, due to the higher risks involved, steeply pushed up the prices charged by the corrupt. At a more serious level of argument, a more authoritarian government is hardly the proper climate for a decline in bureaucratic corruption; you cannot make a group of people less corrupt by making them collectively more powerful. Indeed, had this been true, most Third World tyrannies would have set examples of moral probity.

It is hardly surprising that non-accountability made government agencies persist in their irrationalities. The absence of the usual requirements of public scrutiny and criticism meant that tendencies towards centralization and the personal concentration of power could grow unchecked. Instead of efforts at building the party, Congress went through a curious policy of inducting members into the Youth Congress, providing a platform for the rise of Sanjay Gandhi. This not merely led to the well-known unconstitutional uses of power and irrational excesses of the family planning and beautification drives, which naturally fell most heavily on the poorest; it also carried to its extreme the internal reallocation of power within the Congress elite, leading to the gradual decline of the group of more professional advisers around Indira Gandhi. This meant not only an increase in arbitrariness but also a loss of consistency, for midway through the Emergency the government started discussing the advantages of a more conservative form of economic policy. Under normal conditions of democracy, political initiatives, when they show unpopular or dysfunctional consequences, make for their own abandonment. In an authoritarian regime such dysfunctionalities could continue unchecked; for it is inconceivable that any political regime would have continued with the excesses of the sterilization drive or could have been so uninformed or insensitive towards popular opinion. Authoritarianism made the government behave more ignorantly.

In another sense, the Emergency performed a demystifying function in the political system. After the 1969 split, after the destruction of the Congress machinery, there had been a growing tendency towards bypassing the regular consultative political process, and its replacement by a bureaucratic and administrative manner of decision-making, withdrawing in effect the most significant decisions about the country's development from the public political process and its institutions of formal accountability. Its cause was the massive majorities of the ruling party. This had a terrible, but subtle, consequence: withdrawal from the regular consultative processes within party and parliament made the political process more violent. For the only way of being heard was to create a noise. Ironically, although much of the rhetoric in undermining bourgeois democratic institutions was derived from old socialist arguments about the social conservatism of the judiciary, actually the subtle eclipse of parliament went much deeper than the explicit eclipse of judicial institutions. This is because the judiciary is given some powers of institutional self-defence by the constitution, but parliament is helpless against its own sovereignty. Marginalizing the opposition, not letting it speak effectively, had unfortunate consequences for constitutional politics as a whole. For this meant that grievances and dissent, deprived of channels of legitimate articulation and hearing, would erupt more violently; and increasingly on a larger number of issues, the space for discursive politics would be given up, and government and dissenting groups would face each other more violently.

Ironically, however, the destruction of the opposition also destroyed the justification for the Emergency. In course of time both arguments for the Emergency faded into insignificance. Though the Emergency itself could be seen as a degeneration of ordinary democratic government, it turned midway into a degeneration of this degeneration.

Earlier, to the politically gullible, this could have appeared as a move against rising fascism, though its own ways of fighting fascism were very intriguing indeed. After the opposition movement was effectively contained, the argument about political insurrection could not be sustained with the same liveliness (despite some good work by the Congress propaganda machinery, which printed posters showing Indira Gandhi parting anarchy from utopia—much like God separating light and darkness in Renaissance paintings); this deprived the regime of the reasons it had given for its existence. The second, supposedly economic, reason was belied by the performance of the government in the later part of the Emergency, which was not significantly different from any other unruly democratic year. It seemed increasingly that the entire apparatus of authoritarian rule was preserved to secure immunity from criticism against the rise of Sanjay Gandhi, and the increasing violence of the state against the unsterilized and unbeautified poor. People were also irritated by constant sanctimonious lecturing by an inefficient government about more work and less talk—again a characteristically self-referring admonition. For grocers, peasants, workers, fishermen, for instance, were not exceptionally garrulous communities; the only people who could afford such diversion during their hours of work were government employees. They were therefore supposed to apply these high ideals of purposeful existence to themselves—the paradox, again, of the government needing the Emergency to govern itself rather than an uncontrollably talkative country. The arguments snatched from the opposition also cut less ice, as India, as it went deeper into discipline, did not seem to become a dramatically less corrupt, inefficient, costly, or poor country. Under such circumstances, it could appear to everyone that the loss of bourgeois democracy had been a waste.

Signs of Irrationality

In 1976 two parallel developments began which were to end the Emergency eventually. With public discussions suspended, some of the worst features of our ancient culture began to assert themselves—openly dynastic suggestions, gratuitous abasement of political leaders, medieval sycophancy. The 'relocation' of poor people for reasons of offending middle- or ruling-class aesthetics, and the use of massive force in sterilization campaigns all showed the state was becoming used to conditions of unaccountability—the usual insensitivity of third world authoritarianisms. Obviously, this pursuit of sterility and beauty created intense opposition to itself, and made an equally violent retribution to itself inevitable. As resistance to its policies grew, it was beset with the inefficiencies of authoritarianism. First was the paradox of censorship. By destroying press freedom, the government simultaneously destroyed the credibility of its own—the only available—media. This had some subtler consequences. Rumours of disturbance are more powerful than news of disturbance. Since there was no news of disturbances in the censored press, rumours began to circulate of improbable and exaggerated resistance. Censorship became entirely counterproductive in its political function. Only if its purpose was the simple and perverse pleasure of denying information was it successful; if the object was political, i e. to deny news to keep people quiescent, it failed. The party structure became so ossified it could not mediate between any political forces at all. Finally, even vital government agencies beagan to fail—for excellent structural reasons. Members of the elite around Indira Gandhi had a purely derivative existence; they had no political base of their own, bases which they could lend to her in case of her need. Except for Devaraj Urs, all those who rose to eminence in the new Congress turned out to be liabilities. They had no control over politics in their regions even in the odious way in which the earlier conservative Congress leaders had. The politics of the Congress had come to its logical extreme point: centralization meant that the point of resistance and gravity, to use a different metaphor, was simply one indispensable individual.

Administratively too, the Emergency regime showed signs of irrationality. It was of course increasingly overloaded at the top. Much of the ostensible loyalty of party men who gratuitously asked Indira Gandhi to decide the most trivial of local issues, while an example of abjection, concealed a gesture of political abdication. Naturally this led to a clogging of decisions at the top, an already overloaded centre taking more and more decisions about things of which it knew less and less. It is rumoured that when the government called for elections, its own intelligence system misled it to believe that it would win these elections—which is possible, since in times of authoritarianism it is not wise to carry anything except good news. It leads to a censorship in reverse. The Emergency had also given rise to an invincible coalition against itself—of the urban and intellectual grievance at the abrogation of civil rights and the indignation against the terrifying form in which this was taken to the rural poor.[19]

Assessments of the Emergency experience must turn on some minimal questions. First, what was it about? Were there any long-term redistributions of power or economic benefits through that interlude? For obviously, in a situation in which public debate is in abeyance, such redistributions can take place quietly, swiftly, and finally. Secondly, what were the lessons of the Emergency for Indira Gandhi: how did it affect her politics in later years?[20]

I have already said that I agree with a structural explanation of the Emergency, but I wish to modify this on one point. To say that the Emergency was directly a result of structural strains can lead to an embarrassing implication for this theory. For, a corollary which would seem to follow would be that by the end of the Emergency such structural strains must have eased considerably for the Emergency to be revoked. And since the ruling elements have never had to take recourse to such straightforward measures again, it would imply that, whatever the crisis in the mid 1970s, it did not exist afterwards. I wish to suggest, on the contrary, that the crisis of politics has carried on. Consequently I prefer the idea that structural tendencies are not meant to explain individual events in history, and the Emergency had contingent causes. So the fact that the Emergency was revoked did not mean that the political crisis had ceased. The Emergency, in retrospect, was not deliberately meant to rework the structure or the internal weights inside the dominant coalition.

But how was the coalition doing in the meantime? The coalition of ruling classes was of course internally uneven, and because of their strategic situation and economic dominance, business and urban interests had a greater share of the fruits of inequality than the more politically quiescent rural groups. Since agriculture largely stagnated in the Nehru years, the major beneficiaries of development were the industrial

[19] For further details of the actual politics of the Emergency, Frankel 1978, ch. 13.

[20] For an example of Indira Gandhi's response to the Emergency in retrospect, see Carras 1979: ch. 9. Also, chs 1, 2, and 3 in Gandhi 1984.

bourgeoisie and the urban professionals. However, the logic of coalition creates a situation in which every move of every group has a dual value, for it is not only a move against the elements outside the coalition, but also, to a lesser extent, against those inside. As the power of the agricultural groups increased, there were more intense demands for a renegotiation of inequality or of payoffs inside the ruling bloc. Occasionally, disgruntled members of the ruling bloc can make temporary alliances with groups outside the coalition, weakening the bloc. If the 'voice' option does not work, they can pretend to use the 'exit' option to force a renegotiation of the terms of the class coalition.[21] In class terms, this is precisely what seems to have happened with rich peasant groups. After the late 1950s, a sustained efflux of these groups from the Congress is visible, beginning with Charan Singh in UP. For the next ten years or more this trend continued in at least North Indian states. However, by the 1970s it was clear that their move had achieved in part what they had demanded—a renegotiation of the terms of the coalition, or, to put it differently, their 'fair share' of the coalition's benefits. Every threat to leave the coalition was also an offer to remain if the benefits of inequality were more equally shared. Further pursuit of their objective could not happen by staying permanently out of the government party, but by rejoining its fold at a higher price, as it were. During the Emergency one discerns a tendency for rich farmer interests to be rearticulated within the Congress, helped now by the much greater hospitability of the ruling party to these groups. This was probably due to two related circumstances. First, after a certain level of secular growth in the economic power of this social group following the green revolution in North India, it became too important a segment to be neglected by the ruling party. Their influence spread across all political parties, including the government. At the same time, the suspension of the ordinary party system during the Emergency meant that the earlier means of exerting pressure on the government by qualified defiance would not work. Now, the only politically sensible thing was to get back into the Congress fold if they were not to be left out in the cold. Both the Congress perception of their indispensability and their perception of indispensability of the Congress made for their re-entry. Since this change did not take place dramatically, through open politics, but through quiet adjustments, it is often

[21] To use terms from Hirschman 1970.

neglected. But the growing trend of the Congress losing support of rich peasants and the emergence of farmers' parties as pressure lobbies is gradually replaced by a more mixed picture. But this development, though important and relating to the basic class nature of politics, could not be traced to a deliberate redistribution of power and influence through the Emergency.

There was, however, another important shift during the Emergency. Although it did not change the nature of the coalition in dominance, it did show some signs of changing government policy. Midway through the Emergency the government began to talk about a more 'pragmatic' economic policy, diluting the earlier Nehruvian commitment to a reformist bourgeois programme and social design in favour of a different policy with less emphasis on the public sector, import substitution, administrative planning, and with an accordingly greater reliance on market forces, price mechanisms, a strategy of export-led economic growth. In the later stages of Indira Gandhi's rule, some of these measures for economic liberalization were implemented.

Whatever its general impact on Indian society, the Emergency experience did not change Indira Gandhi's politics. After the initial shock of the defeat there was a slight element of contrition in her assessments of the Emergency period, but the particular form of the countermeasures that the Janata administration took removed much of the point of the Janata victory. The choice of Desai and Reddy as prime minister and president seemed to emphasize a conflict of individuals rather than principles. Through its messy and undistinguished record the Janata administration let down its mandate badly and failed to state with clarity the questions of principle implicit in the national experience of the Emergency. Consequently, Indira Gandhi never had to face squarely the necessity to analyse, justify, or exonerate the Emergency to the national public. For the gradual slide of the Janata coalition into incoherence put other questions than the Emergency before the electorate.

IV

If Indira Gandhi's defeat in 1977 was surprising, her victory and return to power in just three years was perhaps more so. Part of this transformation was of course due to the skill of the opposition in out-playing itself. Much of its three years in power the Janata government spent in debating what to do with Indira Gandhi rather than what to do with the country. It was the Janata phase which actually showed the extent to which Indira Gandhi dominated Indian politics. However, the manner of her return to power showed that all the longer-term tendencies in Indian politics we have analysed before remained; indeed, they had intensified. It reconfirmed the structural crisis of Indian politics. This revealed itself in at least three different ways. First, the options of bourgeois politics seemed to be exhausted between the two packages offered by Janata and Congress—between incoherence and repression. Each package seemed to reach a limit point after a time, and set off a reaction towards its opposite strategy. Oscillation in electoral fortunes seemed simply to reflect this exhaustion of alternatives. There was a crisis, in a second sense, in precisely the absence of a viable alternative to Indira Gandhi, despite some of her obvious failures in her evident indispensability under this dispensation—a form of politics in which she was both the problem and the only available solution. In a more fundamental sense, the crisis was reflected in the simultaneous presence of contradictory tendencies in the system. It failed to produce the political preconditions for the Nehru model of development.

However, crisis tendencies could configurate differently at different times. In 1975 they were expressed in the confrontation between two large national coalitions. Afterwards they have been replaced by a more insistent form of regional confrontation. An assessment of what Indira Gandhi has meant to Indian politics must involve an analysis of the nature of this regionalism.

Regionalism of the recent type is different from the regionalism of the 1950s. This regionalism is often misrecognized as a recurrence of its earlier form. If that were true, then these could be solved by repeating moves which were successful during the Nehru period. Movements for regional autonomy or self-assertion in the 1950s were really protests against the irrationalities of British administrative arrangements, which had put together territories into administrative units with utter disregard for linguistic and cultural formations. Such large administrative regions helped some regional elites to establish their pre-eminence in the presidencies. Bengalis in eastern India, and, similarly, strategically placed groups in other presidencies gained pre-emptive control of occupational openings against other groups.

Understandably, after the end of British rule there were demands for ending such sub-imperial domination and for linguistic rationalization of the administrative machinery of the state. No doubt among the regional elites who led these movements cultural indignation was subtly and inextricably mixed with concupiscence in relation to government jobs. Nehru, it appears, was presciently hesitant about granting the linguistic state idea.[22] Of course, the idea had two powerful arguments in its favour: it was right in an abstract moral sense, and also administratively convenient. Still, he had apprehensions about its long-term effects. Some of those fears have turned out to be justified. A first difficulty was the unevenness in its applicability: in large parts of the country the principle could be applied, but there were some areas where the principle made less statistical or political sense. Besides, it left large linguistic minorities in every state, and, given the political advantages of being a strident minority of any sort, this could be a recipe for endless trouble. Finally, the creation of linguistic states increased fears of regionalism in the centre and has helped the case for centralization as a counterweight. Correspondingly, a stronger centre has given legitimacy to regional forces, sometimes giving a regional complexion to what are not really regional demands.[23]

The new regionalism is neither a legacy of the British nor a product of something external to the system. It is produced by inequalities created by the operation of our political economy. Unevennesses which have caused regionalism during Indira Gandhi's time are structural because they are there not despite the structure, but precisely because the structure is what it is. Indifference to regional inequalities created by our form of capitalist development has often led to intense regional grievances. In the short term, such difficulties are sought to be solved by either a co-optation of the leadership or by a politics of concessions.[24] Co-optation naturally does nothing to solve the problem, except to buy a political reprieve. If unsolved, these grievances tend to re-emerge

[22] Gopal 1979, 1984.

[23] For instance, the conflicts between the centre and the Left Front government in West Bengal are not often strictly regional contentions; still, they get structured that way.

[24] Both these solutions were untidily tried out in the cases of Andhra Pradesh, Assam, and Punjab.

with greater violence and are more intractable to solution, because the local leadership which could have figured in it is already discredited. Even if one particular irruption is solved by concessions, it tends to turn up elsewhere, and concessions are by definition not generalizable. If everybody is given the same treatment, it ceases to be a concession and loses its meaning; secondly, the resources needed for generalizing such treatment usually do not exist.

Sometimes, these structural problems were compounded by shortsighted electoral calculations. It is widely argued that the creation of a fundamentalist faction within Punjab politics was due to Congress encouragement, because of the obvious electoral advantage a split in Akali votes would give to the Congress. This shows how the attempt at a short-term electoral gain can lead to deep crises in political life, crises which gradually get out of control. Thus, over the years the regional problem has assumed a particularly intractable form. There are incompatibilities not merely between centre and the states, but, what is often unnoticed, between the demands of the states themselves. It is apparent that demands of two types of regional movements—of which Punjab and Assam are examples—are incompatible. For the Punjab demands, in purely economic terms, are for retaining the differentials of regional inequality in their favour, while the Assam demands are against the policy of genuine economic neglect of the area.

Their incompatibility appears clearly if one considers hypothetical policies which might help meet them. The Punjab demands would require a greater insulation of regions and leaving them, especially the more prosperous ones, to the logic of their own economic operations—a sort of *laissez faire* of regions. Satisfaction of grievances against regional underdevelopment on the other hand, can be done only by some redistributive effort on the part of the centre. There is hardly any policy which can satisfy both demands equally, although, ironically, both movements see the centre as their common adversary. Effects of the green revolution, an excessive accent on productivity increases through inequality and insensitivity to its political costs, and the continued neglect of outlying regions by buying out their elites—have gradually led to a configuration of regionalism which the political system simply cannot control. The system finds it impossible to rectify its causes because they are tied to the reproduction of the system itself.

Most alarmingly, the events leading to Indira Gandhi's assassination show a reappearance in Indian politics of the power of communal ideology which was certainly underestimated by the evolutionist political thought that informed both our state institutions and our political debate.[25] At her death, Indira Gandhi left an extremely mixed inheritance, some of the contradictions of which are yet to unfold.

V

What did the period of Indira Gandhi's rule mean for Indian politics, a period she dominated so completely? Surely, a general assessment would have to take into account India's political economy, and the relative successes and failures of her strategy of development, something that I have kept out of my picture. Despite occasional deviations, like the Emergency or the large IMF loan, there is no doubt that she wished to continue the basic frame of policy laid down by Nehru. In comparative terms, the advantages of this strategy over satellite capitalist development are easy to see. Politically, despite strains, India has retained a democratic framework of government, although it has not spread effectively to transform political relations in the countryside. India has also retained its politico-economic sovereignty, and perhaps expanded its room for choice and manoeuvre in a world which is still inhospitable to third world development. However, it could be uncharitably said that these are all consequences of the Nehru strategy, which Indira Gandhi simply continued—and in some cases she showed historical incomprehension of the basic theoretical design.

Although in the very long run, perhaps, Indira Gandhi's regime will seem historically indistinct from Nehru's, in the shorter term there are some obvious differences. To put it schematically, Indira Gandhi retained the general framework of political economy laid down by Nehru; but her handling of questions of power increasingly destroyed the institutional and political preconditions for the effective pursuit of that strategy. The federal structure of the Congress was destroyed, giving rise to a more centralized but less effective state apparatus—particularly because of her equation of the strength of the nation with the power of the central government. Nehru perhaps had less power

[25] Kaviraj 1984.

as a prime minister, but he presided over a political system that was more effective; Indira Gandhi was more powerful as an individual, but dominating a system which was less politically viable. Power in political life is of two kinds; one is the power to deal with individuals and parties; and the other, which should really be called effectiveness, is the ability to attain and achieve more impersonal and longer-term goals. In Indira Gandhi's regime one finds a paradoxical split between these two types of power. Through the initiatives she took, Indira Gandhi certainly became an extraordinarily powerful individual, and people sometimes marvel at her transformation from a gentle, apparently unspectacular, individual to such a powerful ruler. The solution to this minor riddle should not be sought in the hidden reserves of strength in her personality, or in her traumas—which Arun Shourie is so good at finding out[26]—but in the nature of the political structure in a society that lacks institutions. She turned from a gentle and minor politician to a fearsome leader via the entirely unmysterious logic by which teenagers became builders of empires in medieval times. A highly centralized system of decisions invest individuals, if they are there for a long innings, with nearly mystic powers of indispensability. Gradually people become substitutes for institutions, because they do what institutions do elsewhere. Around such personalities myths of indispensability get built, which become the conditions of their real political indispensability. As a result, after her death, for some people who had a strong dislike of her, she became the substitute for all serious explanation. She became the uncaused cause of all evil.

The decline of political institutions meant a corresponding growth in the size and power of bureaucracies. Although it is fashionable to talk about the bureaucratization of socialist societies alone, there is probably equal or greater bureaucratization of society in the third world. Third world bureaucracies are larger, less accountable, and socially more powerful than those elsewhere; for in both socialist and advanced capitalist societies there are effective countervailing organizations. In developed capitalism, the imperialist urges of the bureaucracy are contained by limitations of cost effectiveness and the market, and partly by a culture permanently suspicious of accretions of political power. In socialist societies, bureaucracies are subordinated to

[26] Shourie 1978.

the party which sets its goals. Bureaucracies in the third world are so powerful precisely because many of these discrete functions are concentrated inside it—of setting goals and policies, the instrumental realization of such goals, and even the monitoring of costs, outlays, and achievements. With the virtual decimation of any second-level group of politicians, the bureaucracy has extended its control over Indian public life, increasingly suffocating society by a self-reproducing, obstructive, unproductive, and unrepresentative apparatus.

Finally, the difficulties that have been left at Indira Gandhi's death represent a structural crisis of the capitalist strategy of development. We must state clearly what is meant by a structural crisis. Marxists are often criticized for overplaying the crisis argument. If a system is considered to be always in a crisis, and the crisis apparently deepens without ever coming to a head, it is said there is something wrong with the idea of crisis itself. I believe that such objections are not as decisive as they appear. Crises are of course special types of difficulties which can threaten but not necessarily result in the destruction of a system. All illnesses that become medical crises do not end in fatalities; otherwise, the concept of crisis would have been redundant and indistinguishable from a collapse. Crises of political systems or social forms can arise from various kinds of sources—external, contingent, structural.[27] The suboptimal decisions of political leaders can be so crucially wrong as to result in crises. But here we are concerned with the sense in which marxists speak of structural or organic crises. Marx speaks of crises only when difficulties show certain special attributes: first, it must be self-produced, i.e. related to the reproduction of the basic dynamics of the system. These are in that sense not contingent or accidental things, and unless something is done to stop them they go on piling up and becoming more intense. In other words, they are not usually cancelled out by the normal fluctuations of a system's performance. Secondly, a crisis of this type occurs when we find that two processes, x and y, are equally necessary for system S, but each hinders and exacerbates the other and produces problems of resolution or compatibility. This leads to a three-way problem: there is an incompatibility between x and y which are equally and necessarily produced by S; if they are both produced indefinitely they may,

[27] For a theory of organic crises, see Gramsci 1971: 210–18.

through their conflict, put intolerable internal strain on S and make its survival doubtful; it is therefore necessary for S to do something about this x-y incompatibility to survive; but if something radical is to be done to it, S cannot remain S. This seems to me to be the meaning of the idea of long-term crisis tendencies in a social form. This, if the reading is correct, also seems to fit the present crisis of Indian capitalism.

What is remarkable about the period of Indira Gandhi is not the occurrence of serious problems, but their insistence. Individual political problems are sometimes got over, but a general crisis never seems to go away. From 1966 onwards, the periodization I have suggested is basically a sequence of crises. And every time political difficulties have reappeared sooner and in more intense and intractable forms, and in different ways extracted high political costs. Thus, the difficulty could be called structure-related in two senses. First, because of their sheer persistence, because the theory that this is a case of an uninterrupted run of bad luck is too thin. A more interesting idea would be to ask—why do the difficulties not go away, or ease, or stop altogether? Are these difficulties arising in spite of the system, or rather because of it? Schematically, these seem to arise out of the asymmetries of backward capitalism, the inability of its weak impulse of development to rework the cultural and social levels of the social form, a failure to rectify existing inequality and prevent new distributive irrationalities of the growth process, and a tendency to destroy the political and institutional preconditions which are necessary for this strategy. It is impossible to outline a larger theoretical argument of this kind here. But its phenomenal expressions are clear in the story that we have traced. It is shown in the questions which were central to the referenda—in 1971 it was whether poverty was to be removed, in 1977 whether we should have democracy, in 1980 a minimal basic order, in 1985 whether India could exist as an integral unit—surely an intriguing way of moving forward. Defenders of her regime would often say that, over the last years, in some ways, the economy did quite well. But it could well be that there are limits to such relative autonomy of the economy.

There is no doubt that we are inside a period which is still dominated by her initiatives and which will be known by her name. Her death and the elections afterwards did not mark the end of her period, but only showed its continuity. Despite her assassination, her image was crucial to the last elections. It was the last election, or referendum, she won for the Congress—most decisively and most tragically. The first election for Rajiv Gandhi is yet to come.

References

Bardhan, Pranab. 1984. *The Political Economy of Development in India*. Delhi: Oxford University Press.

Buci-Glucksmann, Christine. 1980. *Gramsci and the State*. London: Lawrence and Wishart.

Carras, Mary C. 1979. *Indira Gandhi in the Crucible of Leadership*. Beacon Press, and Bombay: Jaico.

Frankel, Francine. 1978. *India's Political Economy 1947–1977*. Princeton, NJ: Princeton University Press.

Gandhi, Indira. 1984. *The Tasks Ahead*. New Delhi: S. Chand and Co.

Gopal, S. 1979. *Jawaharlal Nehru*. Volume II. Delhi: Oxford University Press.

———. 1984. *Jawaharlal Nehru*. Volume III. Delhi: Oxford University Press.

Gramsci, Antonio. 1971. *Selections from the Prison Notebooks*. New York: International Publishers.

Hirschman, A.O. 1979. *Exit, Voice and Loyalty*. Cambridge, Mass.: Harvard University Press.

Kaviraj, S. 1980. Apparent Paradoxes of Jawaharlal Nehru. *Mainstream*, November–December.

———. 1984a. On Political Explanation in Marxism. Paper for Seminar on Marx, Keynes, Schumpeter, ICSSR, New Delhi, 1984.

———. 1984b. On the Crisis of Political Institutions in India. *Contributions to Indian Sociology*, July–December 1984.

Kothari, Rajni. *Politics in India*. Boston: Little Brown and Co.

———. 1976. *Democratic Polity and Social Change in India*. Allied Publishers.

———. 1984. Will the State Wither Away? *Illustrated Weekly of India*, 8 July.

Manor, James. 1983. Anomie in Indian Politics. *Economic and Political Weekly*, Annual Number, 18.

Miliband, Ralph. 1983. *Class Power and State Power*. London: Verso.

Olin Wright, Erik. 1978. *Class, Crisis and the State*. London: New Left Books.

Poulantzas, Nicos. 1973. *Political Power and Social Classes*. London: New Left Books.

Shourie, Arun. 1978. *Symptoms of Fascism*. New Delhi: Vikas.

Therborn, Goran. 1978. *What Does the Ruling Class Do When It Rules?* London: New Left Books.

Zins, Max. 1978. La Crise Politique en Inde: 1947–1969. These de doctorat d'Etate, Universite de Paris I, 1978.

7

Crisis of the Nation-State in India

To identify the political form of a state with a nation is common in the analytic literature on modern politics, but to ascribe a single nationalism to that nation is deeply problematic. The nation-state has undoubtedly become the predominant form of modern political identity, but this idea brings together in a historically special and unstable combination two dissimilar things—the tangibility of an institutional organization of force in the state which derives its imaginative and moral justification from the idea of a nation.[1] Besides, this political imagination of the nation is rarely an incontestably simple and single idea; most actual nationalism contains within its apparent singularity conflicting interpretations of what it means to be that nation and contest these for space and political expression. The nation-state is thus, despite its pretence to permanence and its claims to an immemorial history, a contradictory historical phenomenon: as a state and a political-institutional form, it aspires to historical stability; yet the body of ideas on which its permanence must be based tends to be internally contested and eternally contestable. It is rarely that a clear line of causality and moral empowerment runs from a single homogeneous self-understanding of a people, called its nationalism, to the sovereign state. Behind the state several configurations of nationalism lie indistinctly and jostle for political realization; the dominance

First published in *Political Studies*, Special Issue, vol. 42, 1994, pp. 115–29. Reprinted in John Dunn, ed., *Contemporary Crisis of the Nation State?* (Oxford: Blackwell, 1995).

[1] For a wide-ranging discussion about the idea and its many trajectories in historical practice, see Dunn 1993: 57–81.

of one of those, which then turns into the ideology of the eventual nation-state, is, though decisive, historically contingent. To understand the historical trajectory of the nation-state in India, it is necessary to set this contingency against the state's conceit of permanence and begin from the ambiguities of Indian nationalism—of its origins, its social support, its various ideological forms.[2]

Nationalism evidently bears a specially intimate historical connection with modernity,[3] because the national community was an identity unavailable in earlier political imagination.[4] But modernity does not merely add the form of the nation-state to the earlier repertoire of identities, it appears to do something fundamental to the structure and nature of identities in general. Surely, before the coming of modernity people had identities, and if pressed may have been able to provide a fairly clear picture of who they thought they were. Yet it is a safe guess that occasions would not have been very common when they would have been asked to face this most pressing of modern questions. Philosophical schools often urged enquirers to 'know thyself', and there was an instructive abundance of serious reflection on this question of all philosophic questions. But such philosophic reflection was never expected to have political relevance. Political life in precolonial Indian society was structured around a peculiar organization of power.[5] First, the impersonal rules of the caste system vested

[2] On the intellectual history of Indian nationalism, see Chatterjee 1986.

[3] One of the most forceful arguments on the connection between nationalism and modern practices comes from Gellner 1983; but its emphasis on the material side of the connection has to be supplemented by the analysis of political imagination in Anderson 1983.

[4] It is necessary to differentiate between the various senses in which the term identity is used in political analysis. There can be a distinction between the identity of a group, which means a cluster of features by means of which they can be clearly marked off from others; and their self-identity, the characteristics by which they recognize themselves. Often, this is a crucial difference for political action.

[5] If we reserve the term 'state' for the sovereign political centres in modern societies, it is difficult to apply that term to traditional political authority. Political authority and control tended to be dispersed and distributed between various levels of authority—a state of affairs that late medieval historians have sought to capture by the concept of a 'segmentary' as distinct from a

some critically significant functions in an 'absent' centre of the system, which governed boundaries and controlled transactions between social groups. Royal authority was entrusted with the task of maintaining and invigilating this system, without being empowered seriously to modify its principles. Most significantly, the state could not expand its powers radically; it had to function under the rigid rules of the caste system;[6] nor did all social demands for preferment or redistribution have to be routed through the state. Political belonging to territorial states was a rather tenuous affair under traditional conditions. Kingdoms and empires constantly collided and expanded at the expense of each other, so that a group of people stably inhabiting a particular space could be part of different kingdoms in a short space of time. The ease with which such political inclusion could be achieved also made such 'belonging' rather thin in contrast to modern practices. It was in that sense impossible to achieve the kind of firm identification between people and a form of politicized space which is presupposed in the political ontology of the modern nation-state.

Not only was the connection between people and states tenuous, identity itself meant a somewhat different kind of social adhesion. The logic of traditional identity appears to have been different from its modern counterpart in several respects. Politically, at least, premodern identities tended to be fuzzy in at least two ways. First, the identity of an individual was distributed in several different social practices; a kind of layering in which the fact of his distinctive belonging to his village, local community, caste group, religious sect, language, kinship complexes, trade associations would have all figured in a context-dependent fashion.[7] An individual was not exclusively one of these things, nor under pressure to yield an undeniable lexical ordering

---

'sovereign' state. It is safer to use the concept of a *power* organization rather than a *state* form.

[6] This is not to deny that the brahminical system allowed occasional liberties with its rules, particularly in the case of successful ruling groups, who always found obliging Brahmins to confirm their belonging to the Kshatriya caste from an immemorial past. But the system was understandably more principled in case of those who lacked political power.

[7] I have tried to explain this argument in greater detail: see Kaviraj 1992: 1–39.

of such features. It was not only individual identity which was plural and flexible; the structure of identities in the world itself was fuzzy in a related sense. Although both modern and traditional societies have to structure social differences in a significant order, they arrange such differences in different ways. Traditional societies arrange identities in the way colours are arranged in a spectrum, one shading off into another, without revealing closed systems with clear demarcatable boundaries. It is a world of *transitions* rather than of *boundaries.* And if people live in such worlds the differentiation between the self and the other remains necessarily a fuzzy, unconcluded, and inconclusive business. Finally, the ontology of the traditional social world, especially its cognitive constituents, was fundamentally different. Traditionally, individuals were equipped with a fairly detailed and sometimes astonishingly intricate system of classificatory categories by which to distinguish the relevantly similar and different, us and them. Still, they simply lacked the cognitive means to generate a global picture of the spaces in which social groups lived. Individuals who could quibble indefinitely about the hierarchical status of two castes in adjacent areas, or define ritual purities with endlessly tedious detail, still had the equipment merely to establish who was a Vaishnava or a Brahmin or when one properly belonged to one among the innumerable and constantly fissile sects. They simply did not have the equipment to know how many Vaishnavas there were in the world, and the means of persuading the members of this group to act together to shape political possibilities in their favour. Conflicts were not rare among religious sects, castes, or other social groups; but in the absence of the fatal knowledge of maps and numbers, they expressed themselves primarily as wars of position in the terrain of everyday life rather than as wars of manoeuvre in the political arena. Conflicts of interest therefore did not take on the scale which modern violence can produce so effortlessly.

British colonial power in India put an end to this traditional social ontology, and replaced it with an ontology of a fundamentally new kind. Colonial control over India was uneven, and in its early years resembled earlier empires, a thin layer sitting rather insecurely on top of an exceptionally resilient social order.[8] But British colonialism

[8] For a brief critical discussion on the debates about the colonial state, see Chatterjee 1993: ch. 2.

commanded historically unprecedented resources in military, political, administrative, and cognitive terms; and some of its political initiatives started off a comprehensive social transformation. British administrators brought with them an entire cognitive apparatus from modern Europe, especially mapping and counting, and produced an image of India as a geographic and demographic entity which far surpassed in tangibility and precision the hazier notions with which people transacted business in earlier times. The fundamental transformation involved a picture of the social world in which the organization and perception of social difference was altered: irreversibly changing peoples' images of their collective selves and their occupancy of the social world. Ordinary peasants may be entirely unable to count, but, despite this small technical infirmity, they knew exactly what it meant to be a member of a majority or a minority community, and how to act appropriately in these social roles. The political consequences of this new ontology were decisive: this made possible a membership of individuals in abstract religious identities like Hindus and Muslims, and, by corollary, a new kind of impersonal and abstract violence, as people began to ascribe to them an untraditional capacity to have intentions and undertake action. Once this new ontology of social/political being comes into existence, it becomes impossible to escape the logic of its consequences.

Enumeration processes began in the early nineteenth century, as did the establishment of Western-style education for producing a new, collaborating middle class. By the middle of the century, the first unintended consequences of this process of enumeration had become apparent. Sections of the new intelligentsia which were more disgruntled or imaginative than others already grasped the sources of power this enumerated space provided. By the end of the century, the idea that 350 million could not be politically helpless had gained such currency that popular patriotic songs constantly reiterated such empowering arithmetic. Still, in the nineteenth century a curious ambiguity remained at the heart of the early sentiments of anti-colonialism. Paradoxically, the earliest writers to create an anti-colonial sensibility had only resolved to defy colonial power, but had not yet chosen their nation. Among the first Bengali 'nationalist' writers one detects a strange ambivalence about whether the nation that they belonged to was a nation of Bengalis, of Hindus, or of Indians. Each one had its distinctive appeal, the decisive advantage of an Indian nation being its enormous size and its shared resentment against foreign rule.

It is common in modern social science to assume a dichotomous classification of identities between modern and primordial. This assumption is subtly fallacious: I should like to argue that the logic of modernity pervades the map of identities: there is no identity that it leaves untouched. People were indeed Muslims or Hindus before; but, under conditions of modernity, their way of being Hindus and Muslims changes fundamentally and acquires new, unconventional implications. First of all, from the traditional point of view these huge blocs of Hindus and Muslims were entirely new inventions of *political* agency; relevant groups for traditional religious practices were small self-recognizing sects.[9] Modern identities are either directly or potentially political.

Despite its internal complexity, the dominant political imagination of the Indian national movement went primarily in favour of a constructed modern Indian nation, an identity in which both the principle (of modern state citizenship) and its *symbolic* markers were modern. Yet it would be wrong to follow some hasty followers of Nehru and give to this movement a deeply anachronistic sanitized history that recognizes secular modernist nationalism alone as 'truly' nationalist and in effect retrospectively derecognizes other, less appealing, exclusivist trends. To understand the full range of political possibilities in the future, it is essential to admit the full range of possibilities that existed in the past. In historical fact, Indian nationalism consisted of a number of competing, jostling constructs of political imagination: one of these was severely modern and secular, but it was

[9] We can perhaps make a rough distinction between formal and practical/agential identities. A formal identity is one like being a Hindu, which would have been logically intelligible to an actor in a past society, but which would not have had any practical purchase; i.e. that group of people, though logically classifiable, would not be seen as a category for practical action. Agential identity would be one which is not merely formally understandable but which forms part of the generally accepted range of strategies of social life. Thus, worshippers of a particular Vaishnava sect would have their temples, their religious centres, and occasionally their distinct system of donation collections, etc.: the group of Hindus would have none of these and would thus be politically inert.

surrounded by others which had much more ambiguous attitudes towards democracy, secularism, social justice, and the entire programme of modernity.

Most nationalist politicians were in love with the narratives of Western modernity, especially its dominant hegemonic form which saw the nation-state as an agency of collectively intended social change. Although this narrative made the achievement of a free national state intensely desirable, some aspects of the trajectory of European nationalism could not be replicated under Indian conditions. If the nation-state had to be culturally homogeneous by definition, it did not fit the cultural reality of the Indian subcontinent: and one of the central divisions within nationalist ideology was between a homogenizing and a pluralist trend. Nationhood, the first view held, gave strength because it was the great force of homogeneity and identity. But the more dominant and persuasive strands in Indian nationalism opposed this construction, and interestingly Gandhi and Nehru were one in upholding a distinctively pluralist idea of the Indian nation, though their detailed constructions were vastly different. All cultures in India were of a similar family, and the responsibility of the new state would be, on this view, to provide a political template which could accommodate this enormous diversity, turning this diversity precisely, economically, and culturally into the main strength of the future nation. Eventually, it was this political imagination which was translated into the founding institutions of the Indian state with several parallel and mutually reinforcing principles of pluralism. Secularism provided for a pluralism of religious practices; federalism encompassed the pluralism of regional cultures, and democracy allowed the expression of plural political ideals. The constitutional form of this nationalism was civic, based on a secular, republican citizenship rather than belongingness to any mystical cultural or ethnic essence; at the same time, with characteristic prudence, it provided for an expression of more ethnic identities within limits. Interestingly, there was no way, in this political arrangement, for any person to be *only* Indian and nothing else; indeed, one could not be an Indian without being some other things at the same time. Being a Bengali or Tamil or Punjabi, or Hindu, or Muslim, or agnostic was not contradictory with being an Indian. Indianness was a complex and multilayered identity which encompassed other such identities without cancelling them.

Translating this humanistic complex imagination of a political community into legal rules was a difficult task, but it was achieved by the heroic labours of a constituent assembly which produced a document that was among the longest and most complex in the world. The enormous intricacies of legal rules which this elaborate construction required, because it did not wish to hurt any sensibility and tried to mediate between different partially conflicting pictures of justice,[10] made the constitution a technical rather than a popular document. Thus there was a mixed, complex, ambiguous imagination of nationalism standing behind the new state. It appeared in 1947 that the secular, pluralist, version had won a final victory; but this history always pursued its uneasy career, empowering the secular pluralist option but also menacing it. It was not wholly surprising if the Nehruvian form of nationalism failed, its other forms, sent into hiding by its triumph, would reappear and contest its claims.

After Independence, the nation-state followed, broadly, three major goals. The first and minimal one was to maintain its own integrity, but the principle of democracy added an implicit rider that this securing of territoriality must imply some exercise of consent.[11] In the context of the post-war political economy the second, equally significant objective was to defend political sovereignty, preventing a drain of real decision-making authority through absorption into the military systems of the Cold War. Nehru was particularly convinced, against the shared common sense of the Soviets and Americans, that the world appeared more bipolar than it actually was, and acting as if it was not bipolar

[10] One of the major conflicts was between the right to equality and the right of some groups to escape from traditional disabilities, a question that has repeatedly erupted into political turmoil, the most recent being the disturbances following the declaration by the central government that the recommendations of the Mandal Commission would be implemented. But there were other conflicts as well: for instance, some of the rights were conferred and conferrable only on individuals; some others, especially those relating to minorities, could be enjoyed by individuals only by virtue of their being members of particular communities. This can lead to difficult problems at times.

[11] The fact that India practised a form of democratic governance added to her problems in retaining territorial control over disaffected areas. This was reflected in the recent attempts by the Indian government to hold elections in the disturbed state of Punjab.

would in fact make it less so.[12] The third objective of the nation-state, generally termed economic development, had a complex connection with its explicitly political goals; and its economic aims themselves were complex and involved internal trade-offs. A dependence on more advanced nations for capital and technology was seen to be the major reason for depletion of sovereignty; and the first strand of development, therefore, was to be industrial self-reliance through a strong drive to develop capital goods industries. The amelioration of extreme economic inequality and destitution was immediately necessary as well for the political stability of the new regime. Happily, a strategy of state-led industrialization could answer both needs: the state was the indispensable centre of planning for capital goods industrialization; it was also the primary agency for redistributive policies. For the first generation of nationalist rulers, the nation-state they had established could acquire legitimacy in two different ways: its political legitimacy depended on its constitutional structure being considered fair by most social groups; but its legitimacy would also depend, it was widely acknowledged, on how it performed on the economic indices of import-substituting industrialization, increasing production, and supporting redistributive processes.

The Indian nation-state did remarkably well in the first twenty years in terms of the objectives it had decided to pursue. Although India's economic performance is routinely derided, compared to the size of the problem of poverty, and the considerable complexity of the goals, its performance during the Nehru era was impressive by any standards.[13] The constitutional structure absorbed some initial shocks from regionalist movements against the ruling Congress Party; but these were not so much against its policies as its forgetfulness about past promises of the linguistic reorganization of states, which was not pursued energetically. But these problems were largely settled by a general territorial

[12] Nehru showed the greatest political astuteness in his analysis of international relations. This is borne out by the initial difficulties but eventual success of the non-aligned movement. Ultimately the non-aligned idea was a victim of its own success, when inclusion of all third world states, from Pakistan to Cuba, made it politically formless.

[13] For a generally sympathetic account of the achievements of Indian economic planning, see Chakravarty 1987; for a more critical and more recent assessment, see Bhagwati 1993.

reorganization of the federal structure in 1956. Upper-class professionals often grumbled privately against the reverse discrimination practised in favour of socially backward groups; but hardly anyone questioned the principles behind these policies.

Apart from overtly political events, several more silent and less newsworthy processes provided the foundation for the stability of the nation state. During the colonial period, the British administration had, for their own interests, created three major structures for the support of the subcontinental empire. Foremost among these was the British Indian army, a highly disciplined force recruited from all parts of the country, and permeated by an all-India rather than a provincial character. It was complemented by the celebrated bureaucracy of the British Raj which, by the time of Independence, was largely manned by well-trained Indian officers. Finally, and not least significant, the British had patronized the enterprise of indigenous enthusiasts in developing an educational system which worked with a common curriculum all over the country. The elite produced by this educational structure was essentially bilingual, using English for communication across vernacular boundaries. More than its formal curricular structure, this system produced a common culture of educated manners and taste which was appreciated and intelligible across the country. Nationalists under Nehru's leadership in a sense nationalized these British institutions, now using their non-parochial (i.e. pan-Indian) character effectively to nationalist purposes. The army remained instrumentally effective, despite humiliating defeats in the border war with China, and coped quite successfully with initial military skirmishes with Pakistan. More significantly, it maintained, despite its effectiveness and prestige among certain circles, a scrupulous loyalty to the civil political leadership. The structure of the colonial bureaucracy was altered on crucial points by the constitution, which carefully retained and strengthened its national character, systematically insulating it from temptations of regionalism.[14] Higher education was expanded by massive investments in the teaching of high science and technology,

[14] Recruitment to the Indian Administrative Service is through a national examination; and administrative careers consist of transfers to posts across the country and occasional secondments to serve at the centre. This is meant to provide officers with both the equipment and the incentive to decide on the basis of national rather than regional considerations.

producing both an educational and a labour market for modern professional skills. Transformed by deliberate nationalist engineering, these structures of erstwhile colonialism performed efficiently for the endurance and legitimacy of the national state in the first twenty years.

But the nation-state inherited the teeming expectations of the nationalist movement. 'To wipe every tear from every eye', even when restricted to socially relevant tears, is not a very practical programme for a new state. Nationalist rhetoric endlessly repeated the idea that colonialism was to blame for economic backwardness and social injustice. The amorphousness and ambiguity of nationalist ideology meant that the state it created had to strive simultaneously to meet several types of expectations, not any single consistent set to the exclusion of everything else.[15] At least three types of state functions which now emerged were condensed into the new nation-state. It had to perform with almost unconscious fluency the sovereignty functions that absolutist regimes in Europe took two centuries to outline and learn how to perform. This involved, because of the very different organizing principles of the caste system, a massive transfer of social practices from the province of social regulation to state control.[16] Simultaneously, it had to take on the expectations arising out of a democratic process, much like the ones described by Tocqueville for nineteenth-century Europe.[17] Finally, it was also a conscious emulator of the social democratic strategies of the Keynesian state of modern Europe, which added to its political responsibilities the unprecedented

[15] It appears in the light of research in comparative political economy that democracy might impede fast capitalist growth; and certainly the countries of East Asia have done better than India economically, at least in part because their search for economic rationalization was not hampered by the democratic rights of their populations. It is of course a different matter that, after achieving growth, these countries might be forced to democratize politically.

[16] The most remarkable instance of the assumption of this new, historically unprecedented, power was the legislation abolishing untouchability. This was not merely an unprecedented social policy; this could be attempted only through an utterly different conception of the state.

[17] The most relevant Tocqueville text for Indian democracy appears to be the *Recollections*, which describes the ferment produced by democratic aspirations in a highly unequal society. For a perceptive analysis of India's democratic experiment, see Khilnani 1993.

role of engineering economic growth and redistribution. In European history—the paradoxical paradigmatic text that the leaders' imagination wished to re-enact—these processes did not happen at the same time: the winning of modern state sovereignty, the slow wrenching of universal suffrage from reluctant aristocracies, and the preparation of the welfare state through the conversion of the principles of democracy from the political to the social realm happened in sequence, not in simultaneity. Logically, at least, it could be argued that these processes were not entirely symmetrical or self-evidently consistent with each other; if happening simultaneously, one might in fact impede the progress of others. It is not at all apparent that the logic of secularization and of democracy, or of democracy and primitive accumulation for capitalism, are effortlessly consistent and compatible with each other. The pursuit of such complex objectives evidently made the Indian state's success more difficult by its own acknowledged criteria of politico-economic judgement.

Nevertheless, the record of the Indian nation-state in the first three decades was fairly respectable, if not impressive. Political sovereignty, as Nehru believed, was successfully defended through difficult times of hard bipolarity through a non-aligned foreign policy and its intelligent connection within development strategy. The basic format of development planning in the Nehru years was fairly internally consistent. Planning was organized by the state, which allocated certain spheres of industrial production exclusively to state control but allowed ample room for free enterprise to India's commercial and industrial bourgeoisie, assisted by generous protectionist laws.[18] The state monopolized capital goods industries like steel, heavy engineering, petrochemicals, and military equipment production, while private enterprise expanded energetically in production of consumer goods and small producers' industries. In the first three five year plans, India achieved a rate of growth which was unspectacular in gross terms, but

[18] It is often forgotten in debates about liberalization of the economy that indigenous enterprise benefited from state control in some ways and lost in others. Licence controls by the state obstructed its entrepreneurial spirit certainly, but protectionism shielded businessmen from external competition. The indigenous bourgeoisie's admiration for the free market and trade is not wholly consistent.

this was offset by its impressive differentiation of industrial production, especially self-reliance in heavy industries. Unfortunately, the structure of the world economy changed rapidly from the 1970s, creating opportunities which India's self-reliant industrialization made inaccessible. Since the state performed three vital functions relating to the economy: setting out general targets through its powers of planning, fiscal controls to exercise supervision over free market operations of the private sector, and physical production of critical capital goods, this led to a constant expansion of the state bureaucracy. The expansion of the state sector in turn impelled greater demand for the production of personnel who could fill these roles through an education system which had to be comparable and equal across different regions, a recruitment which spanned the whole territory, and their final integration into an appropriately nationalist bureaucratic culture.[19]

The forces of the market, ironically, pulled remarkably in the same direction of a greater and deeper integration of Indian society into the organizational structures of the nation-state.[20] Indian capitalism had enjoyed remarkable growth during the last years of colonial rule, partly due to the difficulties of international commerce during the prosecution of war. And the years after Independence saw a sharp growth in capitalist industrialization, leading again to the growth and integration of the vast territory into a more meaningful national market for goods and for professional and skilled labour. The logic of economic modernity in both its forms, the market and the developmental state, contributed to a greater integration of the national structure of state and economy.[21] Occasional crises in foreign relations, especially wars with China and Pakistan, and serious conflicts with the United States over economic and political questions, reinforced this sense of national integration instead of undermining it. Crises created a sense of danger to the

[19] I use the term 'nationalist' in such cases not to indicate an access of intense patriotic emotion, but to note the much less dramatic fact that they thought and acted in pan-Indian (i.e. national) rather than regional terms. Usually, this is the sense in which everyday political discourse in India differentiates between national/nationalist and regional political parties.

[20] Indian industrialists appreciated the importance of the nation-state for their own purposes quite early in their historical career. See Chandra 1977, and Bagchi 1972.

[21] Although their economic functions are dissimilar, the sociological boundaries between the occupational groups serving in the state and managerial

nation-state and produced paroxysms of patriotism at difficult times; but probably such sentimental intensity was based on the fact that these occasions of crisis called forth an exceptional mobilization of resources of precisely these professional groups in society and their various skills: the army, the bureaucracy, the press, the intelligentsia, and the managerial elites. Thus the nation-state in India during the Nehru years experienced a general consolidation, although its career was never free of trouble. The two types of trends which have imperilled the health of nation-states recently—the internationalization of production and control, pressing from above as well as local resentments undermining it from below, were not absent; but they did not produce the kind of fatal corrosion evident in later years.

It was a mark of the solidity of the nation-state that it could easily absorb the effects of low-level political instability and discontent. The electoral hegemony of the Congress in all parts of India provided an important source of political stability and order, since the federal character of the party allowed some dissatisfactions to seek recourse inside the party rather than through external opposition. But there were intimations of a new kind of impermanence in this political world in the bitter conflicts of succession after Nehru's death, and in more aggravated form after Shastri's. Although Indira Gandhi's accession to power provided an appearance of continuity, in fact she inherited a political world of very different construction.[22]

Ironically, serious difficulties for the Nehruvian system ensued from its successes, not from its inability to achieve the targets it set for itself. Indeed, what happened in Indian political economy is an especially emphatic example of the recursive requirements of political rationality. A scheme of policies presupposes a world within which it is calculated to succeed. But the historical successes of those policies themselves alter, sometimes quite fundamentally, the structure of that world and its conditions. Strategies, consequently, begin to offer diminishing returns, not because they were misconceived in the first place, but because of the more ironical paradox of the necessary obsolescence of success. Politicians and policy-makers can, and usually do, maintain plausibly that it would be extremely odd to change policies which have

---

bureaucracies are porous; and they collectively constitute a single occupational culture.

[22] I have analysed Indira Gandhi's regime in Kaviraj 1986: 1697–1708.

been successful; yet watchful scepticism is the condition of long-term successes in the constantly reforming world of modernity.

In its own historical world, Nehru's regime registered some signal successes. Within a relatively short time, it accomplished a kind of forced march of heavy industrialization, and the complementarity of the state and market brought into secure existence a new, modern burgeoning economy which, because of its close connection, both structural and personal, with the decision-making bureaucracy, could bring the rest of the sprawlingly diverse economy under its regulative control. Secondly, this economic change was brought in within the framework of a democratic structure of governance, admittedly limited in its reach, depth, and dependability, yet remarkable in the context of the high rates of infant mortality among democracies in the South. Again, remarkably, the Nehru regime was able to receive its legitimacy through periodic elections, without becoming obliged to scatter scarce resources in short-term populist policies. Its legitimacy was sufficiently deep to allow it to make decisions which required long gestation periods—something that a government could undertake only if it was under no immediate pressure to distribute imminent financial benefits in exchange for electoral support. Yet the dominance that modernist processes of economy and politics achieved over other sectors of society was flawed and insecure in several crucial ways. The dominance of state or market capitalism was primarily a regulative one. It did not generate sufficient momentum to transform the rest of the primitive agrarian and artisanal economy into capitalist production; it merely succeeded in imposing the demands of capitalist accumulation on other sectors which remained, in their productive logics, largely untransformed. Capitalist transformation of the whole economy homogenizes the economy and society after a period of social turbulence; capitalist subsumption, which captures more truthfully what happened in India, fails to homogenize the economy's structure, and social turbulence simmers on instead of coming to a forcible solution. Eventually, a situation of this kind comes to combine the disadvantages of modernity with those of the society it has disturbed without supplanting. In its size, depth, and scale the modern economy in India was an enormous organization, a world in itself; inside its secure, comfortable interior space India's social elites and their supporting professional classes could live out their existence; but in fact it sat uneasily poised over a statistically vaster, backward, populous, agrarian economy which was riven by more intense contradictions precisely because of the demands that the modern capitalist sector insistently made on its resources. Also, this interior world of middle-class comfort was surrounded by processes of modern destitution and squalor, anger and resentment, symbolized by cities increasingly submerged by slums. Besides the classical terms of trade disputes between the two sectors, cultural resentment gradually surfaced. Large parts of the submerged population in the rural economy learnt to make demands on the state through the continued use of democracy, and expressed their resentment against the fact that the benefits of development were monopolized almost entirely by urban, modern bourgeois classes to their total exclusion. The only rural group which secured benefits out of the development process was the large farmers whose compliance was bought by heavy subsidies, the absence of income tax, and their slow co-optation into governmental power. The ruling coalition of the bourgeoisie, high managerial elites, state bureaucracy, and agrarian magnates came under serious strain as capitalism in agriculture spread unevenly and produced a class of rich farmers who controlled substantial resources and felt unjustly cheated out of their fair share of the privileges of political power.[23] From the mid 1960s, electoral politics in India showed a rearrangement of the political coalition of dominance, the rich peasants defecting from the Congress and leading a resentful coalition of rural interests under the flag of peasant parties.

Within twenty years after Nehru's death, the central conflicts of Indian politics and the discourses expressing them changed unrecognizably. Politics in the Nehru years appeared a tolerable imitation of Western political styles, in which the main disputes occurred between ideological groups of the left, right, and centre. In the 1980s, it appeared that these were unsubstantial differences within a modernist bloc of privilege which was opposed with increasing energy, vehemence, irritation, and insolence by a bloc of social groups who were outsiders to the etiquettes of Westernized modernity. Politicians of this bloc spoke derisively of English-speaking modernists in a truculent vernacular, wore indigenous costumes; and they understood, tolerated, and at times revelled in premodern rituals of political power.[24] They

[23] For a discussion about the ruling coalition, see Bardhan 1985.

[24] In recent years, successful politicians were honoured by their caste groups or constituencies by being weighed against money. Sometimes they used a

created politically innovative coalitions which defied description in terms of either modern or traditional alphabets of politics to bring to bear the pressure of numbers on their adversaries and intended victims. Electoral instability played an important part in this change. Politicians like Indira Gandhi, who felt electorally insecure after the 1967 defeats of the Congress Party, invited these forces onto the political plane; but once they came inside it was hard to banish them again to the margins of democratic politics. They came in through a typically opportunistic welcome which was not meant to be permanent; but once inside they were too powerful numerically to be extruded. On the contrary, they tended to rewrite not merely the agenda but also the language of democratic politics in India.

Ironically, the logic of democracy has often worked against the stability of the nation-state in recent Indian history; though both nationalism and democracy speak in the name of the people, they invoke it in different ways, with widely different implications. In the period after the Emergency, 1975–7, what initially appeared a crisis of government has slowly spread to become a crisis of the Indian nation-state, at least in its current institutional form. A crisis is a kind of persistent difficulty of self-maintenance produced by the operation of the system itself, from which the system cannot come out untransformed. The crisis of the Indian nation-state has several dimensions. Planning, in its early stages, simply got remarkable results by rationalizing resource utilization and giving some direction to the economy. But once that plateau was reached, traditional forms of physical planning, based on direct state production, failed to produce growth. On the contrary, the entrenchment of vested interests among both public sector managers and a relatively privileged labour force made these industries indefensibly wasteful. Bureaucratic shielding of their performance and government protection made them immune to criticism, and they gradually became expensive white elephants which undermined not merely the balanced budget but, more significantly, the moral authority of the state sector. The state sector, originally fashioned to counterbalance the mercenariness of the private

---

symbolism particularly paradoxical in a republican state—presenting successful parliamentarians with crowns.

capitalist, gradually came to represent an economic sphere whose function slipped unnoticed from a predominantly economic to a political one: from distribution of welfare by producing low-cost inputs for industries, these became producers of unaccountable funds used by politicians and pliable bureaucrats. Ideologically, this made it appear that it was the welfare function of the state which was bound to produce corruption, and its excesses could be rectified only by the harsh, if purifying, sanctions of an unrestricted market.

A second success of the Nehruvian development design also started turning sour. Industrialization after Independence helped strengthen the national economy, but at the cost of intensifying regional inequalities. With the opportunity provided by democratic institutions, resentment against regional unevenness tended to find quick translation into regionalist movements. The response of the central government to these demands fluctuated from uncomprehending repression to attempts at co-optation.[25] Although the central government was occasionally successful in transforming guerrilla leaders into instant chief ministers, such transactions inevitably tried to head off widespread social resentment by private satisfaction, often leading to a quick isolation of the leaders who defected into a dishonest constitutionalism—to the disapproval of their militant followers. Anyway, this pattern did nothing to produce long-term political stability. To most cases of threat to political stability the standard answer of the nation-state has been a stern centralizing response. Yet political democracy meant that political troubles arising out of regional resentments had to be provided a consultative solution. Given India's great regional diversity, which is bound to express itself politically in an increasing differentiation of interests, only a transformation towards more decentralization can, in principle, produce a political order based on democratic consent.

[25] In a large number of cases, one comes across the same sequence of central response: starting with repression, moving to reluctant concessions, finally an attempt to co-opt the leadership by offering the allurement of political power. Such 'solutions' usually bring short-term reprieves at the cost of long-term problems. Democratic politics tends sometimes to encourage such shortsightedness, since the incumbent party can enjoy the brief glory of the reprieve, expecting others to come later and count the costs.

Unfortunately, however, the politics of the parties who have controlled the central regime has inclined in a different direction. Due to India's great size, it is always in principle possible for a party or an interest coalition to gain an absolute majority in the central legislature by winning the support of a major part of the country, leaving some enclaves permanently incapable of channelling their grievances into the significant spaces of decision-making. Indira Gandhi successfully pursued policies of isolating resentment in Assam and Punjab, outmanoeuvring regional opposition through a formal democratic process. But such operation of formal democracy strengthens the government while weakening the state. Disaffected groups enjoying large regional support become gradually convinced that their interests will remain permanently outplayed and marginalized through the democratic electoral process itself, and they will be reduced to a permanent enclave of helpless resentment. The operation of elective democracy can thus be seen not as a process of representation, but a means by which representation is craftily taken away. It is not impossible to convince people in those regions to turn away from formal processes of electoral democracy because for them, plausibly, these mean permanent disfranchisement. Consequently, the festering of regional sores of this kind in Punjab, Assam, and Kashmir have tended to make politics in those states reach a level of volatility which is impossible for democratic norms of restraint and conversation to contain. What is remarkable is the rapidity with which the curve of regional resentment rises from electoral defeats straight to armed militancy, instead of the trend common in the 1950s and 1960s of spilling over into large street demonstrations and popular movements. The rise of armed militancy of course does not increase participation; it reduces its scope still further. Punjab offers the best example of a situation where the people of the state were reduced to a state of utter redundancy between two combatants speaking in the name of contrary nationalisms: Indian armed forces preserving the Indian nation-state and armed militants trying to create a new Punjabi state of Khalistan.

It is possible to combine the main lines of causality in the trajectory of Indian politics, the silent, insistent movements of political economy, the logic of capitalism working through the state and the market, and the voluble, visible turbulence at the level of cultural expression. The fundamental process at work appears to have been a form of capitalist development which intensified both class and regional inequality and intensified anger against a modernist elite. The loyalty of this elite to its own acclaimed values of democracy, secularism, and equity may have been suspect and practically inconsistent; yet it is not its disingenuousness that is attacked, but the values themselves. Democratic governance made it possible for the enormous grievance against such cornering of the benefits to express itself. Democracy also encouraged the slow rise of a new idiom of politics which constantly invokes majorities of various kinds to justify a bending of benefits towards some large groups which can hope permanently to outnumber others. Three majority arguments have broken out with great violence in Indian political discourse recently: the majority of Hindus, of backward caste groups, and the less evident one of Hindi speakers: in all of these there is an implied belief that majority can sanction the sacrifice of equity. If a majority legislates rules which are evidently harmful to others, democratic principles of governance can legitimize them; and all of these trends wish to turn the level plane of rights of citizens into slopes which favour their own constituent members. Naturally, the response to such threatening language of majoritarianism is an instant reflex to seek spaces where the groups whose seclusion is sought can find a sanctuary in an answering majority. If some linguistic, religious, or social groups believe that in a united India the rules of political game and economic distribution will be skewed permanently against them, they will naturally try to create political spaces where they can constitute similar majorities and practise, in retribution, similar iniquity towards others. Under the pressure of these contending majoritarianisms, and the possibility of a convex majority which might combine principles from all these, the original political imagination of independent India is in danger of disruption. These are not proposals for abandoning the nationalist imagination altogether, but for replacing the Nehruvian imagination of nationalism with other forms.

Thus the central contradiction of the history of the Indian nation-state seems to be, at this point at least, between the logic of economic development and the logic of political identities. Economic change through the centralizing state and the homogenizing market works towards large entities like the commodities and labour market. Associated institutions of the modern, highly technically sophisticated armed forces, the large and powerful bureaucracy, a massive managerial and professional middle class the size of the population of big European nations, can understand the advantages of scale; they enjoy the surpluses that only India's scale makes possible. But the processes which produce this coalition of modernist groups and their advantages also produce, in their dark underside, equally constant processes of exclusion, resentment, and hostility to undeserved privilege. Since this elite speaks the language of national integration and unity, the latter speaks the negative language of localism, regional autonomy, small-scale nationalism, in dystopias of ethnicity—small, xenophobic, homogeneous political communities. This does violence to the political imagination of the Indian nation-state, which emphasized diversity as a great asset and enjoined principles of tolerance and mixing as the special gift of Indian civilization. That narrative of Indian history may have been romantic, but its politics was certainly praiseworthy and it produced the most noteworthy spell of democratic governance for about a fifth of mankind for close to half a century. The present stage marks a crisis in the life of the Indian nation-state in both senses of the term. It is brought on by the unfolding of its own inner tendencies, and therefore it cannot escape from the crisis by a policy of masterly negligence, precisely because this is not a result of policy failures, but rather of its limited successes.

Secondly, it cannot, it appears, emerge out of it untransformed; a simply singleminded pursuit of centralization is apt to make its strains only worse; its apparent suppression at one point would make it erupt elsewhere. The nation-state as it emerged through the Nehruvian design of the 1950s can survive only if it allows its dominant imagination to admit amendments, and strive to achieve greater equity between classes and regions; and try to surmount and heal the great cleavage of dispossession caused by processes of the cognitively arrogant, socially uncaring, brutal form of modernity.

But the crisis of the Indian nation-state as it is imagined at present does not of course indicate a depletion of the attraction of the abstract idea of nationalism. The structure of the international system forces all dissatisfaction to seek articulation, however inappropriate, through the obligatory pretence that each minority, each disgruntled group of people, are a nation-in-waiting that must break away from one erstwhile nation only to create another. With heroic unreasonableness they also believe, in the face of history, that their nation will not repeat the tragedies of others. If the present Indian state suffers disintegration, its space will most likely be occupied by a number of smaller, more homogeneous, less democratic states with their own insecure narratives of being a nation from immemorial antiquity. However threatened the future of the Indian nation-state, the age of the nationalist imagination is far from over. The world of political possibilities in India seems to be simplifying into the frightening choice before most of the modern world's political communities: to try to craft imperfect democratic rules by which increasingly mixed groups of people can carry on together an unheroic everyday existence, or the illusion of a permanent and homogeneous, unmixed, single nation, a single collective self without any trace of a defiling otherness.

References

Anderson, Benedict. 1983. *Imagined Communities.* London: Verso.

Bagchi, A.K. 1972. *Private Investment in India 1900–1939.* Cambridge: Cambridge University Press.

Bardhan, Pranab. 1985. *Political Economy of Development in India.* Delhi: Oxford University Press.

Bhagwati, Jagdish. 1993. *India in Transition.* Oxford: Clarendon.

Chakravarty, Sukhamoy. 1987. *Development Planning: The Indian Experience.* Oxford: Clarendon.

Chandra, Bipan. 1977. *The Rise and Growth of Economic Nationalism in India.* Delhi: People's Publishing House.

Chatterjee, Partha. 1986. *Nationalist Thought and the Colonial World.* Delhi: Oxford University Press.

———. 1993. *The Nation and Its Fragments.* Princeton, NJ: Princeton University Press.

Dunn, John. 1993. *Western Political Theory in the Face of the Future.* Cambridge: Cambridge University Press.

Gellner, Ernest. 1983. *Nations and Nationalism.* Oxford: Blackwell.

Kaviraj, Sudipta. 1986. Indira Gandhi and Indian Politics. *Economic and Political Weekly*, XXI: 1697–1708.

———. 1992. The Imaginary Institution of India. In P. Chatterjee and G. Pandey, eds, *Subaltern Studies VII.* Delhi: Oxford University Press.

Khilnani, Sunil. 1993. India's Democratic Career. In John Dunn, ed., *Democracy: The Unfinished Journey.* Oxford: Clarendon.

8

The Politics of Liberalization in India

Liberalization is an excellent subject for the study of political economy, the necessary entanglement of economic policies with political conflict. Liberalization, strictly speaking, refers to a set of internally interconnected economic policies. But the introduction of these policies is, in most cases, an intensely contentious political process. Liberalization of an economy never happens in isolation, but always against the background of some already settled ways of ongoing economic life. The changes collectively called 'liberalization' happen in the context of previous conventional, settled habits of policy formulation by governments and the general economic conduct of ordinary people.

There are a great variety of states in the modern world, and different kinds of states follow significantly different orientations towards the economy. Thus, what liberalization would actually mean for citizens of a particular state would depend to a large extent on the kind of relation that already exists between the state and the economic sphere. In economic terms, states in the modern world could be classified into four groups. In some cases, like the United States, the society conventionally worked on the basis of a very limited conception of the state's economic role. The state usually provided law and order, the enforcement of contracts, and minimal conditions for the efficient operation of a capitalist economy. State intervention in economic life was deeply disapproved of as inefficient, bureaucratic, and also as inducing an economic culture opposed to self-reliance. Diametrically

First published in Simon Bromley, *et al.*, eds, *Making the International: Economic Interdependence and the Political Order* (London: Open University and Pluto, 2004), pp. 133–72.

opposed to this model were the economies of former communist states in the Soviet Union and Eastern Europe, which were run by state planning. In these economies, the state not merely assumed overall direction of the economic activities as a whole, but also engaged in the direct management of production. Thus, the vast majority of people were direct employees of the state, and the state was the primary producer of goods and services. It was also the provider of a comprehensive system of welfare. European states of the late twentieth century developed a deliberately complex form which admitted structures from both of these models, without surrendering the entire functioning of the economy to either the unrestrained logic of the market or the total control of the state. These were characterized as 'mixed economies'. Despite considerable divergence in the exact mix of the two elements, and the precise fashioning of the institutional structures, these represented a recognizable third form.

However, despite their disproportionate influence, the world system consists not merely of Western states, but also a vast number of non-Western state forms. In economic terms, non-Western states would seem to belong to a fourth category. In these contexts, the states or political regimes simply did not develop capacities to regulate economic life in any comprehensive sense. Economic activities—ordinary peoples' livelihood, mercantile exchange, market organizations—all proceeded without much reference to the state. Usually, the state exacted a certain revenue from the society's economic activities, where it could; but in premodern economies its taxing and regulatory capacities were extremely limited. In our analysis, one particular distinction is of crucial importance. Both in the first and the fourth types, the state leaves much of the economic activity alone; but these should not be confused. In the first case, the state has the capacity to interfere; and it occasionally does—for instance, in cases of war or emergency. In the second case, the state simply lacks the capacity itself.

'Meanings' of Liberalization

Given this diversity among states, and their divergent relations with the sphere of economic activity, liberalization can mean quite different things. (i) First, liberalization can occur in economies that are already following liberal free enterprise policies as a settled habit of economic practice. Such societies are already organized on 'liberalizing' principles. These either do not require 'liberalizing' policies or feel minimal disturbance in their experience of economic life when they are introduced. But in all other types of states, the experiential impact of liberalization can be radical. (ii) Secondly, liberalizing policies can be introduced in socialist/communist economies in which ordinary people's economic life was entirely controlled by the state, and centred on its institutions. The effects of liberalization in such contexts mean nothing less than a total reorganization of economic life. Historically, however, the conversion of communist societies to markets have led to very different trajectories of social change. This process affected completely state-planned economies like the former Soviet Union the hardest, taking away secure jobs, destroying social security, creating highly unstable quasi-markets which often collapsed into open lawlessness. However, there were other examples of more successful and orderly transitions, in cases like Hungary and Poland. The most intriguing and paradoxical example came in China where a secure, unchallenged communist regime has supervised a phased introduction of a booming market economy. (iii) Third, liberalization occurred in economies where the habits of policy were relatively non-liberal, where the people expected large economic benefits from the state's activity, and consequently the state habitually intervened substantially in economic life either by regulatory structures or by direct management of economic enterprises. In Western Europe, where mixed economies flourished in the 1960s, this meant cutbacks in welfare spending by the state, a reduction of the political power of trade unions, and large-scale privatization of state-managed companies providing public utilities. (iv) Finally, liberalization can happen in societies that had a large, premodern economic sector unacquainted with modern controls of economic life, where economic and productive activities took place in unregulated spontaneity, with the state being indifferent and irrelevant to much of ordinary economic life. This is very different from the two dominant forms of modern economic life: in the liberal version the state leaves enterprise free but enforces contracts, prevents and punishes malpractice, and provides the legal framework for capitalist industries; in the socialist version it regulates economic life, ensures substantial redistribution, and at times manages direct economic production.

In the last two types of contexts, liberalization of the economy means nothing less than an alteration of the settled forms of economic practice.

Often economic liberalizers seek to insulate such changes from political conflict by claiming that these changes are 'technical' economic questions, a matter of simple determination of the most effective means for achieving narrowly economic objectives. However, it is, in fact, never so simple, or so clearly a-political. These changes affect the life-chances and life-structures of major social groups who are bound to respond powerfully to such reforms: and this means that liberalization is always serious politics. Liberalization might appear to be 'freeing the spirit of enterprise' of economic individuals and groups, but, contrary to ideological images of the process, there is nothing spontaneous or natural about it. Treating people as 'economic individuals' with atomistic self-interested inclinations is not a natural human trait but a cultural construct. In the second and the fourth kind of economies, it means serious reorganization of economic life, which only the state has the legal ability and the sheer social power to carry through. This leads to the first paradox of liberalization: though the eventual and ideal objective of liberalization is to reduce the state's role in economic life, ironically, it is only the state which can reduce the functions of the state. Or, to put it less paradoxically, economic liberalization in most cases requires a significant use of political power.

Since we shall be concerned primarily with liberalization of the Indian economy, let us see where in this typology we can place the Indian case. The Indian economy is extremely diverse and internally complex, but its segments are a mix of the second, third, and fourth types. In a case like India, liberalization could not be anything but a deeply contested political affair. This essay cannot go into the details of the economic policies through which liberalization of the Indian economy was carried on, starting from 1991; it will discuss the *politics* that went before liberalization and prevented its happening earlier; that went on around it and made it feasible; and the politics of its likely future. Liberalization will be seen not as an economic but a political process.

The process of liberalization of the Indian economy has to be understood in terms of two contexts. First, the impulse towards liberalization came, in part, from outside the country—from international agencies and a strand of highly influential contemporary economic thinking.[1] Secondly, it is essential to ask two questions specific to Indian political economy: (i) what kind of economic structure did India have earlier, which liberalization was meant to dismantle and transform? and (ii) why were those earlier policies adopted? What were the arguments for their justification?[2]

The Global Context

It is a commonplace today to link changes of any large magnitude in national economies with the process of globalization. But how revealing or analytically useful this statement is depends on the exact meaning placed on the term. At times, the contemporary trends of globalization are presented as historically unprecedented; but clearly, on a longer view, the present phase of globalization is an accelerated process of a historical tendency continuing for two centuries, at least since the rise of modern industrial capitalism in the West. Globalization as a concept can be construed narrowly or broadly. In the broad sense, it refers to the process of intensifying interdependence and emergence of networks of regular transaction between economies and states across the world that began with European colonization and the rise of the

[1] This directly implies that this strand of thinking was not influential before. Indeed, the study of how and why individual economic doctrines become dominant and begin to shape government policies is an intriguing but neglected field of academic research. At the time of Indian Independence, immediately after the Second World War, economic thinking was dominated by theories—like socialist or Keynesian ideas—that were critical of the market mechanism.

[2] Of these two questions, obviously, the first is descriptive, and the second set is evaluative. The second set of questions raises further ones, by implication: were earlier political economic policies wrong from the start, when they were adopted? Or were these superseded by historical changes in the Indian and the international economy? Did the early Indian elite adopt these policies for purely economic reasons, or for a combination of economic and political objectives? For discussions about some of these crucial issues in India's political economy, see Chakravarty 1984, and Bardhan 1984. Some of the political implications are analysed in Kaviraj 1994.

modern world economy. This process was clearly discerned by the more historically perceptive theorists of the nineteenth century, like Marx.[3] This general process, however, went through several distinct stages, keeping pace with the development of productive technology and the evolution of new techniques of political organization, which theorists like Michel Foucault characterize as 'disciplinary power'.[4] Both technology and disciplines of bureaucratic control vastly expanded the capacities of economies and states to affect the lives of social groups, sometimes at great distances. Undoubtedly, this long-term historical process has recently gone through a qualitatively new phase of acceleration, in which such interdependence and capacity to produce reciprocal effects has gone further than ever before. Narrowly, this is called 'globalization' since the 1980s. This has been caused by the growth of new technology, based on digital communication, and corresponding developments of political and economic institutions, which can at least encourage and monitor, if not regulate, the networks created by these technological leaps. For a historical understanding of what is happening to our world, it is essential to guard against two common errors—the first is to believe that nothing like this ever happened before, the second to think there is nothing new in the present stage. From the 1970s, there was wide realization that the structure of the world economy was changing, and intensive trade practices had fundamentally altered the structure of the world economy that emerged from the world wars. States veered round to the view that greater, more intensive economic exchange between societies was inevitable, and each state had to find a way of turning it to its benefit. From the late 1970s, another unexpected development accentuated this trend. It became increasingly clear that the Soviet system in Russia and Eastern Europe was in serious economic difficulty. The utter collapse of these states removed the imaginative attraction of an alternative economic model. It became possible to simplify this historical trend as 'the end of history', when only one single economic and political model was left standing. Widespread reforms towards

[3] Marx's *Capital*, vol. III, contains a sketchy but powerful analysis of the emergence of a world system through capitalist development in the West.

[4] Particularly useful is Foucault's discussion of the idea of 'governmentality'. See Foucault 1991.

liberalization of economies occurred in this international setting. But to understand liberalization in India we have to ask: what was the structure of the Indian economy before the reforms began, and why was it the way it was? What were the intellectual justifications, in other words, of Nehruvian political economy?

The Indian Context

The complex of policy changes collectively called liberalization represent, without doubt, the most radical change in overall policy orientation in the Indian economy since Independence. These policies were brought in explicitly to transform, alter, and reorder very different policies the Indian state had followed for over four decades. The earlier set of policies can be seen at two levels: the first is the level of intellectual discourses of political economy, i.e. the arguments put forward by economists and public intellectuals; and second, at the level of governmental policy-making—the attitudes and decisions of major political actors, the bureaucracy, political parties, pressure groups. In the first case, we should analyse how economists formulate policy directions on the basis of more technical considerations about economic objectives, and how these technical ideas are taken up by political groups who derive their support from particular social constituencies. To have serious political effect, those 'technical' economic ideas must go through a popular translation. Political parties give those ideas a more accessible, less technical form, so that these then become part of political discourse reflected in public meetings, parliamentary debates, and journalistic arguments. At the second level, we must study opinions and interests inside the bureaucracy, the formation of party policies, and pressures brought on the government by organized interests. These constitute the non-electoral side of democratic politics, which is sometimes neglected by an exclusive focus on elections and government responses to their verdicts. Actual political events are determined by both discourses and interests. It is wrong to believe that individuals or social groups have some kind of immediate, pre-theoretical understanding of their own interests, that they can understand their interests the way persons feel pain. Rather, persons and groups 'perceive' what is in their interest through the languages of political discourse. These discourses shape the horizons of popular imagination about what is regarded as desirable and possible. The more mundane politics of interest-pursuing actors occurs in the context of such possibilities already shaped by discourse.

After Independence in 1947, the Congress Party ruled India uninterruptedly for nearly forty years. This long period of Congress rule can be divided into two phases. In the first, Congress followed a reformist (some would call it socialist) programme of industrial development devised by a relatively radical elite around Nehru; but in the period after his death, when leadership of the party passed to Indira Gandhi and Rajiv Gandhi, Congress policies changed in significant ways. In the period of Jawaharlal Nehru's leadership, from 1946 to 1964, a fairly coherent and well-reasoned structure of policies was put in place through a discourse of political economy that achieved almost complete intellectual hegemony and which became a kind of social 'common sense'. Over the next two decades, these policies subtly changed their character, leading to serious unintended and undetected consequences which eventually undermined those policies. By the early 1980s, that old, reformist, redistributive, state-centred intellectual consensus had lost its persuasiveness. A vague but distinctly discernible new kind of 'common sense' emerged in economic circles, and began to circulate in the political public sphere through academic discussion, journalism, media debates, and the unceasing flow of political gossip which often plays an important role in opinion-making. Initially, through the decade of the 1980s, this remained a subtle change in the climate of elite opinion, without achieving much tangible policy consequence. But in 1991, due to some dramatic turns in political life, a new government took office that decided to introduce policies of economic reform.

The Legacy of Economic Nationalism

The nationalist movement that brought Independence to India was a wide, broad-based coalition of social groups, economic interests, and ideologies. The Congress Party, which formed the centre of this mobilization in its final stages, represented this large, coalitional, ambiguous nature of Indian nationalism. Although we speak of Indian nationalism in the singular, in fact several strands inside this broad movement entertained strikingly dissimilar views on what to do with state power once it was won from the British. Since the late nineteenth century a group of political economists had advocated a 'drain theory' about Indian poverty.[5] It claimed that British dominion led to an economic impoverishment of Indian society. They were particularly scathing about what they saw as a process of de-industrialization in which British industrial goods slowly ruined Indian artisanal crafts, and extraction of revenues from the Indian colony fuelled British economic growth. There existed highly significant differences between various nationalist strands on economic policy; but until Independence became a serious prospect, these remained primarily theoretical disputes. From the late 1930s, however, economic policies were discussed with a new seriousness. Interestingly, Congress always had strong relations with political leaders of the Indian business community. A few years before Independence, a group of politically minded industrialists published an outline of the kind of economic policy they thought the state should follow after Independence. It was popularly known as the 'Bombay Plan'. Although primarily a platform supported by industrialists, it advocated policies derived from the tradition of economic nationalism and advocated two key ideas—surprising for a capitalist group. Not surprisingly, the Bombay Plan initiators advocated a strong protectionist policy for the development of indigenous industries, shielding them from competition from more powerful Western business. They wanted this policy to apply to industries not merely located in India, but actually controlled by Indian business. Indian business, as a social class, saw clearly that while the nationalization of industries could go against their interests, protection against foreign competition required a large role for the state; and a weak state could not pursue economic nationalist policies. They also supported the idea that the state should play a significant role in running industries which capitalists could not support, and provide economic infrastructure. Leftist nationalists, influenced by Marxist and Fabian ideas, had already pressed for such policies. Thus, there was an interesting convergence between discursive advocacy of leftist opinion and the hard interests

[5] The major authors of this school were Dadabhai Naoroji, the author of *Poverty and Un-British Rule in India*, and a member of the British Parliament for a time; and R.C. Dutt, a high civil servant who wrote a more academic, but no less critical, *Economic History of India*, vols I and II.

of the capitalist class, which promoted an incipient political consensus in favour of an interventionist state. True, leftist forces and capitalist groups supported the state on the basis of radically different principles, and expected rather different things from its intervention; but they did support the idea of an active state. Such discursive facts often play a very significant role in political life. In India, this consensus got written into the founding political institutions of the state, and shaped the political imagination of elites and ordinary people, structuring political life in particular ways.

In countries with a democratic political set-up, the movement of ideas and the formation of public opinion are crucial in the determination of long-term policy, though in the Indian case, due to widespread illiteracy, this effective 'public' was highly restricted. The Gandhian national movement had mobilized huge masses of the people on large general issues like the right of self-determination; but illiteracy reduced ordinary voters' ability to influence more specific questions of policy. In the first two decades of democratic politics, ordinary voters were mainly politically quiescent, leaving unusually large room for initiatives by political elites and intellectuals. In India's post-Independence history, there were broadly four stages of development of politico-economic ideas. In 1947, gaining freedom from the British empire seemed a magnificent political achievement. It was hardly surprising that, immediately after decolonization, the overriding concern for the new nationalist elite was the protection of this newly won political sovereignty. Indian nationalists had since the early twentieth century contributed to a strong sense of economic nationalism. They were convinced that Indian poverty and British affluence were both based incontrovertibly on the colonial 'drain of wealth'. From the mid-1930s, this tradition of economic thinking, developed by giving an ingenious nationalist twist to Scottish political-economic doctrines,[6] was increasingly linked to analytical frames drawn from Marxist critiques of imperialism. Jawaharlal Nehru's own economic understanding played a significant part in producing a form of 'common sense of

[6] The major writers on the drain theory drew most of their main principles from British political economy, the works of Adam Smith, Ricardo, and later John Stuart Mill. But these texts were regularly and widely read by Indian intellectuals from the early nineteenth century.

the state'—an underlying strand of thought which helped shape state policies at a fundamental level. Nehru was critical of the political practices of the Soviet Union, but he applied a primarily Marxist framework to the understanding of international politics. In contrast to the standard 'realist' view that relations between states could be explained in terms of their single-minded search for power, the Marxist theory believed there was a deeper underlying field of causality related to productive and economic forces. Power came out of the institutional organization of economic capacities. The protection of political sovereignty was thus not just a narrowly political question. It depended heavily on India's place in the complex structure of the world capitalist system. This was a highly plausible theory, which saw the industrialization of the West as the real source of its colonial power; it argued that if ex-colonial societies were to move out of their crippling dependence on the West, they had to industrialize themselves, rather than agree to the disingenuous ideas of comparative advantage. Continued specialization in agricultural production, which had been their conventional strength, would lead to a perpetuation of economic backwardness because of the adverse international terms of trade between industrial and agricultural goods. Significantly, even simple industrialization in consumer goods was not likely to dispel Western economic domination, as this would continue the dependence on Western technology and machinery. Nehru and nationalists feared, like elites in other post-colonial societies, that the West might use its economic leverage to reduce political sovereignty, and turn them, despite formal Independence, into effective satellites. Sovereignty depended on economic independence. True economic independence could emerge only if India could develop her own heavy industries.

Several major policy directions followed from this theoretical perspective. Since indigenous Indian capitalists simply did not have the kind of capital required to establish these large industries, this could be done only by the state. Following this line of reasoning, the state in independent India assumed a large role in direct economic production in certain sectors, particularly in steel, heavy engineering, petrochemicals, power generation, and distribution—all lines of economic production regarded as essential for the development of other, consumer-oriented industries. Although this model of economic growth gave the state in India a large and in some ways determining economic role, it was also fundamentally different from Soviet-style planning. India was seen as a 'mixed economy', with economic activity left largely to private enterprise, though, because of the theoretical mistrust of private enterprise in socialist economics, the state was also given large regulatory powers.[7] The economic ideal of the Nehru regime could be called 'socialist' in a broad sense, because it used an eclectic mix of various leftist ideas; it certainly included a Marxist understanding of the working of the capitalist world system, and a Fabian concern with redistribution of income, but within a democratic political framework. Its economic ideal was the creation of an economy that was self-reliant, not autarkic.[8] In early public debates, there was considerable voluble discussion about the state's role in income redistribution and social justice. Nehru recognized that the new state's resources and tax base were just too small to attempt serious redistribution, or sufficient provision of welfare.[9] In fact, welfare in the strict sense was limited in Nehru's times to programmes intended to help the urban poor by providing low fixed-price food through state distribution channels called ration shops. By the time the Nehru regime had worked out its economic growth model in some detail, by the mid-1950s, the state had established a large role in the economy in two ways—its ability to impose regulatory controls through bureaucratic institutions, and its role in directly running crucial productive industries, which provided infrastructure or essential inputs into other industries.[10]

[7] The idea was very widespread that capitalist enterprise, left to itself, led to 'anarchy of production', crises of overproduction, large-scale unemployment, and increased social inequality. Not merely Marxists, socialists, and communists believed in these arguments—so did many liberals.

[8] This was a major difference between Nehruvian thinking from communist economic ideals of either the Soviet or the Chinese variety. It was always seen to be functioning primarily within the structure of the capitalist world economy, not a separate or oppositional model.

[9] Even in his most romantic moments, for example, when he was devising a programme for long-term economic development and social justice, in the Avadhi session of the Congress Party, Nehru proposed cautiously a 'socialistic pattern of society' instead of a socialist one.

[10] The railways had been a wholly state-run industry since colonial times. New industries set up as public corporations included steel-making, heavy electricals, and petrochemicals.

This was the overarching intellectual frame for economic policies, but the actual pursuit of these objectives in the real world contained surprising, unintended developments. Interestingly, there was little serious intellectual opposition to this basic policy from any organized social group. Organized labour, under the influence of communists or left wing Congressmen, welcomed them in any case. The middle classes were large intellectually persuaded by the cogency of these arguments and a realistic expectation that this policy of industrial growth would materially benefit them by the creation of management and technical jobs: engineering education became a great favourite of ambitious middle-class families. Bureaucracy was enticed by its nationalism and the prospect of immense increases in its own size and powers of control. Even business, as we saw earlier, supported this brave protectionist vision of industrial development, resulting in something like a rare economic consensus. But the actual pursuit of these objectives led to surprising events.

Nehru was always a socialist, but never, after the 1930s, an admirer of its Stalinist model. He admired the Soviet Union's astonishing industrial growth but was repulsed by the methods of terror used to achieve it. Under Stalin, the Soviets heartily returned his dislike, calling him, at times openly, 'an agent of Western imperialism'. Despite his very early, but short-lived, admiration of Soviet society (which was incidentally shared by many Western socialists in the 1920s) a convergence of policies between independent India and post-War USSR was highly unlikely. In spite of sharp criticisms of Western societies for their colonial past, and continued gentleness towards European colonialism, in Nehru's thinking Western states like the UK and the USA were the most likely allies of independent India. Realities of the post-War political world soon altered this perception. Serious friction began between India and the Western powers on both political and economic issues. Immediately after the war, the US-led Western coalition began a frenetic search for allies across the third world for containing communism, by establishing a ring of interconnected military alliances around the perimeter of the communist bloc. Nehru thought these treaties contributed to increased tension, and decided to follow a policy of non-alignment, a strategy condemned initially by both the superpowers as a devious way of siding with the other camp. Western powers also used their economic leverage to pressurize Nehru on this question, which simply increased his suspicion that they wished to compromise India's political freedom of decision-making.

On the economic side, Western governments, especially American ruling circles, looked upon his statist policies with deep suspicion and feared that they could be a prelude to a comprehensive nationalization of foreign and private industries. When Nehru's government sought technology and capital to develop his primarily state-led industrialization plan, American response, from government and business circles, was hostile and negative. But this led to a mutual misunderstanding of motives. The West thought it had enough reasons to treat Nehru as little better than a communist; Nehru thought the West was little better than imperialist.

Foreign Policy and Development Strategy

Nehru's regime had two options—either to abandon its ambitious plans for industrialization, or to look elsewhere. The change of regime and fundamental shifts in Soviet policy after Stalin made this possible. The end of the Stalin era led to not merely some internal changes in the Soviet system, but also to a comprehensive revaluation of Soviet policies towards the world. The Khrushchev regime slowly began to change its attitude towards newly decolonized states, and made cautious overtures towards them. In part, this was also driven by a crucial and more realistic assessment of the structure of world power. The inflated ideological discourse of bipolarity often confused the real condition of the world. It stated correctly that there were only two superpowers who dominated the world, but often went on to imply incorrectly that their powers were broadly equal. In fact, the bipolarity of the post-War world was marked by an asymmetry between the West and the Communist world in terms of economic strength and political influence. Only in military power was there something like an equality of conventional arms and nuclear deterrence. But the asymmetry meant that the objectives of the two sides were determined very differently. The West generally expected its allies to give full support to its military and political objectives. The communist system, as the weaker player, would have been content if countries like India did not follow the lead of the West, and the post-Stalin regimes recognized this in their policies. In other words, the Soviet objectives were lower than the Western; and therefore this created a possibility of a convergence between Soviet and Indian objectives, without ideological agreement.

A combination of this kind of economic thinking and short-term political moves eventually shaped the outline of the political economic structure India was to follow for nearly three decades after Independence. It was undoubtedly a mixed economy, with a sprawling private sector, loosely or insufficiently regulated, but dominated by a highly visible public sector in crucial industries like steel, mining, heavy engineering, petrochemicals, oil exploration. Much of the technology and some of the capital needed for this drive towards heavy industrialization came from the USSR. The coincidence of Soviet and Indian policy towards Kashmir and other international disputes sometimes made this convergence of interest look far worse in Western eyes, and among some panicky bourgeois groups inside India. Equally, Western hostility to legitimate ambitions of industrial growth and the mysterious ways of Western foreign policy made Indians increasingly mistrustful of Western declarations.[11] What Indians found particularly strange was how the Americans, who were in theory fighting for the free world, in practice preferred army regimes in Pakistan over elected ones in India.

The creation of the new public-sector industries led to the elaboration of a system of public administration, which classified industries, somewhat in the line of British thinking at the time, into four kinds. There were private enterprises wholly owned by capitalists; but besides these there were, legally, three types of government involvement in industries. 'Joint enterprises' had shared private and state control, usually with a majority share with the state. 'Public enterprises' were funded by the state, but their managements were supposed to enjoy managerial autonomy of decision-making. These were, in administrative theory at least, sharply distinguished from 'ministerial departments' like the railways or the post office which were entirely controlled by state ministries, and were regulated by ordinary rules of bureaucratic management. In the Nehru period at least, public-sector industries enjoyed some serious autonomy of managerial decisions from the bureaucracy. And the initial performance of public-sector industries

[11] Western foreign policies seemed from the Indian point of view marked by an inconsistency between principles and practice. Western governments claimed to be fighting a war for the safety of the free world, but seemed unaccountably attracted towards openly dictatorial regimes.

was encouraging: first, they successfully established these industries in the Indian economy and reduced dependence on external sources of heavy industrial goods; and secondly, even their economic performance in terms of productivity and costs was fairly respectable. As a whole, the policy generated industrial growth, though at a relatively modest rate; it created an economy with a large and versatile production base. Most significantly, from the Nehruvian point of view, it helped India, in the thick of the Cold War, to remain impervious to pressures from outside to alter its political policies. India remained more independent of international, particularly of Western, pressure, compared to countries like South Vietnam or South Korea which were seen derisively as Western satellites. For three crucial foundational decades Indian political economy followed this fundamental design.

Assessments of Nehru's Policies

Historical assessments of Nehru's policies diverge widely. There are two main lines of evaluation. Some economists have argued forcefully, since the 1970s, that the state-led heavy industrialization policies were flawed from the inception, in their very design, and not surprisingly they delivered a sluggish long-term growth.[12] Raj Krishna, a leading economist, famously derided it as the 'Hindu rate of growth', though what this rate of growth has to do intimately or causally with Hinduism is unclear. This line of thought believes typically that the criteria for assessment should be exclusively economic, in fact narrowly income-oriented and based on stringently narrow calculations of 'economic growth'. Other economists who support less narrow conceptions of economic development, and advocate wider and more complex criteria like 'quality of life', judge Nehru's policies rather more positively.[13] Another line of thought still asserts the correctness of Nehruvian policies, and blames its two main disappointments—widespread poverty and slow growth—on failures of implementation. Interestingly, from a theoretical point of view both these judgements depend crucially on comparison between actual states of affairs and counterfactuals.

[12] One of the best, and certainly most influential, arguments, is in Bhagwati 1993.

[13] Among the most well-known analyses of India's political economy are Bardhan 1992, and Dreze and Sen 1998.

Consequently, these judgements always leave a certain margin of uncertainty. It is possible to suggest a third, more mixed, judgement. If the criteria used are mixed—combined economic and political ones—and assess growth objectives, some of which can be decomposed individually and others which are indivisible public goods, then the historical judgement on the first stage of policies is bound to be more complicated, at least less pessimistic. Collective and non-economic goods like political freedom of decision-making and political non-dependence would show the performance of Nehru's policies in far better light. But even those who advocate this historical line of judgement must admit that in its two main functions in the economic sphere the state's involvement began to yield diminishing and eventually counter-optimal returns over the longer term. Even after decades of Nehruvian planning, the Indian economy remained plagued by the two problems of slow growth and large-scale poverty.

The problems with the Nehruvian economic design were probably twofold, again some economic and others political. First, as some economists suggested, planning itself went through a first, relatively easy, phase in which the initial effort of inventorying resources and their direct use by the state brought some quick and impressive results. But once this period of 'easy planning' based on more rational use of physical resources was over, there was a need for the political-economic design to change. In fact, the relative success of this kind of planning was altering the structure of the economic world in which it was taking place, making its continued success more difficult. Paradoxically, precisely because state policies were 'successful' in the short run, and their objectives realized, these policies should have been changed. However, it is clear that from the point of view of politics and bureaucratic decision-making this would appear odd, to say the least. It was implausible to ask politicians and bureaucrats to change policies which had been successful. By the mid-1970s there was widespread perception in the political public sphere, in journalistic debates, and in the popular mind, that state-run industries were running uneconomically and inefficiently, running up huge losses which eventually fell on the state. The second aspect of state intervention, its system of regulatory controls, increased bureaucratic power and too easily degenerated into corrupt practices.

But the degeneration of the public sector and its growing disrepute was not entirely an economic phenomenon. Political processes were equally to blame. After Nehru, the administrative distinctions in management styles and structures between ministerially controlled industries like the railways and post office and relatively autonomous public corporations producing steel were slowly eroded by political interference. Indira Gandhi's attempts to centralize government resulted in increasingly direct bureaucratic and ministerial interference in their affairs. By the mid-1970s, there was hardly any discernible difference between the two types of enterprise: public sector industries were run as bureaucratically as ministerial departments. Everyday political commentary and popular gossip was full of speculation about politicians surreptitiously using the resources of state enterprises for their own political purposes or for straightforward financial malpractice. Thus the degeneration of the 'public sector' was a somewhat complicated affair. There was no doubt that the public sector had degenerated; but it was, equally truly, not the same kind of public sector. This had two highly significant results: first, the economic performance of the public industries became uniformly poor, and began to be universally derided, not merely by economists preferring the market, but also by ordinary commentators. Secondly, it became increasingly clear that the Nehruvian discursive justifications for the sector, for its contribution to the economic strength of the country and preventing concentration of economic power, had ceased to apply. Some larger international developments contributed to the decline of intellectual support for this economic policy. The USSR collapsed with its model of rational comprehensive state control over economic life, leading to a serious philosophical decline in the general credibility of socialist arguments. Finally, and perhaps most significantly, the structures of the world economy and the international state system changed sufficiently to make the 1950s' fears of neo-colonial subjugation appear outdated. This altered political and economic context made 'liberalization' a realistic agenda which could be taken up by political actors.

The Short-Term Context of Liberalization in India

Yet, interestingly, it needed a serious foreign exchange crisis to start serious policy change. By the early 1990s economic arguments for liberalization were not new or unconventional. In the 1960s, to argue against the state sector and in favour of large-scale privatization required some courage, because it was to go against a political consensus about the economy. By the mid-1970s that consensus had lost conviction and was becoming decrepit as an ideology. Some other significant changes had also taken place in the Indian economy. Nehruvian political-economic thinking had regarded agriculture primarily as a sector to be used to encourage industrial growth—by encouraging productivity increases and enabling a transfer of surplus labour from agrarian to industrial occupations. Government policy therefore treated agriculture differently. Industrial production benefited from government activity, agriculture from non-action. Nehru's government had, in accordance with its socialist convictions, been convinced that agricultural productivity could be boosted dramatically by land reforms, rather than by technological fixes. Instead of relying on technological improvements in agriculture, which were likely to increase inequality among the peasantry, Nehru's regime enacted legislation which helped the state to fix ceilings on land proprietorship.[14] The excess land held by rural magnates was to be redistributed by the state to land-hungry poor peasants. It was generally believed that poorer peasants or agricultural labourers, when given land to own, despite their small farm sizes, would raise production enthusiastically. From the mid-1950s, the Congress Party, under Nehru's pressure, enacted land reform legislation.

In the long term, this policy was a mixed success: it both succeeded and failed. In the short run it seemed a failure, because richer farmers managed to retain most of their land by a creative use of legal provisions. Only an insignificant amount of land was eventually redistributed. Over the long term, however, agricultural policies were seen to produce an enormous social transformation in the countryside. Nehru's legislation expropriated the zamindars, a class of absentee colonial landlords who had flourished under British rule and stifled the agrarian economy by their high rent demands. After their rapid demise, the

[14] In the Indian constitution, agriculture falls under the legal jurisdiction of state governments, not of the centre. Nehru's government at the centre did not enact land reform legislation. The Congress Party asked its state governments to introduce land ceiling legislation, which they obediently did.

way was left open for a class of richer farmers to emerge—to replace them as the dominant class in the countryside. They benefited from the startling absence of agricultural income tax, and the general non-existence of regulatory legislation. By the mid-1960s, rich farmers had become a major political interest group in some parts of the country. In the 1960s, government policy too began to turn in their favour. Agricultural productivity remained stubbornly low despite the land-reform legislations in the Nehru years. After Indira Gandhi became prime minister, the government decided that the land-reform strategy had failed, and changed over dramatically to a new 'green revolution' policy of supporting technological change in agriculture. This required preferential treatment to farmers through a raft of measures—subsidized farming inputs, assured prices for agricultural produce, the provision of energy at low prices. These reforms led to an increase in socio-economic inequality in the countryside, but accompanied by a general rise in productivity. The success of the green revolution in the wheat-producing areas released the government from its crippling dependence on food aid and import, and increased its range of freedom of decision-making. Sociologically, Indian society had undergone significant changes: while industries were more widespread and stronger, and spawned a larger, ambitious, politically voluble professional class, a new class of rich farmers had come to dominate rural society with much greater wealth and consequently political ambition.

In retrospect, the causes that produced liberalization in the 1990s were not new. Dissatisfaction with Nehruvian policies, or their mis-implemented form, became increasingly widespread after the mid-1960s. Bureaucratic impositions were criticized increasingly by a minor section of the intelligentsia, capitalist entrepreneurs, private managers, aspiring small businessmen, and ordinary people who had to deal with bureaucratic delays because of the constant overelaboration of Byzantine procedures. Large social groups, who had great electoral leverage, and influential and strategically placed elites who commanded wealth and connections, increasingly saw bureaucratic controls over the economy as serious obstacles to their growth. But the old policies retained solid support from other social groups—the bureaucracy, which enjoyed immense powers from these regulations; the political class, which indirectly or corruptly benefited from its assets; and organized labour, which profited from vastly improved working conditions.

The interest convergence, which had led to the Nehruvian policies without much serious opposition, started fragmenting. The politics of discourse also began to change, but more slowly and more subtly. Intellectually, a major part of the political intelligentsia still defended a state sector that functioned very differently from Nehru's times by wholly anachronistic reference to high-minded Nehruvian economic ideals. But both politicians and common people recognized that the state sector represented a large vested interest rather than a welcome counterweight to the power of private capitalists. The genuine policy consensus of the 1950s and 1960s was thus already in jeopardy. Early suggestions towards liberalization mainly stressed two policy recommendations: reducing state controls over the licensing of new industries, and bringing market forces into sluggish sectors of the economy, thereby ending state monopoly. The climate of opinion changed slowly: though a larger section of economists began to argue forcefully for reduction of state control and greater freedom of the market, they met with a stodgy dismissal.

But there were discernible changes in practical orientations of economic policy. In any case, Indira Gandhi showed, from the start of her prime ministerial career, a more flexible and pragmatic approach to macro-economic policies than her father, certainly less constrained by ideological convictions about development or redistribution. The first major change in economic policy she initiated, the shift to the technical fix in agriculture through green revolution strategies, showed how easily she could abandon the egalitarian conviction behind the earlier policies of land reform and institutional change.[15] For the benefit of sharp rises in productivity, she was prepared to accept large-scale inequalities. More subtly but fundamentally, Mrs Gandhi's attitude towards planning was very different from Nehru's. Under her leadership, economic planning changed in character. Though the Nehruvian rhetoric of planned development was retained, from the Fourth Five Year Plan onwards the government, in imperceptible degrees, gave up the intention of directing economic growth

[15] For detailed discussions on agricultural policy changes, see Frankel 1971, and Mellor 1966. For an excellent account of the political side of agricultural policy, see Varshney 1998.

purposively. Planning slowly became a process of setting down targets and large-scale objectives, and the vast apparatus of planning kept itself busy in statistical exercises.

During the short period of the Emergency (1974–6), in an interesting interlude, a section of the Congress leadership, encouraged by Mrs Gandhi's second son Sanjay Gandhi, began to suggest heretically that India should abandon planned development and adopt 'the Brazilian path', a transparent code for more liberalized economic policies. With the gradual decline of Nehruvian economic thinking behind real control regimes, these policies lost their ideological resilience and crumbled morally from inside. As a result, the control system did not collapse, but it became a gigantic, arbitrary, Byzantine mass of rules capriciously implemented, more to extract bribes or inconvenience adversaries than realize defensible policy objectives. The control system became more repressive and less justifiable at the same time. Already, a certain change in economic thinking was discernible in government circles in the last years of Indira Gandhi's rule. Economists with pronounced liberalizing views were appointed to highly influential and visible advisory positions in the economic ministries. Their presence indicated incipient rethinking in political circles and the high bureaucracy. These economists also made strong attacks on the inefficiency of the conventional state sector and licensing controls, slowly altering the intellectual climate in which government economic policy was formulated.[16]

Arguments for liberalization and market-friendly reforms did not re-emerge in serious public political debates until Rajiv Gandhi came to power. Rajiv Gandhi had a shorter term in power, but his economic tendencies were even more eclectic than his mother's. He clearly pushed for an incorporation of high technology in particular sectors of the Indian economy, especially telecommunications and computers. Although general policies were not radically revised, government attitudes were seen to be friendlier towards risk-taking entrepreneurial initiative. Since high technology could not easily come into the Indian economy without market-friendly reforms, this was seen as a natural entailment of his policies. But Rajiv Gandhi was assassinated

[16] For a view of this kind, see Ahluwalia 1999.

before his initiatives could form into seriously worked out general policies.

Liberalization of the 1990s

The latter half of the 1980s were highly significant for Indian politics. Though analysts and commentators generally remember them for a period of messy, infructuous government, in fact, the political universe of Indian democracy was moving from one historical stage to a very dissimilar one. The central government was always controlled securely by a majority party, the Congress. In 1991, for the first time, Indian society faced the startling fact that no party could secure a majority at the centre. In the elections of 1989, after Rajiv Gandhi's death, Congress, riven by internal factional fights, failed to get a majority. Yet there was no party which could replace it on a stable basis. Congress had declined, but not enough to disappear electorally; the BJP had emerged strongly but not enough to form a government. Historically, this was an interregnum between strong central governments by powerful, all-India political parties and much weaker ones based on coalitions between regionally powerful forces which were obliged by the electoral arithmetic to seek support from others.

Full-scale liberalization, when it arrived, was full of paradoxes. The government that P.V. Narasimha Rao formed was the weakest central government in modern Indian history. In parliament the government did not command a majority. Its survival depended on voting support from some opposition groups, mainly leftist and lower-caste parties. Rao was not secure inside his own party, with a major section of political leaders openly declaring their loyalty to Rajiv Gandhi's widow, Sonia Gandhi, and obstructing his policies. Rao was the weakest prime minister both in parliament and inside his own party. Yet his government undertook what was undoubtedly the most radical reform of the Indian economy since Nehru's times. How was this possible? How could the most radical reforms be carried out by the weakest regime since Independence?

Four types of reasons could be advanced to explain this paradox. First, economic changes from the 1950s had led to a slow, imperceptible recomposition of social classes, altering the balance of economic power in society. The most significant change was the rise of new capitalist farmers in the green revolution areas who were the main beneficiaries of the absence of agricultural income tax, and some of the regime of subsidies. The professional middle classes, initially the prime beneficiaries of industrial growth, because they monopolized the new job opportunities in both private- and public-sector industries, and the bureaucracies that supervised them, increasingly felt their economic life had reached a point of stagnation. Until the 1960s, these upper-class groups were entirely dominant in the political world; but from the 1970s their exclusive control of the political field was successfully challenged by politicians coming from rich-farmer and lower-caste backgrounds. As this class became less dominant in the political process due to growing democratic participation, they became more receptive to liberalizing ideas, expecting new opportunities of income growth from global economic changes. A highly skilled section of the Indian professional classes gradually got access to the international economy, and developed much greater aspiration for wealth than the earlier structure of policies allowed. Secondly, the structure of the global economy and the nature of economic relations had changed radically. These changes seemed to make fears of neo-colonial control by ex-colonial powers unrealistic, and therefore policies meant to guard political sovereignty unnecessary. In addition, countries that were derided as satellites showed through their prosperity the great economic advantages of intensified trade and a policy which opened economies out to the world rather than closed it in the name of self-reliance. The spectacular economic growth of the East Asian economies was analysed by Indian observers, and this fuelled speculation that, given proper government policies, Indian business could emulate their prosperity. Ideologically, the global collapse of communist systems seemed to undermine the philosophical legitimacy of socialist economic thinking in general, and thus nationalistic arguments that relied on those concepts carried a fading power of persuasion. Even without a concerted intellectual campaign to open up the Indian economy, the slow dispersal of the Nehruvian consensus in favour of import-substitution, state interference in the economy, and redistributive policies led to the emergence of a new, weaker consensus in favour of liberalization. Curiously, no one argued strenuously for the market, except for a small group, but mistrust of the state grew so immense that it amounted to the growth of a new economic 'common sense' which even the leftist parties could not resist with conviction.

However, this kind of consensus by default, which exists as a background common sense among economic and political elites, cannot translate into economic policy without some political agents to carry it through. Although it is sometimes casually asserted that political democracy and economic liberalism have an elective affinity as both are based on principles of unrestricted choice, in actual historical contexts this relation does not hold so simply. The mere existence of democracy is no guarantee that voters will choose liberalizing policies. It is more likely that voters will reflect on the possible effects of liberalization on their own economic interests, and that large social groups which rely on benefit from state action will vote against liberalization initiatives. In India, despite this widespread feeling of the inefficiency and unpopularity of state-centred policies, pushing through liberalizing reforms was widely seen as a hazardous, unpopular business. Liberalization, if fully implemented, would help some groups and injure others, and consequently large political parties shrank from taking the first step. Organized political groups would have agreed to allow liberalization policies to go through only if others enacted them, and they could avoid the responsibility. Here an extraneous, non-economic factor intervened. The Rao government came to power without an absolute majority, and it used its position of relative weakness with masterly political skill. In 1991 the balance of payment situation came to such a crisis that radical decisions could not be avoided. Rao's finance minister, Manmohan Singh was a distinguished economist who became a bureaucrat and eventually a minister, but not a career politician who had to cultivate an electoral constituency. He fashioned a powerful, cogent, and eloquent intellectual justification for these reforms, bringing the vague drift of opinion among elites to a clear focus. Liberalizing reforms were unpopular to a large section of the Congress Party itself. But they could not produce a counter-strategy to deal with the immediate crisis. Rao, as prime minister, resolutely protected his finance minister from pressures from inside his party and from the opposition in parliament. Ironically, other parties had, in their own way, come round to similar conclusions about the long-term economic strategy, though they were unwilling to admit it publicly. For them, it was in fact advantageous that Congress was forced to take the initiative, and would take the blame. It is remarkable that although in the intense debates in the political public sphere both the Hindu nationalist BJP and the leftist parties criticized the Congress and warned about the effects of liberalization, no political group opposed it hard enough.

There was also an entirely non-economic but politically compelling reason. Although the debate about liberalization was a mainly economic one, it did not happen in a vacuum. Academic analysis separates out single problems—like liberalization in our case, and seeks explanatory accounts. People do not live in the comparative luxury of such single issues in real political life; they live within tangled webs of interconnected exasperations. What political actors decide to do about one issue is sometimes determined not by what they think about that problem but what they think about others. Similarly, the actual decision of Indian political parties in 1991 was determined, ironically, not by their thinking on the economic consequences of liberalization, but the possible effects of a takeover by the BJP, the Hindu nationalist party which began to emerge into prominence from the 1980s: this cast its shadow on all other questions in Indian political life, including liberalization.

Briefly, as a party the BJP is both old and new. After Independence, the Jana Sangh was the major party of Hindu nationalism which wanted India to become a Hindu rather than a secular state. Its political campaigns have always been strongly anti-Muslim. Interestingly, the Jana Sangh never had a clearly defined economic programme, though its major political support came from lower government employees and small businessmen in northern India. But the Jana Sangh was never able to go beyond modest gains in electoral terms. In 1977 it decided to join the coalition of opposition forces against Indira Gandhi and merged into the Janata Party. Ideological rifts soon began in the Janata Party, and when it broke away it assumed a new name, Bharatiya Janata Party (BJP), presumably to emphasize its 'Indianness' and indigenism. In the elections of 1984 the party's fortunes fell to a record low of two seats in parliament. It began a highly visible and divisive campaign over the destruction of the Babri mosque at Ayodhya and the building of a temple in its place, alongside a broader campaign for rebuilding many other temples after destroying mosques. The campaign was surprisingly successful and rebuilt the BJP's electoral base. By the time of the liberalization initiatives by the Congress, it had started to threaten to launch a bid for power at the centre.

From the mid-1980s the BJP enjoyed a startling electoral revival: in successive general elections it stormed to ever-larger share of seats, and by the time Narasimha Rao became prime minister, Congress dominance had been more seriously eroded than ever before. Narasimha Rao was not a strong politician, but a wily one. With long political experience, he knew how to calculate on the weakness of his enemies. He played the interconnection of the two issues with masterful political adroitness. All political combatants realized that if the BJP was able to form a government at the centre, it would probably re-structure Indian politics in a fundamental way, changing both the constitutional thrust of secularism and the common sense of everyday politics. For opposition parties, therefore, the choice was invidious. They could seriously threaten Rao's reforms only by letting the BJP into power. The left parties disliked liberalization, but they disliked the prospect of a communal takeover at the centre even more. Rao gambled, as it turned out quite rightly, that if he pursued liberalization policies forcefully, the left would merely criticize him, but not topple his government. By enacting legislation for liberalization, he dared them to dismiss his ministry. Understandably, the leftists and other opposition parties thought liberalization was a lesser disaster than the BJP's accession to power. Predictably, they stopped short of voting Rao's government out of office.

The Content of Liberalization: The Fixing of Sequences and Priorities

In politics vagueness is often an unanswerable strength. Liberalization went through successfully partly because of the ambiguity of its meaning and the great variety of expectations. Different groups meant different things by liberalization. At least some interested social groups or political parties believed that they would allow some aspects of liberalization to take place and delay or stop others. There was also another underlying irony. Seen from any angle, liberalization sought to reduce the role of the state in the economy; but it was only the state which could reduce the power of the state.

Intellectually, those who advocated liberalization, the Congress government and its general supporters, understood its internal logic clearly. Liberalization meant the adoption of a structured set of interconnected policies, the success of each part of which depended on the other parts. Segments of this policy structure could succeed up to a point, but not entirely. Just as Nehruvian planners slowly realized that the structure had an indispensable internal coherence, liberalizers understood the coherence of this alternative set of policies. Liberalization meant several radical changes in the received structure of the economy, and consequently in the settled forms of economic practices in everyday life. All observers saw some constituents of liberalization as crucial: reducing the labyrinthine regime of industrial licensing, reducing tariffs, particularly on import goods, reducing subsidies, the creation of a flexible labour market giving greater power to managements, and finally, in cases where state-sector industries were running at a loss, privatizing them. Obviously, each one of these measures went directly against the settled policies of the Nehruvian design of political economy; therefore, their adoption would have meant, irrespective of the tact or skill with which they were handled politically, a radical change in the overall character of economic life for all social groups.

We need to understand how each component policy of liberalization reforms was likely to affect large social interest groups. Social groups have complex and not always predictable relations with political parties. Thus the translation of group interests into political sentiments is a complex affair, as is the further transfer of these into party policies.

Social Groups and Liberalization

Indian liberalization, it is generally acknowledged, proceeded slowly, compared to China and some cases in Africa. Accordingly, its economic and political results were also quite different. This slow progress was not merely because of obstacles, but for deliberate political reasons. The Congress Party was itself divided about liberalizing reforms, and a large segment opposed it—out of habit, if not conviction. The part of the leadership which had to push them through therefore had to conciliate not merely the opposition, but sections of opinion in their own party. Secondly, the reforms progressed slowly out of deliberate political calculation. Some more acute observers of the Indian liberalization programme have noticed that in effect the decision-makers made deliberate distinctions along two separate axes: some policies could have effects only in the long term, others almost instantly.[17]

[17] Sridharan 1993.

Predictably, liberalization policies did not affect all social groups equally, or equally quickly. There are some paradoxes here. Liberalizing economists tend to assume casually that business interests unequivocally favour opening the market; but that, evidently, is not true under all circumstances; it depends on whether business expects to do well because of the market opening. While for international business corporations the opening up of the immense Indian market was a tempting prospect, for Indian business it meant, crucially, an end to protection. Competition by international business could drive some indigenous industries to the ground. Thus, the business response was mixed. On the whole, entrepreneurs welcomed the opportunities for cheaper imports, fewer licensing controls, lower or more rationalized taxes, and openings for easier collaboration with large international corporations that had capital and the latest technology. But they had reason to fear unrestricted competition as well as the great volatility of the international capital markets, which soon afterwards led to the crash of the East Asian economies. Some specific industries, like software manufacture, which were knowledge-intensive and unhampered by the constraints of bad infrastructure, quickly turned these openings to best use. But the success of these industries was partly because of their peculiar nature, their ability to exploit India's social and economic strengths, and the specific conditions of the world market. Other industries could not emulate them so easily. Old-style industries, used to protectionist laws, comfortable with outdated technology, selling to undemanding captive markets, had less reason to rejoice at this impending triumph of the market.

The Indian business world is highly fragmented and stratified. Small businesses formed a different social group and a distinctive political constituency, with a history of support for right-leaning opposition to the Congress. In North India, they had conventionally supported the Jana Sangh and the BJP. These groups, which had complained most bitterly against small-time bureaucratic controls leading to extortionate practices and corruption, stood to gain moderately, or at least to lose nothing. At least in the foreseeable future, big international corporations were not going to swamp their businesses.

Professional managerial groups, which play such a significant role both in directing decisions and opinion in Indian society, were also likely to approve, due to a peculiarity of opinion-formation in social groups. Of course, because of the nature of the Indian economy, this group was divided. Private managers were always in favour of market-friendly policies; bureaucrats and public-sector management in favour of controls. But it is important to recognize that sociologically they constitute a single social group. Although divided by their specific interests, they are tied together intimately by familial and social relations, and the common climate of opinion in classes earning similar incomes. As a result of liberalization, bureaucrats as a special group may face a relative loss of their regulatory or discretionary power. But general group opinion often transcends calculations of narrow individual self-interest. Often, bureaucrats would have family or kin in private management or other professional occupations likely to benefit disproportionately from these reforms. Professional-managerial classes could realistically expect a long-term expansion of their economic prospects as a social class, if not as individuals or families. However, what bureaucrats would lose was often an illegitimate penumbra of power, not legitimate authority, and certainly not their jobs. The bureaucracy thus did not have either strong motivations of group interest or the ideological conviction to resist liberalizing policies.

However, the initial impact of liberalization affected this group in a specific fashion, by opening up utterly unprecedented income differentials within the upper middle classes. Salaries in private management always tended to be higher than government salaries. Now, the more fortunate section that got access to international companies got a vertiginous rise in their incomes, with no chance of bureaucratic salaries catching up—leading to some envy. But social opinion of the group could come to the entirely rational conclusion that what one section lost could be more than compensated by what others gained, and the expectations of long-term gains for the class as a whole.

The likely impact of liberalization on the livelihood of farmers was equally complex, again partly because of the internal differentiation of the Indian peasantry. Farmers who benefited from the green revolution often invested their surplus income into small local or regional businesses. This fraction of their interests was to coincide with those of other small- or medium-scale business interests. But there were two central elements of liberalization which went directly against them. In all liberalization packages, there is a reduction and eventual removal of subsidies. This would have meant a serious reduction of state support for the entire rural sector, particularly its wealthier sections. Apart from conventional arguments against subsidies and their effects on government finances, there was an added problem in India. Since agriculture constituted a much larger sector of the economy than the industrial and service sectors, this meant that a smaller sector of the economy was subsidizing a vastly larger one. This was very different from the European case, where a larger and powerful industrial sector subsidized the agricultural. In the second, European kind of case, subsidies could continue; but in the reverse case, i.e. India, such policies simply could not go on indefinitely. The elimination of subsidies—of the large government subsidies in agro-inputs and energy—threatens a major source of their prosperity. Any proposal for rationalization of the tax structure was also likely to raise the spectre of an agricultural income tax. If the wages of labour in agricultural jobs went up, as liberalizers expected, agriculturists, as net users of hired labour for their farming (especially during the harvest season), were going to lose very heavily. So, liberalization was bound to get a mixed reception from the farming interests. Recently, the scene has become muddied by competitive bargaining among political parties for the rural vote; some parties in a recent election in Punjab have promised to provide farmers electricity entirely free of charge. There is an enormous paradox/contradiction here. Economically, reducing subsidies is a fundamental part of liberalization. But because farm lobbies influence votes in the countryside, it is the hardest measure to implement politically. In this case, liberalizing policies were difficult to implement precisely because the political process was democratic: and the state has to find a way of expropriating people with their consent.

Organized labour, a social group that is powerful because of its numbers, organization, and strategic location in the industrial economy, looked at liberalization with the greatest anxiety. They expect to be the most serious losers in a comprehensive liberalization of the economy. Due to labour legislation influenced by socialist thinking, employment in the organized sector is permanently secure, irrespective of productivity. Reform of the labour market, in line with liberalization policies, will certainly entail retrenchment and prospective unemployment on a fairly large scale. Liberalization will affect the working conditions of workers in the state sector in particular, where labourers have enjoyed large social benefits, not to mention permanent employment. Disinvestment in public-sector industries is bound to end in large-scale redundancies and new labour rules entailing much greater uncertainty for workers. An additional factor is the great reduction of trade union power which is bound to follow. In India, as elsewhere, the opinion of the working class is sometimes confused with the opinion of trade union leaders, to the benefit of the latter. Not surprisingly, liberalization policies were most strenuously opposed by the representatives of the organized working class, and by the political parties which ran the biggest trade unions. But the conventional left parties, communists and socialists, have steadily declined as a force of effective opposition since the 1960s. Now they simply lack the political strength to stall liberalizing reforms; in addition, their overriding anxiety about the Hindu nationalists capturing power through an electoral opening has constrained them to give their grudging consent to Manmohan Singh's initiatives. Even in the states where leftist parties control power, and do not face an immediate threat from the BJP, the parlous state of government finances has forced them to ask for assistance from international agencies and invite industrial capital, all of which is contrary to their deepest ideological beliefs.

But this is a very incomplete political sociology, because the majority of citizens in India are not businessmen, managers, bureaucrats, rich farmers, and organized labourers. They are mostly poor unorganized labourers in the cities and the countryside, or poor peasantry, small craftsmen, and artisans. Women in very large numbers are housewives, and are affected by policies through the changing economic fortunes of their families. This vast mass of people, who are not organized through professional interest-articulating institutions, have no regular or uninterrupted contact with policy-makers. Their only opportunity for letting governments know what they think of their reforms is during elections. Both political parties and organized groups therefore try to couch their own demands in such a form that they can appeal to a vast number of these unorganized people. But exactly how these people have reacted to liberalization is hard to analyse, since the only data collected is through secondary questions at election surveys.

Liberalization and Political Parties

Policy-makers who introduced the reforms based their moves on political calculations derived from such perceptions of group interest. How the parties moved depended on their sociological support-base and institutional structure. Both Congress and the BJP (which had by the 1990s emerged as the major opposition party) were socially universalist, i.e. they wanted to attract support from all social groups, not just some powerful sectional interests, as the communist and peasant parties did. Thus, they had to make sure that the introduction of liberalization did not inadvertently produce a grand coalition of social interests against them and destroy their chances of winning elections. They chose their priorities and the sequencing of policies with the greatest care.

Observers have pointed out how the liberalizers selected some policies for early implementation and pushed others down in their priority. As the economic crisis that brought liberalization on was mainly due to a foreign exchange shortage in July 1991, the first moves were to stabilize the economy. Stringent restrictions on foreign exchange were lifted, and tariff regimes were relaxed in the early phase. The actual implementation seemed to separate out policies which were likely to yield short-term results from those which required a long period to succeed. Politically more significant was a distinction between policies, which brought immediate benefits for some groups without affecting others adversely, and those which would mean serious costs to large organized social constituencies. This explains why economic reforms in India have not merely been slow, but selective, or rather why their slow progress has been due to their selectivity and deliberate sequencing. The easing of foreign exchange regulations immediately benefited businesses and the upper classes. The import of capital goods and technology became easier and made export-oriented industries and upper-class consumers happy. Relaxing licensing rules dealt with a long-term complaint of entrepreneurs. It also helped small entrepreneurs whose main capital was technological skills; its best example was the burgeoning software industry in South India. These changes, though quite radical against the context of past policies, mainly allowed new developments without negatively affecting others. Some liberalization policies were politically different, because they would cause serious pain to economic groups. If the government allows more flexible labour markets, permanent employment in the public sector will have to be sacrificed. The closure of loss-making public sector firms will lead to unemployment. Reduction in subsidies was urgently required if the government had to impose fiscal discipline and cover its costs by making financial economies, instead of simply covering the deficit by printing money and pushing up inflation. But such subsidy-reduction policies would have serious adverse effects for agricultural groups, and if the agricultural sector acted as a single political interest, instead of breaking up into class fractions, they had the immense power of numbers on their side. The only way of avoiding a grand overwhelming coalition of political forces against liberalization was thus to select and sequence its constituent policies—to make sure that these groups were not antagonized by adverse policies at the same time. However, economists advocating liberalization pointed out that the success of liberalization depended on an implementation of the whole package. Breaking up and sequencing the various parts were bound to make the changes less effective. This was another paradox for politicians: to succeed economically, the policies had to work together; to succeed politically they had to be pursued separately and in parts.

The actual progress of liberalization in India has been very interesting. While economists have often deplored the fact that the whole package of policies has not been implemented, and therefore that their full beneficial effects have not been realized, others point to their remarkable success given the unpromising initial conditions. In fact, the political history of the period immediately following liberalization was highly volatile. Four successive governments have come into office, run by parties of very different character. The Congress government, which began the reforms, was followed by a coalition of assorted 'leftist' groups.[18] It drew its main support from parties which had been sharply critical of liberalization; but when they came to office did little to obstruct or reverse them. After a brief and ineffectual period, the coalition went out of office.

This led to the most serious ideological change in Indian politics since Independence, as the BJP finally found a way to power at the centre, even if as the major constituent within a coalition. This was not an insignificant replacement of one coalition by another. The BJP

[18] The coalition was composed of the Janata Dal, a centrist conglomerate, lower-caste parties which supported radical changes in caste-based reservations, and the Communist parties. It was led by I.K. Gujral a veteran politician long associated with the Congress. These groups were strongly opposed to the Hindu nationalist ideology of the BJP.

had always challenged the hegemonic vision of secular nationalism advocated by the Congress; and its electoral success was built directly on the campaign around the demolition of the mosque at Ayodhya.[19] Oddly, however, it had continued the economic indistinctness of its precursor, the Jana Sangh. But as its role changed, and it transformed from a regional North Indian party into a serious contender for central power, it was forced to define its economic policy more clearly. In the event, it developed two somewhat contradictory lines of argument. In line with its general ideological indigenism, it began to appropriate the traditional Gandhian economic ideals of swadeshi—a policy which supported cottage industries, the voluntary restriction of consumption, a simple rural lifestyle, and above all the rejection of foreign-made goods. This was incongruous for a party which was directly linked to the RSS organization—one of whose members had assassinated Gandhi. Yet, the strand of indigenism was quite strong in some sections of the Hindu nationalists, and they increasingly made more assertive claims for swadeshi policies. But the BJP, crucially, wanted to entice the upper and middle classes from their traditional habits of supporting the Congress because of its policy of economic modernism; and the BJP has strenuously sought to dispel the idea that it was a backward-looking fundamentalist force, opposed to modernity. A large section of its social supporters and leadership advocated strongly modernist economic policies, and claimed that under their leadership the economy would come out of mismanagement and stagnation. Ideologically, therefore, the BJP did not have a clear line towards liberalization.

Both the left parties and the BJP fiercely criticized the Congress for initiating liberalizing reforms; but when they came to power they did nothing to stop or reverse them. After the 1998 elections, the BJP ruled at the centre with fluctuating and at times unruly coalition partners in a strange mixture of broad stability alongside small instability—because it was never certain about its allies. Predictably, to keep the coalition together, the BJP had to tone down its ideological stance alongside its deeply anti-Muslim agenda. On economic issues, however, it had

[19] In December 1992 activists from Hindu nationalist groups demolished the structure of the Babri mosque at Ayodhya leading to widespread rioting in the whole subcontinent.

a free hand, as none of the coalition parties were strongly opposed to liberalization. In fact, some of its coalition partners, like the dynamic chief minister of Andhra Pradesh, Chandrababu Naidu, used the opportunities created by liberalizing policies to produce an economic interpretation of federalism and press for faster regional development. The BJP's own formal attitude towards liberalizing policies was surprisingly conciliatory. Although it criticized the Congress at the time of their adoption, it kept its own position vague. After the economic situation started to show remarkable improvement on several counts—overall GDP growth, the reduction of inflation, an improvement in export earnings, etc.—others sought to steal some of the credit. Not surprisingly, in character with its general expertise in chauvinism, the BJP, or some sections of it, have kept up a fierce rhetoric of economic nationalism against 'foreign interests', generally unspecified.

But the rhetoric has not threatened to invade actual policy-making. Internally, Hindu nationalists have always been friendly to business, especially small business groups which were their loyal constituency in the first three decades. Big business did not traditionally support them, preferring the more comprehensive modernism of the Congress. But instead of alienating big business or the professional classes when it was making electoral strides towards power, the BJP sought to woo them by promising greater efficiency, less corruption, and by making it clear that it was not advocating a comprehensive re-traditionalization of Indian society. This had two reciprocal effects. As its electoral strength grew, and the prospects of its power improved, upper-middle-class and big business interests became more interested in it; and reciprocally, the party put into more prominent roles its more modernizing leaders. Now the party often fronts individual leaders who try to cultivate a highly modernist image, suggesting a politics which is knowledgeable about international trends, friendly to business and markets, and interested in high technology. This is a partial makeover of its indigenist image, and a very real strand of its quotidian politics. The BJP has also come to realize that international economic pressures demand a continuation of liberalization: it appointed a committee for disinvestment, followed by a special ministry to look after the necessarily contentious process of dismantling government enterprises. And even leftist governments like the CPI(M) in West Bengal have admitted that loss-making state industries have to be closed. As the finances of state governments near collapse, the central authorities can use the situation to force through liberalization.

But the emergence of the BJP and its stable control of the central government also led to other significant shifts. One of the most significant was the slow redefinition of India's national interest. Nehru, and Congress under his influence, thought of foreign policy as primarily an instrument for protecting sovereignty and securing economic development. India's influence in the world was expected to come from the persuasiveness of its suggestions and the moral validity of its position on issues like arms control, apartheid, imperialism, etc. Already, in Indira Gandhi's times, this had changed significantly towards a clearer orientation towards power; and Indian policies clearly sought regional hegemony. The BJP's orientation towards the international society continued and intensified those tendencies. Nehru did not seek nuclear weapons; the BJP dramatized its acquisition of new nuclear weapons. Given its ideology, it naturally emphasized the idea of sovereignty, but interpreted it utterly differently. Its understanding of sovereignty implies a more assertive stance based on increased military power, and, more dangerously, an internal connection of sovereignty with an exclusivist Hindu definition of Indian nationalism whereby the power of this redefined 'Hindu' nation is used to threaten internal minorities. Some of the BJP government's foreign-policy initiatives strengthened the drive towards economic liberalization. Its attempts to improve political relations with the United States, for instance, accelerated liberalization. If foreign investment into India's economy is to be radically increased, its first condition is greater liberalization of economic controls. But the strand of swadeshi cannot be dismissed entirely. Although the supporters of economic swadeshi are not in dominant positions, they remain a major part of the Hindu nationalist formation. Advancing liberalization is bound to exacerbate internal conflict within the BJP on this question.

It appears then that the logic of liberalization has developed a life of its own. Irrespective of which political party comes to office, and what they say rhetorically, their economic administrations are constrained to enact legislations which carry forward into the logical next step the 'logic' of liberalizing reforms. That, after all, is the central objective of the liberalizing policies—to emancipate the economy from control by the state and the uncertainties of electoral politics, and to render this entire process irreversible. It appears that in India, despite large and unpredictable complexities in this process, the state has gone some way in freeing the economy from itself.

References

Ahluwalia, Montek Singh. 1999. India's Economic Reforms: An Appraisal. In Jeffrey Sachs *et al.* Eds. *India in the Era of Liberalisation*. Delhi: Oxford University Press.

Bardhan, Pranab. 1984. *Political Economy of Development in India*. Delhi: Oxford University Press.

———. 1992. *The Political Economy of Development in India*. Delhi: Oxford University Press.

Bhagwati, Jagdish. 1993. *India in Transition: Freeing the Economy*. Oxford: Clarendon Press.

Chakravarty, Sukhamoy. 1984. *Development Planning*. Delhi: Oxford University Press.

Dreze, Jean, and Sen, Amartya. 1998. *India: Economic Development and Social Opportunity.* New York: Oxford University Press.

Foucault, Michel. 1991. Governmentality. In *The Foucault Effect: Studies in Governmentality*. Eds. Graham Burchell, Colin Gordon, and Peter Miller. Chicago: University of Chicago Press.

Frankel, Francine. 1971. *India's Green Revolution*. Princeton: Princeton University Press.

Kaviraj, Sudipta. 1994. Dilemmas of Democratic Development in India. In Adrian Leftwich. Ed. *Democracy and Development*. Cambridge: Polity Press.

Mellor, John. 1966. *The Economics of Agricultural Development*. Ithaca: Cornell University Press.

Sridharan, E. 1993. Economic Reforms in India. *Journal of Commonwealth and Comparative Politics.*

Varshney, Ashutosh. 1998. *Democracy, Development and the Countryside*. Cambridge: Cambridge University Press.

Index